The Creation of Reality

For Jörg Hennig

The Creation of Reality

A Constructivist Epistemology of Journalism and Journalism Education

Bernhard Poerksen

Translated by
Alison Rosemary Koeck and Wolfram Karl Koeck

imprint-academic.com

Copyright © Bernhard Poerksen, 2011

The moral rights of the author have been asserted
No part of this publication may be reproduced in any form
without permission, except for the quotation of brief passages
in criticism and discussion.

The German original was first published under the title *Die Beobachtung des Beobachters*, Universitätsverlag Konstanz, 2006.

English translation by Alison Rosemary Koeck and Wolfram Karl Koeck

Published in the UK by Imprint Academic
PO Box 200, Exeter EX5 5YX, UK

Published in the USA by Imprint Academic
Philosophy Documentation Center
PO Box 7147, Charlottesville, VA 22906-7147, USA

ISBN 9 781845 40 2099

A CIP catalogue record for this book is available from the
British Library and US Library of Congress

Contents

Preliminary note vii

Introduction 1

A. Foundations

I **Premises and Postulates** 13
  Extreme Epistemological Positions 13
  Variants of Constructivism 15
  Figures of Thought in the Discourse of Constructivism . . . 23
  Anatomy of a Debate: Accusations and Reservations 29
  Fundamental Problems of Constructivist Theory Development . . 40
  Recapitulation of the Argument 48

B. Educational Objectives

II **Deepening Critical Awareness of Science** 53
  The Inevitable Presumption: Indispensable Scepticism 53
  The Idea of Science: General Reflection I 58
  Methodology and Method: General Reflection II 62
  Points of Reference for Knowledge: General Reflection III . . 73
  The Results of Scientific Enquiry: General Reflection IV . . 75
  Scientific Literacy 78

III **Deepening Critical Awareness of Language** 81
  Linguistic Registers: The Sum Total of Choices 81
  The Language of Neo-Nazis: An Extreme Example 86
  Generalisation of The Findings: The Linguistic World View . . 94
  Against Linguistic Realism: Constructivist Considerations . . 98
  Linguistic Realism in Journalism:
    A Proposal for a Systematic Approach 103
  Understanding and Improving 106

IV Deepening Awareness of Media-Epistemology 109
The Programme of Media-Epistemology: Sketch of an Idea ... 109
Event and Message: Programmes of Construction I 116
Schemas and Genres: Programmes of Construction II 125
Media Epistemology as a Theory of Distinctions:
  Programmes of Construction III 131
The Practice-Relevance of Media-Epistemology 135

V Deepening Ethical Awareness 137
Epistemology and Forgery: Tom Kummer's Apologia 137
Ethics of the Second Order: Excursus I 142
Consequence Theory of Truth: Excursus II 149
Journalistic Ethics: Key Concepts and Core Questions 157
The Question of Autonomy:
  Discourse-Generating Contradictions 161
The Question of Fact and Fiction:
  An Observer-Relative Re-Formulation 164
The Question of Responsibility: Ethical Awareness 171
The Indispensability of Trust: Idealistic Closing Note 176

C. Ways of Learning

VI Deepening Awareness of Autonomy 181
The Formal Anthropology of Constructivism 181
Paradigmatic Considerations and Consequences 187
Role Models and Self-Images 202

VII The Reality of the Study of Journalism 215
The Distinction Between Theory and Practice 215
The Management of Contradictions: Informing Irritations ... 224
The Parable of the Blind Spot 231

VIII Summary in the Form of Theses 233

Bibliography 243

Preliminary Note

The words making up the title of this book, *The Creation of Reality*, play on a polarity. On the one hand, *reality* is held to be what is given, what is encountered directly, what exists, as we usually say, independently of an observer, of a knowing subject. On the other hand, the concept of *creation* suggests a contrary impression: what we are dealing with is not something encountered directly, something given, but something made, fabricated, manufactured. Proponents of this position assume that reality does not exist in itself, but is created, constructed, by the observer.

One might now be tempted to get rid of this toying with differing or contrary connotations in favour of only one, the definitive interpretation, to set up a mono-perspective as the only and absolutely adequate one, and to affirm as a result: reality is the point of reference of all efforts of knowing, which exists independently of us. Or in reverse order and with comparable force: what we call reality is merely a construct, a more or less arbitrary emanation of the mind.

However, such a rigidly dogmatic position and a corresponding commitment to a realist, constructivist, or some other, orthodoxy would militate against the central concern of this book. The book much rather seeks to promote a style of thinking that involves changes of perspectives and modes of observation and may thus help to keep twisting and turning so-called certainties, ultimate truths, big and small ideologies until their edges become fuzzy, until we are able to see more than before. The creation of reality and the construction of certainties are the core topics and the key problems of constructivism that will here be applied — with the intention of the practice-related application of an epistemology — to journalism, journalism studies, and university didactics. My central thesis is that our understanding of journalism and, in particular, the education and training of journalists, can profit from the insights provided by constructivism. These insights instigate an original kind of scepticism; they provide the underpinnings of a modern kind of didactics oriented by the autonomy of the learners, and they provide the sustaining arguments for a radical ethic of responsibility in journalism.

Among my academic dreams is the wish that scholarly books might perhaps lose the character of a more or less sterile monologue at some stage after their publication and instead turn into a source of stimulation for others and for the author so as to improve ideas and theses through disputation and dialogue.

Bernhard Poerksen
Tübingen, April 2010

Introduction

The Practice of Parody

Two of my students were among the first to demonstrate to me that constructivism can directly stimulate the didactic imagination and that it is, therefore, perfectly suited — at least in the halls of a university — to serve as an irritation theory in the education and training of journalists. The two students had put their names down for a presentation in a seminar on practices of the media, and were supposed to talk about the stylistic characteristics of a squib, to elucidate the defining differences between commentary and squib, and finally to link their presentation with the critical discussion of a text that had been distributed to the participants a week before. They did none of these things or, if at all, then only in a very indirect way. At the time they were expected to start their presentation, they walked up front busying themselves with slips of paper; one of them wordlessly installed a cassette recorder, then sat down on the floor and thus rendered himself invisible to the audience for as long as the seminar lasted. The other student pushed the button that moved the blinds up and down. The room went dark. All one could still see in the brief flash of light allowed in by the opening door was the student leaving the room with his slips of paper in his hands. Brief nervous laughter in the darkness, the ringing of a mobile phone that was not switched off by anyone. The lecturer in charge of the seminar, I myself at the time, decided to wait and see what might happen. After a few minutes, the actual presenter re-emerged. He began, with skilled dilettantism, to handle the overhead projector, dazzled the audience intermittently, and then — operating with increasing speed but still wordlessly — placed transparencies of some sort on the projector glass, which were practically illegible and some of which had obviously been copied the wrong way round. In the meantime, the partner sitting on the floor had switched on the cassette recorder. One could hear a monotonously delivered presentation: 'The squib is a special form of commentary; it works with the instruments of parody, of travesty, and of alienation. Among its central characteristics belongs the fact that the squib is funny, that it exhilarates and shocks.' After that, the endless loop of a repetition: 'The squib is a special form of commentary...' The mobile phone rang again. Nobody switched it off. Transparencies kept emerging, which were at least legible. They carried messages from another reality: 'Ever more!', 'We are the best!', 'What is your reality?', 'We are the presentation!' Exceptionally beautiful the transparency with the inscription: 'It cannot be that you leave here without taking something with you.' At the end – in place of the customary summary – the transparency master served a question in capital letters: 'Did you feel the squib?' This signalled the end of the presentation and he again disappeared. 43 dumbfounded students and a speechless lecturer remained behind sitting in darkness.

Sceptically minded readers might well ask themselves at this point why I have decided to select this particular example for introducing both a heuristically designed theory of journalists' education and training, and an epistemology of journalism studies. The answer is: this performance by an artistic talent – and that is what the presentation actually was – realises an approach and an attitude that will be the topic of discussion here. What happened in this seminar can certainly never be repeated in the same way; it is, however, of exemplary significance. It cannot directly be turned into a recipe but it nevertheless appears to be the expression of a particular attitude that merits a closer look. The two students played with entrenched patterns of communication in a highly intelligent way; they copied the contents of their presentation onto the media of their performance and translated the theory of the squib into the practice of parody, all at the risk of total failure. The motto of their action could have been taken from a piece of work by Niklas Luhmann: 'Irritation is precious'[1], he is supposed to have said once. This is to mean: Irritation brings about a new dynamics, opens up opportunities of understanding and appreciating new perspectives, as long as it does not lead to annoyance and rejection; it encourages intellectual flexibility, it is basically anti-dogmatic, it creates sensibility for the ineluctable contingency of any experience of reality. In one word, irritation must be exploited as a productive force in university didactics, particularly in the preparation for a profession that is essentially characterised, or should so be characterised, by scepticism and curiosity, quick and undogmatic thinking, and the permanent confrontation with ever unfolding new realities. It is the profession of journalism that can profit greatly by such systematic kinds of irritation. The academic discipline, the study of journalism, may correspondingly be conceived of as a kind of study by means of irritation.[2]

Obviously, this raises the fundamental question as to how irritation and the stimulation of intellectual creativity can be given a systematic place

---

1 Quoted in Kahl (2001), p. 81.
2 See Weischenberg (2004a), p. 10.

within an ideal-type study of journalism. How could one, to return once again to the two students, make the best use of their hazardous presentation for the purpose of stimulation? How can one inspire lecturers in journalism studies or, better still, how can one help them to inspire themselves so as to exploit the truly strange fact that university teaching is not taught at all and can and must be turned into an occasion and an opportunity for realising imaginative curricular and didactic conceptions? Questions of this kind, which do indeed express a somewhat strange desire to seek and find a recipe for creativity, aim towards a different attitude with regard to university teaching that would lend contours to concrete action and simultaneously direct such action in an unobtrusive way. The goal can be neither the ultimate recipe nor a rigid method. It ought to be the furthering of a procedure that allows for the adequate adaptation to changing situations; the goal is an attitude, as Heinz von Foerster would have said.[3] This altered attitude can be vindicated and illustrated by the epistemological school of thought, which is nowadays called constructivism. University didactics and, in particular, the didactics[4] of journalism studies can derive profitable inspiration from this school of thought, as will be shown in detail later on.

The analysis of the course of action of the two students makes clear that they practically acted as constructivist lecturers in the hour of their performance, whether they were aware of it or not. Some of the features and goals of a didactics inspired by constructivism have thus already become apparent, however vague they may still appear to be, and they will have to be delineated more precisely with regard to the academic field of journalism studies and the profession of journalism.[5] Evaluating this key example still further, we can see:

- a close connection between knowledge and action, theory and practice, reflection and craftsmanship,
- a struggle for cognitive flexibility and a creative, multi-perspectival handling of contents,
- an interest in such forms of presentation as support intellectual curiosity, cooperative thinking, and dialogue-oriented learning,
- the rejection of a static culture of instruction, a feeling for the skilled management of irritation and for variable perspectives of observation,
- the search for new didactic role models in order to shore up cooperative reflexion and problem-oriented teaching and learning.

The central thesis of this book is therefore: constructivism provides vital impulses for the education and training of journalists in universities; it

---

[3] See Foerster/Bröcker (2002), pp. 64ff.
[4] Didactics is here understood, with Reich (2002a, p. 69), as a theory that prepares, analyses and evaluates teaching and learning.
[5] See also Siebert (2003a, p. 108) on the shaping of stimulating learning environments.

represents a useful programme of irritation for both practice-oriented and also theory-based teaching, and it can fuel the kind of flexible intelligence that is required by the quality journalism of our time. Such a thesis requires adequate grounding and justification. This will be attempted in this book, first by *constructing the appropriate argument,* secondly by means of the *contents treated,* and thirdly by the *chosen manner of writing,* the form of presentation. These three elements of production can be separated only artificially, of course, but they will here be treated separately for the purpose of an introduction that is needed to prepare the ground for what follows.

Construction of the Argument

The construction of the argument makes clear that this book, which involved an intensive study of constructivism,[6] expressly pledges itself to be a contribution to theory work; the concept of theory[7] refers to an 'internally consistent set of concepts, definitions and categories'.[8] In terms of constructivism, we are here dealing with 'observer perspectives that posit distinctions at the expense of blind spots, i.e. which see/generate certain things and not others.'[9] Theory work, in our understanding, implies the following: to devise consistent arguments, to define concepts, categories and models, to introduce terminological neologisms whenever necessary, and to adduce available empirical studies so as to illustrate specific hypotheses if it should thus prove necessary to secure scientific plausibility. With reference to the structure of the present book, the consequence is that I shall first — briefly and by way of a survey — present the variants and the modes of justification of constructivism, then elaborate particular discourse-structuring figures of thought, and finally summarise the sometimes extremely vigorous debate about constructivism in the study of journalism and communication.

The claim that constructivism should be applied to mould the didactics of the university-bound education of journalists in a significant way carries the additional implication that there exists a connection between epistemology and ordinary life, between epistemology and life-world practice

---

6 Cf. the author's publications listed under *D. References*. The frequent quotations from the books written together with Heinz von Foerster and Humberto R. Maturana should generously not be construed as expressions of the vanity of academic self-reference but much rather as an attempt to document to what extent I have profited personally from this cooperation.

7 More precisely, we are here dealing with a so-called base theory. 'Base theories', according to Weber (2003a, p. 19), 'are neither superimposed, potentially totalitarian world views (paradigms) nor theories with a claim to universal or all-encompassing validity (super-theories). They are much rather theories that offer a logically consistent set of concepts, definitions and models, which can be made operational empirically. [...] Base theories offer a pool of concepts, which in appropriate relational linkage yield a model or a logical system which, as a rule, lays claim to representing reality in some structured form.'

8 Weber (2000a), p. 72.

9 *Ibid.*

and, consequently, didactics. This connection is only sporadically, if at all, attended to in the debates about the application of constructivism to the various disciplines and fields involved (pedagogy, didactics, psychology, management science, media and communication studies), it is simply ignored. It is conveniently forgotten although it definitely constitutes a transcendental condition for the pragmatic relevance of constructivist considerations: the condition of the possibility for constructivism to be useful at all is included in the key question of whether, and with what intensity, epistemological reflexions can and should control practical action at all or indeed quite generally.

A typology of possible relations and connections between epistemology and everyday life practice will be proposed here, combined with a plea to establish a *relationship of mutual stimulation* between constructivism and journalism studies. My thesis is that constructivist assumptions (e.g. the orientation by the observer, the abandonment of an emphatic conception of truth, the interest in paradoxical and circular figures of thought, the postulate of the autonomy of the knowing subject) are sources of inspiration for the didactics of journalism and media studies. They exercise stimulation, they provide offers for perception, and they focus attention. They are certainly not thoroughly ineffectual mind games (this would be one extreme); nor do they constitute (this would be the other extreme) premises and postulates which, following the pattern of rigid linear causality, can bring about and enforce specific effects in the field of didactics, in the analysis of journalism etc.

I shall introduce a particular variant of constructivism that I would like to call *discursive constructivism*, in order to demonstrate its irritating potential as fully as possible and to bridge the threatening abyss of self-contradiction and dogmatic self-entrenchment. This brand of constructivism is essentially conceived of as an epoch-specific, potentially most stimulating kind of scepticism, and devoid of any obligation or pressure for commitment. It is not intended to be a new paradigm[10], a school of thought that promises the exact certification of the levels of knowledge attained, nor finally as a kind of meta-dogmatism that is used to terrorise others dogmatically on the grounds of their epistemological errors. In brief: I shall offer varieties of observation, not absolute truths.

Didactics and Contents

Trying to keep the architecture of the theory open on all sides is bound to influence the handling of *contents*. Constructivism does not claim to be a trivial generative programme that automatically produces particular

---

10   This is out of the question also for the simple reason that critical observers of the science system have been pouring scorn on the fact that paradigm changes and the proclamation of ever new paradigms (actually: fashions) seem to have become standard procedure in the practice of science. See Steinfeld (1991), p. 87.

insights; it lacks, consequently, the immediate quasi recipe-based relevance for journalistic practice and the didactics of journalism study. Its basically indirect usefulness consists in its being a reservoir of new perspectives and opportunities of observation:

- Constructivist considerations rob the naive faith in science and facts of its foundations.
- They deepen the awareness of the power of scientific paradigms, theories and methods to constitute realities and, furthermore, of the need for the critical handling of trivial concepts of communication and communication effects.
- They unsettle the fundamentally realist self-image of professional journalism, kindle the interest in patterns of selection, in different forms of presentation, and in varieties of the staging of reality.
- The emphasis on the observer-dependence of all knowledge makes the emphatic ideal of objective news reporting appear illusory, suggests responsibility for personal constructions of reality, and provides arguments for tolerance with respect to other realities (while simultaneously rejecting dogmatic claims to truth).
- Journalists with a constructivist education will at least show deeper awareness of their personal participation in, and contribution to, the production of media realities, and the more or less implicit ontological character of their linguistic descriptions ('it is a fact that …', 'the truth is …' etc.) will become the topic and object of self-and- other-observation.
- The self-referential rules and the autonomy of journalistic reality construction, and the increasing relevance of media to the modern experience of the world, have become more than evident. The manifest processes of *medialisation*[11] have induced some diagnosis-bent observers to formulate the thesis that the realities of life and the realities of the media can no longer be meaningfully distinguished and separated from each other.[12] However, the point must be stated more precisely: everything that happens beyond the immediate horizon of one's own private life-world is brought to one's notice by the mass media and can only rarely be verified by one's own perception; the personal control of authenticity may still be possible in principle but it has become improbable to a high degree.
- The extensive interest in differences and the fundamental decision for plurality, as implied by constructivist positions, have worked as catalysts for deepening critical awareness with regard to the media and society. The systematic curtailing of the manifold variety of realities (e.g. by censorship, press amalgamation and concentration), will inevitably spark off critical reflection and public comment and debate.

---

11 Medialisation refers to the increasing penetration of living conditions by the media and the effects of the media. See Weber (2003a), p. 33.
12 Cf. the discussion between Poerksen (2002a) and Bolz.

By way of an interim summary, and as a preview of the topics to be treated, the following implications may therefore be stated. The voluminous chapter following the initial description of the general state of affairs offers a typology of the different variants of deepened awareness engendered by the epistemology of (discursive) constructivism. It describes these variants more precisely — with respect to relevant competences resulting for students of journalism — and enumerates and elucidates in detail possible learning objectives. The final chapter deals with possible forms of learning and shows in what ways the constructivist perspective could inspire university didactics. The decisive point there is to lay bare the points of linkage and the connecting lines between the epistemological postulates, the didactic methods, and the central requirements of quality journalism, and to describe an application-oriented kind of heuristics. The core concern is to take seriously the autonomy of the knowing subjects (in this case: the teachers and the students) as the fundamental premise of all didactic efforts:

- Knowledge is, according to the assumption pursued here, no thingified *result* of thinking that may be transferred elsewhere but an *event* of thought, tied to an observer, related to particular situations and atmospheres, which are essential for knowledge and insight to come to life and become useful at all.
- The potential learners are moved into the foreground as they are viewed as the active and autonomous constructors; learning cannot be generated, one of the central assumptions runs, but only be made possible. Teachers create environments and conditions so that, in the case of success, even those persons become enthused who have shown themselves resistant to fascination before.
- The principle of knowledge transfer, which derives from a model involving an active sender confronting a passive receiver, is replaced by the rather un-pleasant insight that knowledge cannot simply be transferred but can only be created by the individual. It seems impossible to expect that sentences uttered by human beings would activate in other human beings precisely those thoughts and conceptual nets which the speakers connected with their utterances. Communication is never transport.[13] *Transfer, broadcast,* and *receiver* are misleading metaphors with regard to conceptual content. Successful communication, from a constructivist point of view, appears highly improbable; there is always the inescapable subjectivity of meaning that has to be taken into account. Incomprehension is actually — in this view — the unnoticed standard case: one glides along without realising how little one knows and understands about the partner in the communication process. Only when we recognise that we do not understand each

---

[13] Glasersfeld (2002), pp. 63f.

other do we begin to comprehend that we have not understood each other.
- For university teaching the implication must be that we have to find ways and means to minimalise the improbability of successful communication at least for short-term periods. We need to orient teaching by the reality of the learner, to base teaching on this reality, and to speak in a language of necessary adaptation but also in a language of unavoidable professional independence. The central question is: how can functionally adequate inspirations and irritations be made possible — despite the autonomy of the knowing subject? The answer must necessarily be a modest one: all that can be done is to present the students with opportunities in their own languages and according to their own logics and to offer them reasons and arguments for adapting themselves to new circumstances and changing themselves.[14]

The concrete elaboration of these considerations is carried out in two steps. At the beginning, the basic outlines of a constructivist didactics and pedagogy are introduced. Fortunately, the debate in these disciplines is already far advanced and constructivism has been a most productive influence there. Key concepts of the relevant discourse (knowledge, learning, education etc.) have been re-formulated in constructivist terms. The task is now to work out role-models for teachers and learners at university and to present central concepts of a didactic re-orientation (to press it into a formula: from a didactics of *instruction* to a didactics of *inspiration*). Among the concepts of particular relevance belong, among others, the distinction between trivial and non-trivial machines and the model of context control. In a second step the general premises and concepts, i.e those which are valid independently of particular professional disciplines, will have to be made concrete for the purposes of the didactics of a particular field or discipline. At this point the paradoxes and aporias of the journalistic profession will be analysed and those competences for well-reflected decision-making will be sought out, which derive from the mode of observation of the second order, i.e. the observation of observations. They are — and this is another thesis of the book — of special importance for quality journalists operating in constantly fluctuating professional environments. The title of the chapter, *The reality of journalism studies*, is intentionally ambiguous. On the one hand, reality appears here as an accumulation of limiting conditions that impinge on the contours of the field of journalism studies from outside. Such limiting conditions are, for instance, university reform processes, demands by practitioners, emerging qualification profiles for fledgling journalists etc. On the other hand, the field of journalism studies — especially from a constructivist perspective — is not just the passive recipient of external influences but also itself

---

[14] See Bardmann/Groth (2001), p.15.

an active constructor of realities.[15] These realities, the argument runs, are inescapably of a hybrid nature. They must conform equally well with the demands and requirements of professional practice and the standards of reflexion of the university, they must oscillate between reflection and action, between theory and practice, between education and training — and thus between the acceptance of contingency and the negation of contingency, between the certainty of uncertainty and the necessary ignorance of that fundamental uncertainty intrinsic to all knowledge, which is required by the pragmatics of ordinary life.

Style of Thought and Style of Writing

It is claimed in this book that constructivism as a basic epistemology of university-bound journalist education is useful and that this claim can be validated and illustrated by the construction of the argument, by the contents dealt with, and finally also by the chosen manner of writing. The construction of the argument and the contents have already been sketched out albeit roughly, but the manner of writing has not yet been considered. This will now be done in the concluding section. The core idea is: *styles of thought are styles of writing*.[16] Content and form are — ideally — closely connected; they stand in a relationship of mutual corroboration (and not mutual discrediting). If one does not, as suggested here, consider constructivism as the answer, as the solution, but as a programme of irritation, as a means to combat folk evidence and ever-threatening dogmatic self-insulation, then this must have consequences for the manner of presentation and writing. The problem is: one ordinarily speaks and writes in a way that assigns to whatever is described an existence independent of the observer, one officially breaks off the process of knowing at a particular point and then presents results that accordingly turn into certainties. This implies that one uses a diction of realism, frequently also in constructivist circles, which conceals and even denies what has been said on the content plane. Observer independence is thus linguistically fabricated.[17] The paradoxical structure of constructivism in its entirety (if constructivism is absolutely true then it is false, if it can be proved in an absolute sense, then it is finished) might, however, encourage and inspire us to assert our own statements in a flexible, open and light-hearted manner in order to avoid contradicting ourselves already through the way and manner in which we present our theses. The manner of writing should ideally possess a certain dialogical lightness because in a dialogue the reality of the partner is given legitimate presence, and because one avoids in this

---

15   I owe these ideas to conversations with Siegfried Weischenberg.
16   For the concept of 'style of thought' — understood as a set of assumptions shaping perception — see the early classic on the sociology of knowledge by Ludwik Fleck (1993).
17   Maturana/Poerksen (2004), p. 159.

way to raise implicit claims to truth, claims that one is explicitly negating while writing

It is furthermore necessary to formulate the results of one's own reflections in such a way as to invest them with features of openness and indications of not being ultimately determined. It is necessary to offer opportunities for observation and to exploit perspectival fixations as occasions for intellectual movements that are, however, no longer intended to reach out for some absolute. Naturally, this is easier said and demanded than done — particularly when one is forced to move in the presentation corset of academic communication that is generally organised to be performed as a monologue. It will probably be best to address the dilemma of the adequate form as well as the problem of choosing the form, with which to deal properly with the problem of form, more or less directly from time to time, because we would otherwise overreach ourselves in the process of writing. Whether I have succeeded — at least occasionally — in giving the monologue that now follows dialogical quality and whether I have been able to invest it with the necessary richness of perspectives will now be for those to decide for whom all this has been written, the readers of this book.

FOUNDATIONS

Chapter I

Premises and Postulates

1. Extreme Epistemological Positions

Mediators of Truth in Journalism

In 1992, Klaus Bresser, the former editor in chief of the German television channel ZDF, published a small book with the title 'What now? On television, morality, and journalists.' Already in the first chapter we can read: 'Journalists have to relate what is. They have to separate truth from falsehood, the chaff from the wheat. And much is achieved if they are successful.'[1] In Bresser's opinion, journalists are 'mediators of truth';[2] a sceptical attitude to knowledge, whatever its foundation, seems alien to him. 'In the last few years philosophers have attempted to con us into believing', he writes,

> that the media do not actually inform but merely fulfil expectations, providing reality designs that fit given markets. I insist that the media, including television, are capable of representing reality. Their claim to reality is not naive.[3]

These quotations demonstrate: journalism obviously involves philosophy and will probably need philosophy whenever its professional standards require critical examination. Klaus Bresser takes the position of a realist epistemology, which, as surveys show, is still shared by a majority of his colleagues.[4] It presupposes an observer-independent reality, demands its approximation, and believes that knowledge of truth is possible at least in principle even though it may not always be attainable in a particular case.

---

1 Bresser (1992), p.12.
2 Ibid., p. 13.
3 Ibid., p. 17.
4 Weischenberg/Scholl (1995), p. 218.

The central pattern of such realist thinking is the comparison; media-external reality[5] is compared with its medial representation — in accordance with Ludwig Wittgenstein's statement 2.223 in his *Tractatus logico-philosophicus*: 'In order to discover whether the picture is true or false we must compare it with reality.'[6] Depending on the result and the degree of demonstrable correspondence the representation is then judged to be successful or deficient, untrue in an emphatic, absolute sense.

Between Realism and Solipsism

Evidently, realism marks an epistemological extreme because it claims, in all its guises, that objective knowledge is possible; 'it (pre)supposes that the states of affairs of the mind-independent world can be known, at least partially, as they *actually* are.'[7] Naive realists often promote a concept of truth based on the theory of correspondence (correspondence theory of truth), employ the metaphor of representation (of purported independently existing entities in the knowing mind) or also, when dealing with the gradual approximation of the pole of truth, the image of gradual unveiling; i.e. they conceptualise knowing as a labour of revelation; a veil is removed — and what one sees is the naked truth.

Solipsistic epistemologies, in contradistinction to realist ones, belong to the contrary set of epistemological extremes: they undermine realism by negating the existence of the very objects for which realism claims unconditional apprehension. They believe that everything is chimerical, a product of the individual mind which cannot but be the ultimate point of reference. The existence of the world itself is called into question. The solipsists support the thesis of total cognitive loneliness: they consider it impossible to prove that the entities populating their minds actually exist. Solipsists are alone with themselves and their ideas.[8]

Between these extremes,[9] which have only been roughly and crudely sketched out here, lies the epistemology of constructivism — an interdisciplinary school of thought, a set of research interests, postulates and concepts, with strong scientific, especially biological, roots and of specific

---

5   Media-external reality means in this context: the event in its supposedly still undistorted form or *gestalt*.
6   Quoted in Glasersfeld (1996), p.26.
7   Roth (1997), p. 340 (author's emphasis).
8   From the constructivist point of view, solipsism can be repelled by adopting the so-called relativity principle that provides an argumentative structure by means of which one can speak (and this is the decisive aspect) in observer-dependent way about the existence of an external reality. A more rigorous analysis of the minority position of solipsism in the present context appears dispensable to me; cf. the relevant discussion in Foerster/Poerksen (2002), pp. 26ff.
9   I shall deal in greater detail especially with realist epistemologies in the course of the argument of this book. They are fundamental for the self-conception of journalists, as has already been indicated by the quotation from Klaus Bresser.

relevance to the understanding of realities generated by journalism and media. The proponents of this school of thought emphatically reject representationist theories and realist concepts of perception. They consider objective knowledge unattainable in principle and categorise the question of the existence of an external world that both realists and solipsists seek to answer (albeit with contrary results) as a problem of metaphysics: the decision in question, therefore, concerns an ultimately undecidable question because any attempt to answer it will inevitably remain linked to an observer.[10] Whether or not there is an observer-independent reality unavoidably leads to assertions that can never be definitively corroborated.

The following passages are intended to introduce constructivist thinking by way of an introductory survey. This seems indispensable — despite the large number of similar introductions already published — because constructivism has in the meantime differentially grown into a multitude of constructivisms. It is therefore necessary to establish one's own position within this complex situation, to present variants and ways of justification entwined in the relevant discourses, in order to reach a comprehensive picture of the essential figures of thought that sustain the structure of the entire discourse. These figures of thought (e.g. the orientation by the observer, the abandonment of absolute ideas of truth, the postulate of the autonomy of the knowing subject) are of decisive importance to my own argument: they constitute the reservoir of inspirations and impulses that are apt to throw a totally new light on central concepts of journalism studies and the corresponding university didactics.

The following passages will also show how and in what way these proposals and suggestions have been debated within the professional camp: a typology of the critical objections that have been advanced against constructivism — rightly or wrongly, justified or not — is intended to help avoid certain mistakes and eliminate unproductive distortions. In conclusion I shall summarise the fundamental problems associated with the development of a constructivist theory (the problem of self-contradiction; the problem of constructivism turning itself into a dogmatic ideology; and the problem of practice-relevance), and I shall try to provide ways and means of solving these problems in order to advance my own theory work.

2. Variants of Constructivism

A Formal Definition of Constructivism

Practising science implies trying to solve problems in a method-controlled way. Constructivist observing implies, one may add, to confront the prob-

---

10 See Foerster/Poerksen (2002), pp. 152ff.

lem of knowledge *in a certain way and manner,* and with reference to *some entity or other,* and to try to solve it[11] — by means of a great variety of diverse approaches and methods. In one of the more illuminating definitions, constructivism appears, quite in keeping with the present reflections, as the attempt to clarify, '*how an instance/a place /a unity X generates a reality Y or several realities Y1-Yn* (builds up, generates, composes).'[12] The constructivist core problem, i.e. the observation and analytical description of the genesis of reality as a process, is more or less identical. However, the designation and delimitation and finally the exact examination and investigation of that 'instance X' — focus and attractor of the observations in question – are of extraordinary diversity. 'X' may be specified in many different ways, and the concrete specification indirectly betrays the discipline of a scientist or scholar and reveals different approaches to the justification of constructivism in its totality.

A rough distinction may be drawn between epistemologies based on *naturalism* and epistemologies based on *culturalism*:

> Naturalist constructivists occupy themselves with the construction of reality via perception, brain, consciousness or cognition, their disciplines being biology, physics and psychology. Culturalist constructivists explore the construction of reality via language, communication, media, culture and society.[13]

Such a distinction may appear somewhat surprising at first because constructivist authors, from the outset, have launched their offensive with the claim that what singled out their epistemology was its consistently pursued and practised programme of naturalising epistemology.[14] Any and all representatives of constructivism should consequently be expected to profess naturalism and argue accordingly; this is, however, not the case. On the contrary, we face a plethora of programmes and concepts based on naturalism and culturalism, which may be assigned to philosophy, in particular the philosophy of language, to psychology and the theory of communication, to cybernetics and, in particular, second order cybernetics, to

---

11 It must be noted that I shall not deal with all the different varieties of constructivism. Mitterer's non-dualism, having in the meantime become a subject of intensive debate (see Mitterer 2000a for an introduction), will not be allotted a special chapter section. In the present context, I see non-dualism as the radical (self-) application of constructivist thinking to constructivism itself. Mitterer executes de-ontologisation with utmost consequence. He radicalises the self-application, probes the construction of constructivism, amongst other things, and describes it as the self-contradictory handling and exploitation of ontologically interpreted dualisms like subject/object, image of reality/reality etc.
12 Weber (2002b), p. 24 (author's emphasis).
13 Ibid., p. 23.
14 On the naturalisation of epistemology see Fischer (1992, p. 20) and the reference to the work of Willard Van Orman Quine.

biology and, in particular, neurobiology and, finally, to the sociology of knowledge.[15] They will all be introduced in what follows.

Philosophical Foundations

Constructivists well-read in the history of philosophy (e.g. Ernst von Glasersfeld) have busied themselves with erecting a kind of ancestral gallery: they have been able to show that elements of constructivist thinking can already be found in the work of the early sceptics in the first century B.C. Already in those ancient times, philosophers had put forward the basic argument that it was obviously impossible for a perceiving human being to step behind its perceptions or to step outside itself in order to compare the product of its perceptions with the original entity in its still untouched and undistorted state. It was therefore impossible to create an image of a reality that was independent of human beings. Whatever could be stated at all was inevitably determined by human perceptual and conceptual functions; an emphatically conceived test of falsification was doomed to fail for these very reasons alone.[16] Further prominent philosophical prompters were, amongst others, Giambattista Vico, Immanuel Kant, the later Ludwig Wittgenstein and the linguist Benjamin Lee Whorf,[17] who advocated the linguistic determination of the perception of the world.[18] From the perspective of an informed reconstruction of relevant ideas in the history of philosophy and especially the philosophy of language, constructivism appears to be a kind of epoch-specific variety of scepticism. However, there is a critical proviso: even the doubts voiced by prominent philosophers and the corresponding quotations from authorities do not prove that the doubts they cast upon knowledge are justified and that the reasons given for such doubts are sound. The doubts voiced are merely illustrated, possibly made plausible, but they can certainly not be considered to have been verified by a montage of quotations that, in addition, obscures historical and cultural differences in favour of epistemic similarity.

---

15   Constructivism in journalism and communication studies is the subject of a special chapter section.
16   Cf. Glasersfeld (2002), p. 48.
17   See Glasersfeld (1996).
18   In the famous collection of essays *Language, Thought and Reality*, Whorf (1956, p. 221) introduces his so-called 'linguistic relativity principle': '...which means, in informal terms, that users of markedly different grammars are pointed by their grammars toward different types of observations and different evaluations of externally similar acts of observation, and hence are not equivalent as observers but must arrive at somewhat different views of the world.'

Psychological Foundations

The *psychological foundation of constructivism* derives primarily from the schema theory of the psychologist Jean Piaget[19] and the work carried out and published in connection with the so-called Palo-Alto group with its close links to therapeutic practice.[20] Jean Piaget understands learning, put in very simple terms, as the result of the continual confirmation or disappointment of patterns of expectations, so-called schemas, that are developed in the course of socialisation. The rules abstracted from the regularities of the experiential world are applied persistently although they do not always fit. (Jean Piaget concentrates on the genesis and development of models of reality in childhood). The continual confirmation or disappointment of expectations appears to be meaningful for the process of learning, in any event, because it allows for the stabilisation or transformation of schemas, i.e. the assimilation or the accommodation of the subject.

> *Assimilation* means that the acting subject recognises a given situation as one with which it has associated a particular action or operation although an observer may perceive it to be different. *Accommodation*, on the contrary, designates a reaction of the subject that may occur whenever the result of an action does not match the expectation of the subject. Surprise or disappointment may then lead to a change of action schemas or to the formation of new schemas. In both cases the behaviour of the subject is changed through experience, and one may then speak of "learning".[21]

This means: cognitive change and learning, this is the central assumption, are here understood as the result of the disappointment of an expectation, which is caused by the fact that a schema does not produce the expected result. The ensuing perturbation elicits an act of accommodation, which again restores equilibrium.[22]

The school of Palo Alto, formed around therapists like Don D. Jackson and Paul Watzlawick, also influenced by the work of the anthropologist Gregory Bateson, shares a common goal with the constructivist theorists of learning: the observation of the construction of reality. Its special characteristic is, however, that it does not only seek to observe the emergence of images of the world and of concepts of reality but expressly aims to change pain-inducing patterns of communication and conflict-generating forms of interaction — e.g. through the re-interpretation of symptoms, paradoxical interventions, methods of circular questioning etc. Such a situation, combining practice-oriented and pragmatically directed investigation and theory development, involving at the same time the con-

---

19 See Glasersfeld (1996).
20 Cf. e.g. Watzlawick (1993).
21 Glasersfeld (1997), p. 168. (author's emphasis).
22 Glasersfeld (1996), p. 121.

stant oscillation between concrete vision and abstraction, has quite obviously proved to be extremely productive. Numerous concepts in communication theory—evidently focussed on the communication between individuals—have resulted from the work of the constructivist and systemic inspiration of these therapists. One may only mention the so-called axioms of communication, the discovery of circular patterns of communication, the systematic orientation by interpretations (= realities of the second order in the sense of Paul Watzlawick) and not by truths.[23]

Cybernetic Foundations

A type of cybernetics,[24] re-formulated in terms of a theory of the observer, the so-called *second order cybernetics*, has also been of decisive influence on constructivist thinking and the systems theory of Niklas Luhmann. It breaks with the control and regulation euphoria that was once widespread among cyberneticians, connects the observer with what is to be observed, and analyses the logical and methodical problems which inevitably arise from the observation of the observer, the cognition of cognition, the understanding of understanding. The ur-principle of cybernetic thinking is incorporated in the figure of circular causality, which was intensively explored and made operational for cybernetics by the mathematician and physicist Heinz von Foerster, the founder of the cybernetic variety of constructivism.

What second order cybernetics really means—a dynamic style of thinking, operating creatively with paradoxes and circular theorems—becomes comprehensible in all its complexity only when the history of this meta-discipline is re-examined and re-told, a history that was fundamentally determined by the so-called Macy-Conferences (1946–1953).[25] The vision of the cyberneticians of the first generation did not only encompass the construction of sensory prostheses and the manufacturing of gadgetry for purposes of war, teleological mechanisms and patterns of circular causality. It also pursued much more fundamental projects, in particular the detection of the functioning of living beings, their simulation and eventual replication. The 1943 paper by Warren McCulloch and Walter Pitts, 'A Logical Calculus of the Ideas Immanent in Nervous Activity', which deals with the reception and transmission of impulses by neurons, was expected, it was believed at the time, to permit a logical formalisation of

---

23 Cf. for an introduction: Watzlawick in conversation with Poerksen (2004d).
24 Cybernetics may quite simply be characterised as the science of control in the most general sense. See Winter (1999), p. 125.
25 In this connection the book by Heims 'The Cybernetics Group' (1991) is of interest; a more epistemologically focussed reconstruction is given by Foerster/Poerksen (2002, pp. 101ff.); Pias (2003) has quite recently published all the extant protocols of the Macy-Conferences in a bilingual edition.

neuronal activity.[26] And as the brain consists of neurons, which are connected with each other by synapses and axons, one believed to have found a possibility of the logical-technical reconstruction of the brain. The metaphor of the computer that later shaped cognitive science and represented human beings as information processing systems, thinking as data processing, the brain as a giant parallel computer, and memory as a storage device, is a result of those developments. Accordingly, nobody was unduly worried by the nonchalant talk about building an 'electronic brain'.[27]

It was Heinz von Foerster, who first posed the seemingly innocuous question in this context of cybernetics: What does one need in order to understand a brain? The answer: a brain. The theory, which is required from this point of view, turns out to be circular. It must meet the claim to describe itself; the strict separation of a subject from an object, on which first order cybernetics was based, disappears. In second order cybernetics, the observer and that which is to be observed appear to be inseparably enmeshed. Against this background, Heinz von Foerster's proposed definitions of the two types of cybernetics become comprehensible: first order cybernetics is to be understood as the cybernetics of *observed* systems because the observer is not part of what is observed. Second order cybernetics, by contrast, is the cybernetics of *observing* systems.[28] The dualism of observer and observed is thus eliminated; one has become fully aware that, when observing, one may become one's own or somebody else's object of observation.

Biological Foundations

Biologically, in particular neurobiologically, grounded conceptions of constructivism attracted attention—especially at the onset of the science-internal debate.[29] Heinz von Foerster, for instance, repeatedly highlighted the undifferentiated coding of stimuli and used this long-known phenomenon that sensory cells do not code specifically to substantiate the plausibility of constructivist insights. Only a small part of the already greatly reduced mass of external stimuli that reaches us is finally transformed into the unitary language of neuronal impulses.[30] The specificity of an impulse then results, according to Gerhard Roth, from the topology of the brain or the brain site where the stimulus materialises: these sites of brain activity determine the modality, the quantity, and the intensity of a

---

26 On the significance of this paper cf. Foerster/Poerksen (2002), pp. 105f.
27 See Foerster/Poerksen (2002), p. 107.
28 Winter (1999, pp. 121ff.) provides a detailed comparison of first and second order cybernetics.
29 These proposals will only be mentioned without any further discussion of details.
30 See Foerster/Poerksen (2002), pp. 17ff.

stimulus.[31] Humberto R. Maturana has introduced the concept of autopoiesis (self-creation) as the central criterion of the specifications of life. Living systems form, according to his assumptions, a network of internal and circularly interwoven processes of production, which distinguishes them as unities by continually producing and maintaining them and their autonomy in this manner.[32] Humberto R. Maturana also developed a kind of bio-epistemology.[33] He claims that the nervous system of a living being is operatively closed.[34]

> The nervous system operates as a closed system of changing relations between neuronal states of activity that continually lead to other changing relations between neuronal states of activity. For its operation as a system, nothing else exists but its own internal states. Only observers can distinguish between inside and outside or input and output and can, consequently, diagnose the impact of an external stimulus on internal processes and the organism or, conversely, an impact of the organism on the external world.[35]

According to this conception, cognition can no longer be viewed as the faithful representation of an external world but must be understood as a process of internal construction exclusively governed by principles of its own.

There is, finally, the concept of structure-determinism, which also derives from Humberto R. Maturana, a kind of *systemic grundgesetz* that is closely linked with the constructivist epistemology. According to this assumption, all systems are structure-determined; this means: whatever is happening inside them is necessarily determined by their structure and cannot be determined by anything like external influences. Effects may be

---

31 See Roth in conversation with Poerksen (2004e). (It may be noted in passing that Roth is arguing not only as a constructivist but also (!) as a realist. He combines both positions: he talks about the construction of reality in the brain but simultaneously (pre)supposes the brain to be something real, assigning it to a given world that is independent of the human mind.)

32 This concept has been adapted and promulgated by systems theory, especially in sociology (and thus not in Maturana's native discipline of neurobiology).

33 Maturana's work is, in my view, characterised by four stages. He begins as an empirically oriented biologist and publishes on topics of *neuro-anatomy*. He then develops a *bio-epistemology* that revolves round the question of how a living being generates and produces its own world (autopoiesis). When his critique of the ideal of objectivity and the fanatic quest for truth is published, he enters a stage of *bio-ethics*. He describes how the belief that one is in the sole possession of absolute truth, a belief that is biologically unwarranted, leads to the suppression of dissenting people. In a fourth stage, he occupies himself with the universal foundations of humanness, a kind of *bio-anthropology*: the concern here is the recognition of the other, the fellow human being—Maturana speaks of love—as the basis and foundation of human coexistence and communal living.

34 The counter image and contrasting foil of this view is the assumption that the nervous system is an open system. Accordingly, the receptors react to the excitation by external stimuli and these are then processed and as a result lead to more or less faithful mappings of the real world.

35 Maturana/Poerksen (2004), p. 62.

released externally but they are inevitably specified internally, i.e. inside the system and strictly according to its structure.[36]

To summarise at this point: the core idea of all these varieties of constructivist thinking deriving from biology or neurobiology might perhaps be condensed into the idea or ideal of the autonomy, the self-government by system-specific laws, of the cognitive system. Whether one deals with the neutrality of the neuronal code, the processing of stimuli and the specification of impulses by the topology of the brain, whether one analyses the autopoiesis of living systems, the (operative) closure of the nervous system and the structure-determinism of all systems — one always describes a hiatus between an external and an internal world and focuses the attention on the execution of constructions within a system.

Foundations by the Sociology of Knowledge

The *fundamental questions of the variety of constructivism grounded in the sociology of knowledge* are: how does a self-produced social order arise and how does a social reality gradually harden into stable social arrangements that are then experienced as static and as resulting from natural laws of growth? To answer these questions, Peter L. Berger and Thomas Luckmann, in their classic (1979), illustrate with numerous examples how cultural learning works, how behaviour becomes habitualised and typified, how individual experience is objectified and, under particular circumstances, collectified (in the form of stories and tales), and how the once hardened arrangements of the social order are legitimated.[37] 'One might also say' Karin Knorr-Cetina succinctly summarises,

> that social constructivism attempts a clarification of the ontological status of social reality by recourse to its *pre-history*. It refers to processes and mechanisms (like habitualisation, typification) which, as it were, represent the genealogical *prerequisites* of the existence and experience of a social order as an objectified order.[38]

In this view, reality arises within the framework of a society — and this means that individuals must be seen as entities that can be formed by their society and their surrounding culture. They observe with the eyes of their groups, they see the world against the background of their origins, they are certainly not monads but they can be influenced, in any event, and they are extremely susceptible to external impressions. Thus, to take up a conceptual suggestion by Heinz von Foerster, the *one brain problem* of brain

---

36   This very broad conception of structure and structure determinism in the sense of a universal principle is extensively discussed in Maturana/Poerksen (2004), pp. 69ff.
37   I think it is important to note that both authors do not see themselves as constructivists and, surprisingly enough, do not want to consider their explanatory scheme as a contribution to epistemology: they insist that they practise empirical scientific research, in particular sociology, but not epistemology. Cf. Berger/Luckmann (1997), pp. 14f.
38   Knorr-Cetina (1989), p. 88 (author's emphasis).

research, in particular of the variety of constructivism inspired by neurobiology, turns into the *two brains problem* of education and, finally, into the *many brains problem* of society[39] — so that the necessity arises to mediate between these two variants of constructivism. Integrative conceptions will have to explain how the thesis of cognitive autonomy can be reconciled with the assumption of formative social conditioning and imprinting.[40]

3. Figures of Thought in the Discourse of Constructivism

Productive Heuristics

Despite all these differences with regard to the methods of justification and despite the diversity of the originating and contributing disciplines, the discourse of constructivism is lent contours and coherence by a set of mutually enmeshed figures of thought, postulates and leitmotifs. These figures of thought furnish it with structures and limits. There are three reasons why it is useful to examine them more closely in a comprehensive survey.

1) From the point of view of the philosophy of science, the status of constructivism can be made even clearer in this way as being 'a hybrid being between the poles of super-theoretical or paradigmatic remoteness from empirical domains, and middle (or even lower) range theories that are fully capable of empirical implementation'.[41]

2) A set of figures of thought does not exhibit the compulsory character of a fully fledged mature paradigm but it is — at least in my understanding— rather more like a well stacked toolbox or better still, to formulate it in greater conformity with scientific standards, like a productive heuristics: one helps oneself to whatever one needs whenever necessary, one may flexibly choose particular postulates for dealing with particular problems (and can neglect others for the moment) and can thus try to find out how far this will take one.

3) These very figures of thought and the concepts and key terms associated with them will be used as inspiring suggestions for the theory of journalist education to be be presented here. The concrete relevant figures of thought are the following: the preference of *how*-questions (as opposed to *what*-questions), the orientation by the observer, the abandonment of absolute conceptions of truth, the special appreciation of the differential quality and the plurality of reality constructions, the postulate of the autonomy (of cognition), and the interest in the circular figures of thought. All these characteristic motives of the

---

39 Foerster (1993a), pp. 343ff.
40 Cf. the pertinent discussion in Schmidt (1994) under the title: 'Cognitive autonomy and social orientation.'
41 Weber (2003a), p. 26.

discourse of constructivism will now be introduced by way of a survey.

From the What-Question to the How-Question

The core concern of constructivist authors consists in a fundamental re-orientation: the centre of attention must no longer be held by ontologically intended *what- questions* but by epistemologically understood *how-questions*. The goal of all investigative efforts is a re-orientation from being to becoming, from the essence of an entity to the process of its genesis. It is the conditions that make a reality emerge and actually realise it, which are of prime interest. From such a perspective, nothing can be seen as immutable and simply given; everything can be related to its particular genetic history and be explained with reference to it. Reality is strictly the result of processes of construction. Now ordinary language seems to suggest that construction is a process that is under conscious control, the implementation of voluntary and perhaps even capricious decisions. However, the concept is, as a rule, not really used in this sense. The construction of reality does not appear to be a planned and mindfully directed process, it is not an intentional act of creation, but a process triggered and multiply conditioned by the interaction with a concrete environment, which is shaped by biological, sociocultural and cognitive factors. Construction refers to 'any form of *cognitive-social operation*.'[42] In a formula: 'reality construction rather happens to us than that we would control it'.[43]

Orientation by the Observer

The *orientation by the observer* is always of decisive importance for the entire discourse. Every act of cognition, one assumes, rests upon the constructions of an observer — and not on the more or less exact correspondence of perceptions with an observer-independent reality. The postulate of the relativity of observation takes central place: 'Any kind of knowledge is merely an observation and exists relative to the categories of a particular observer.'[44] The operation of observing may formally be specified — following the logic of distinctions as developed by George Spencer-Brown and adapted and elaborated by Heinz von Foerster and Niklas Luhmann[45] — as the introduction and further processing of distinctions

---

42 Ibid., p. 186 (author's emphasis).
43 Schmidt (1995), p. 240.
44 Baraldi/Corsi/Esposito (1997), p. 101.
45 One could of course claim that these considerations are essentially inspired by systems theory in its modern version as a theory of differences, and that it is therefore not reasonable to classify them as elements of constructivism. This requires two general comments: for one, this book does not distinguish with the same rigour as happens in other publications between classic constructivism and Luhmann's operative constructivism (see Luhmann 1994a, p. 10). However, one particular difference must indeed be especially emphasised. The orthodox

and designations.⁴⁶ Constructivism thus appears to be 'a theory of distinctions'.⁴⁷ In the *unmarked space*, the space still 'unharmed' by distinctions, an observer draws distinctions and so separates a marked state from an unmarked state.⁴⁸ Accordingly, any observation starts out with an act of distinction, which prepares the ground for the designation,

> and introduces a fundamental asymmetry: one can now consider only the one or the other side of the distinction, continue one's operations only here or there and then again apply the distinction to oneself (re-entry).⁴⁹

To observe, therefore, means to distinguish and to designate. Whenever one wants to designate something and then further describe it, one must first decide on a distinction. With the difference between *good* and *evil* – quite independently of the topic chosen – one can observe something different from the distinction between *rich* and *poor*, *new* and *old*, or *true* and *false*. 'Draw a distinction', we can read in Heinz von Foerster's writings, 'and a universe comes into being.'⁵⁰

This means: the choice of the initial distinction is taken to be a fundamental operation of thought, which, in correlation with other distinctions and designations, creates realities that we assume to exist in an external space detached from ourselves. By the distinction chosen, by this ur-principle of reality construction, all observers are connected with what they distinguish, and through the ways and manners of their descriptions, they also unavoidably always produce elements of self-description, which may then potentially motivate other observers to carry out investigations and assessments.

Drawing a distinction, Francisco Varela writes with great precision,

> we separate phenomenal forms from each other that we then take to be the world itself. On the strength of this, we then insist on the primacy of the role of the observer who draws distinctions at any arbitrary spot. On the one hand, these distinctions create our world; on the other hand, they reveal just this: the distinctions that we have drawn [...]. In finding the world as we do, we forget all we did to find it as such, and when we are reminded of it in retracing our steps back to indication, we find little more than a mirror-to-mirror image of ourselves and the world. In contrast with what is commonly assumed, a description, when carefully inspected, reveals the properties of the observer.⁵¹

---

interpretation of systems theory, which has essentially been shaped by Luhmann, insists that all talk about agents must be eliminated, and that communication must be seen as an autopoietic framework of reproduction. Such a position does not appear to be adaptable for journalistic practice and cannot therefore be accepted in this context.

46 A comprehensive introduction to the theory of distinctions of these authors is Winter (1999).
47 Schmidt (1994), p. 20.
48 Cf. Weber (2003c), p. 204.
49 Schmidt (1994), p. 21.
50 Von Foerster (2002), p. 15.
51 Varela (1975), p. 22.

Furthermore, this means: whoever observes the observations of observers, i.e. practices observation of the second order and asks themselves, *how and by means of what distinctions these observers organise their reality*, will realise that every act of perception inevitably obscures a massive residual world of potential perceptions. All seeing is simultaneously blind. When one sees something, one does not see something else; when one observes something, one does not observe something else. Every observation contains a blind spot, in the very process of distinguishing it remains blind for the chosen distinction, which only reveals itself to an observer of the second order who, as a matter of course, equally has a blind spot. Observation of the second order, too—and this is now actually the genuine constructivist perspective—is admittedly itself understood as an observer-specific construction that cannot claim a privileged access to an absolute reality. In the case of self-observation, finally, an operation is carried out that is formally identical with an observation and still appears different: on the one hand, self- and other- observations are grounded in operations of distinction, on the other hand, reflective meta- and self-observations again and again also deal with themselves as objects and observe —operating as observers—their own observations.

Parting Company with the Absolute

If knowledge is strictly coupled with the individual cognitive subject and its peculiar mode of cognition, if the observer, the observed, and the operation of observing can only be imagined in circular linkage, then the craving for certainty is undermined, any claim to knowledge becomes relative, and a further leitmotif of constructivism is made manifest: *parting company with absolute ideas of truth*, and parting company with an emphatically construed ideal of objectivity. This is made plain by realising that one of the qualities of an objective description is that the properties of an observer do not enter into it, do not influence and determine it. The foundation of any kind of judgement—according to this classic-realist understanding of objectivity—is ostensibly situated outside the observing person; it is thought that what is observed can be separated from the observers, their predilections and interests, their cognitive strengths and weaknesses. Heinz von Foerster's cryptically aphoristic definition of objectivity— another key statement of constructivism—can only be appreciated fully against this background: 'Objectivity', he says, 'is a subject's delusion that observing can be done without him.'[52]

The separation of observer and observed is thus called into question, and the observer is consequently established as the factor that cannot be eliminated from any cognitive process.

---

52 Von Foerster (2002), p. 3.

Interest in Difference

Reality in itself — understood as the referential basis of so-called objective descriptions – inevitably changes, if these reflections are accepted, into a multitude of realities, which again entails a specific *interest in difference* and the *plurality of reality constructions*. In this connection, constructivists argue along dual tracks, as it were: epistemologically, on the one hand, and with ethical intentions, on the other. Following epistemological insights one describes, on the one hand, the plethora of possible perceptions of the world, reconstructs their realisation from a biological or sociocultural perspective, observes observers when observing. On the other hand, the protection of difference and the prevention of dogmatism of any kind and shape are considered important ethical concerns; certainties are therefore criticised because they make alternatives of thought and action invisible. At this point Heinz von Foerster's ethical imperative may be quoted: *'Act always as to increase the number of choices.'* [53] Enlarging the number of choices leads, according to this line of argument, to greater freedom of choice and therefore boosts the opportunities of responsible action.

Autonomy and Internal Determination

The discussion of the process of cognition reveals a central basic idea: one might call it the *postulate of autonomy*. Talking about self-regulation and self-control, about self-organisation, (operative) closure and structure determinism, about phenomena like circular self-reproduction (autopoiesis[54]), the transmission of impulses in the organism and the processing of stimuli in the brain, generally shows one thing: the descriptions, in some way or other, always recur to the concept of autonomy — not in the sense of (cognitive) freedom and not in the sense of total environmental independence, but in the sense of an internally directed determinism that may be irritated from outside only according to internal rules and laws. Autonomy does not imply arbitrary or wilful modes of reaction , nor closure in a physical sense: impermeability of such a kind for matter and energy would be fatal. Autonomy means: self-sufficient rule, transformation of attempted extrinsic control into system-typical modes of reaction that make extrinsic control appear as self-control or self-government. The relationship with the environment is, according to this assumption, regulated by the internal mode of operating of the system itself as long as it exists. Such a system is dependent upon what the environment supplies, but it is independent of that environment with regard to the ways and

---

53 Foerster/Poerksen (2002), p. 37 (author's emphasis).
54 Consequently, I understand autopoiesis — in strict correspondence with Maturana – as the specific way and manner in which *living systems* realise their autonomy. Autonomy is thus the more general concept. See Maturana/Poerksen (2004), p. 106.

manners of the processing of external influences. The consequences of an input are determined by the system's specific modes of operating.[55]

The Argument About Circularity

The knower and the known, the observer and the observed, appear inseparably entwined. And it is this circular view of the process of cognition that indicates another topos of constructivism: the *interest in circular and paradoxical figures of thought*. This interest manifests itself in the intensive debate of the phenomenon of *recursion*.[56] This means feeding the generated output of a system back into this system as a new input; the product of an operation is subjected to the same operation, the product of that operation is again subjected to the same operation, and so on. In this way eigenvalues are created.[57] The principle of circularity is also part of the foundations of the concept of autopoiesis: it is, in a very precise sense, the strictly circular self-reproduction of something out of itself.[58] It also emerges when dealing with the concept of *autology*, which means: a concept requires itself in order to be defined.[59] Communication requires communication in order to be specified, consciousness requires consciousness in order to be topicalised, knowledge presupposes knowledge in order to be observed etc. The constructivist key concept of *self-reference* similarly reveals a circular process as it designates the 'relations between operations and events within a defined system (e.g. of thoughts or communications in psychological or social systems) with themselves.'[60] Finally, the extraordinary interest of constructivist authors in paradoxes must be mentioned: paradoxes are the product of circularity (more precisely: of self-reference) in the domain of two-valued, classical Aristotelian logic.[61] There have been various attempts to transcend this kind of logic: the construction of a many-valued logic (Gotthard Günther), a paradoxically organised logic (George Spencer-Brown), and the theoretical integration of self-referential propositions (an example is the *autologic* by Lars Löfgren).[62]

---

55 A very precise description of these relationships is given by Willke (1987).
56 For a definition see also Weber (2000a), p. 84.
57 Eigenvalues—stable values also in the social domain—are described by von Foerster by means of mathematical analogies as the result of circular, in particular recursive processes. See Foerster/Poerksen (2002), pp. 60ff.
58 See also Weber (2000a), p. 86.
59 Ibid.
60 Ibid.
61 Just think of the well-known 'Cretan-paradox', which consists of the following constellation: the Cretan Epimenides asserts that all Cretans are liars. If what he says is correct then what he says cannot be correct. The statement becomes false if one takes it to be true, and it becomes true if one takes it to be false. See Foerster/Poerksen (2002), p. 114.
62 See the summary by von Forester in: Foerster/Poerksen (2002), pp. 115ff.

4. Anatomy of a Debate: Accusations and Reservations

Irritations and Criticism

If one wants to employ constructivism, i.e. the figures of thought, premises and postulates presented here, for the observation of journalism, then this entails first and foremost: parting company with traditional conceptions of journalism in a well-reasoned way. It will still have to be shown in detail that one must keep a clear distance from ontological views and say goodbye to realist concepts of journalism as an enterprise geared towards the representation of an observer-independent reality. Recourse to absolute standards for the assessment of the quality of journalistic products is no longer admissible.[63] Linear models of communication and communication effects, which involve omnipotent journalists and media, powerless recipients, and a direct transfer of information, must be subjected to revision: they negate cognitive autonomy, neglect the individual as the prime instance of processing of media offers, and generally work with a trivial conception of communication.[64] Ideologies of inherited gifts and mythologies of talent ('The born journalist!') have lost their persuasive power because journalistic constructions of reality can and must, according to the constructivist perspective, always be referred to multiple factors of influence. Constructivist considerations change the understanding of *interpersonal communication*; they encourage the specific *interpretation of journalism* and they are, furthermore, of importance to the *investigation of communication and media effects*.[65] The user-oriented approach is thus given an epistemological foundation, and the much-debated key question as to what human beings do with the media and what peculiarities of a media offer are actually acted upon and made use of by particular recipients in a specific situation, is once more brought up to date.

One may therefore note, as this rough sketch suggests, that the postulates and premises that define the constructivist discourse are of great consequence – but the actual research and planning results will not yet be presented here in detail. It is of great importance to make the underlying theoretical position as precise as possible before moving on. For this purpose, the debate in journalism and communication studies will be summarised; the accusations and reservations voiced in this debate require thorough critical analysis and comment before constructivism – relieved of burdening misunderstandings – may be implemented in a theory of

---

[63] See comprehensively Weischenberg (1993).
[64] Großmann (1999), p. 25.
[65] For a survey see Weber (2003b), pp. 190ff.

journalism education and as an epistemology of journalism studies.[66] The reconstruction of criticism is therefore, one might say, an attempt to place the specific proposals in a discursive field, so that they may *also* serve as a reaction and a response to legitimate criticisms and objections.

First a few reference data with regard to the history of the discussions. The dispute about the so-called *Radical Constructivism*,[67] which was at times conducted in an extremely contentious and robust manner, was sparked off by the radio college course on 'Media and Communication' (1991/1992). It became the dominant subject of an annual meeting of the leading professional association in Germany, the Deutsche Gesellschaft für Publizistik und Kommunikationswissenschaft,[68] it decisively affected the reception of the volume 'Die Wirklichkeit der Medien [The reality of the media]',[69] and found its further repercussions in the professional journals 'Medien und Kommunikationswissenschaft' (previously 'Rundfunk und Fernsehen [Radio and Television]'), 'Publizistik' and 'Communicatio Socialis'.

The debate is noticeably marred by a series of grave misunderstandings, legitimate and unjustified objections, which must all be taken up, discussed and, ideally, be eliminated in order to avoid as far as possible potential traps within the argument and theory work proposed here. From the enormous diversity of publications a catalogue of accusations may be distilled, which are still current today and which will now be tackled according to the following pattern: I shall first quote the accusation, then provide an assessment of its justification, and will finally offer and characterise possibilities of a solution.

The Accusation of Trendiness

The *charge that constructivism is nothing new and merely an intellectual fashion* has been put forward by a variety of authors. Calling knowledge into question, it is argued, pervades the entire history of philosophy, as is very well known. To voice and promote the claim of a paradigm change is, therefore, an unwarranted exaggeration. Quite in keeping with the spirit of such considerations, Hermann Boventer[70] notes that the 'discontent with unreflected claims to objectivity and true knowledge has infused the entire history of philosophy since the time of the pre-Socratic thinkers.' His article is entitled: 'The journalist in Plato's cave.' Lutz Hachmeister

---

66 The kaleidoscope of accusations and reservations advanced towards this school of thought is the expression of a number of fundamental problems of constructivist theory formation, which will be the topic of the next section of the chapter.
67 This conceptual designation that originated with Glasersfeld (1996) has not really become generally accepted. Radical constructivism means: epistemology without ontology.
68 Bentele/Rühl (1993).
69 Merten/Schmidt/Weischenberg (1994).
70 Boventer (1992), p. 157.

asserts by way of a thesis that 'the axioms of constructivism' are part of the 'hardly controversial stock of knowledge of the humanities and the social sciences'.[71] And he goes on to say:

> That the cognitive system of human beings structures and categorises impressions of the senses, 'reality' and, consequently, communicative environments, has been a matter beyond dispute no later than Kant and Schopenhauer. The problem whether there exists a reality that is independent of individual sensory perceptions and intersubjective conventions, counts among the contentious philosophical issues ever since the beginning of systematic epistemological analysis and reflection.[72]

Roland Burkart, in his article (entitled: 'Old wine in new skins?') draws the final conclusion: 'in essence, all this is not new.'[73] And Hans Mathias Kepplinger writes:

> Constructivism is just one of these scholarly fashions, and like all these fashions it comprises a lot of intellectual knick-knacks but also a number of correct insights. The fascination engendered by these insights has less to do with their originality than with the fact that they were obviously neglected by earlier fashions of thought.[74]

Such a form of criticism all too easily overlooks, however, that even 'old' theses may exercise a productive influence on scientific knowledge if they are re-introduced in a new guise and in a different, possibly more contemporary and zeitgeist-adequate language: they may make phenomena appear in a new light and supply occasions of thought that can help to clarify the core concepts of a professional field or discipline. And the reproach that what is offered is nothing at all new does not take into account that the protagonists of constructivist discourse (take, for instance, only Ernst von Glasersfeld, 1996) have never ever been inclined to suppress the commonalities with sceptics, Kantians and neurobiologists. On the contrary, similarities have constantly been highlighted — occasionally without pointing out relevant differences — and even quite directly presented as arguments in favour of constructivism. It should be emphasized, however — and this concerns those advocates of constructivism who argue from the history of philosophy as well as the critics of constructivism — that certain conclusions that appear superficially comparable are possibly connected with modes of reasoned justification that rest on completely different foundations involving epoch-specific properties, and cannot, consequently, be taken to entail deeper-rooted conformity. One may, of course, claim, for instance, that constructivism is closely related to Immanuel Kant's epistemology. One must, however, in this case be prepared to refrain from any

---

71 Hachmeister (1992), p. 12.
72 Ibid.
73 Burkart (1999), p. 62.
74 Kepplinger (1993), p. 118.

facile adhering to the flattering shallow consensus with a shining figurehead of European thinking; one must, moreover, acknowledge that profounder scrutiny of Immanuel Kant's work proves that his considerations are directed at the *transcendental subject*, whenever he discusses the inevitable conditioning of all perception and the impossibility of knowing the absolute (the 'thing in itself'). By contrast, the constructivists maintain emphatically that they concentrate in their research work on the *empirical subject*, that they seek to describe the observer-dependence of all knowledge, and that they, therefore, claim quite the opposite, namely that all talk of a 'thing in itself' (and thus equally of an observer-independent reality, even though it may be specified as being unattainable) is meaningless. The existence of a 'thing in itself', for instance, cannot be verified in any possible way because we can only speak of it in dependence on our own individualities and perceptions.[75]

We can affirm, therefore, by way of a general summary, that the question of whether constructivism is 'new' or 'old' can only be decided in connection with the specific perspective of an observer. If one wishes to establish similarities, then differences will have to be neglected. If one asserts sameness, then one is nevertheless forced—in a specious historical argumentation—to argue a-historically because neither the pre-Socratic philosophers nor Immanuel Kant nor Arthur Schopenhauer were acquainted with the findings of neurobiology, nor are Chilean neurobiologists necessarily familiar with the European tradition of the critical analysis of rationality. If one diagnoses distinctions, then one must make clear what they consist of. As I have been trying to show by way of effective examples, they lie in the radicalism of finally coming to terms with the observer-relativity of all knowledge, and they manifest themselves in the fundamental difference between a scientifically and empirically oriented discipline and the domain of a primarily reflection-based philosophy.

The Accusation of Exaggeration

The opinion is voiced repeatedly that no one in the field of communication studies would still seriously support the views of some kind of naive realism, and that no one would speak of a mapping of reality by the media or avow the dignity of absolute truth for their research results. The implication seems to be that the defenders of constructivism are arguing, with great public appeal, against a position based on the belief that newscasts represent or supply images of reality. The critics admit, however, that for-

---

[75] 'How can we claim to know of the existence of that absolute reality and at the same time assert its unknowability? This is just an absurd kind of conceptual acrobatics because all talk about that supposedly independent reality is inevitably dependent on the persons talking.' Maturana/Poerksen (2007), p. 27.

mulations 'of such simplicity can hardly be encountered any longer.'[76] One tries to make one's mark, therefore, by erecting straw dogs and operating with twisted images of the opponents' positions, 'which are all too easy to criticise but are hardly ever seriously advocated in communication studies.'[77] Naïve realism is just such a straw dog—easy to discredit but ultimately irrelevant to the professional debate. Constructivist authors have responded to the accusation that they are directing their criticism at *exaggerations* and caricatures, by insisting on their view that the professional self-image of journalists is still permeated by epistemologically naive realisms. The moderate versions of epistemic realism that seem to be prevalent in the communication studies of the German-speaking countries, which are derived from evolutionary epistemology (Konrad Lorenz) or critical rationalism (Karl Popper), must ultimately be rooted in a kind of naïve realism if they want to remain consistent: they are all connected with the idea of the gradual approximation of the one and only absolute truth.

Konrad Lorenz holds the opinion that there has to be a systematic connection between our perceptions and the real world. His argument is that the perceptual apparatus of humans has adapted itself in the course of evolution through constant and, in the extreme case, fatal trials and errors to the reality of what is given; this adaptation in the process of evolution is then, with a further leap of thought, identified with a gradual approximation of the *thing in itself*. Constructions that clearly fall short of reality would simply be destroyed by the mechanism of selection—and therefore one can assert: 'The adaptation to specific conditions of the environment is equivalent to the acquisition of information about these environmental conditions.'[78] Karl Popper considers the ultimate verification of a hypothesis to be a cognitive impossibility, and he is in this respect asserting something similar to constructivism, but he still assumes that the continual test of falsification will lead to an approximation to an ultimate truth—and he therefore turns into the representative of a variety of realism that may again definitely be referred back to an extreme position. For mere reasons of logical consistency, it may be argued, the gradual approximation of the truth is bound to involve epistemologically naïve realist conceptions if it is to avoid remaining nothing but a speculative assertion. For in order to clarify whether some partial knowledge of the absolute and an approximation of the truth have been successful, one must definitely compare this partial knowledge with the truth itself. This very comparison of alleged knowledge and absolute reality, however, presupposes the possibility of apprehending the absolute truth—how else could the thesis of truth approximation be resolved? The argument is, therefore, that one can only

---

76 Bentele (1993), p. 156.
77 Neuberger (1996), p. 238.
78 Quoted in Glasersfeld (2002), p. 51.

sustain the ultimate truth goal of all knowledge, however far off it may be, if one essentially sticks to a realist position.[79]

The Accusation of Confusing and Misleading Terminology

The accusation of exaggeration is formulated whenever two of the core concepts of the entire constructivist discourse are focused upon: the construction and the invention, of reality. Günther Bentele considers 'the central metaphor'[80] of the construction of reality to be a confusing and extremely simplistic concept and writes:

> Neither earthquakes nor hunger catastrophes, nor train accidents, burglaries, chemistry accidents or summit meetings, are *constructed* by the media. What is actually "constructed" is the manner of reporting these events, which leads to a form of reality in its own right, i.e. to a media reality.'[81]

Christoph Neuberger argues that the concept of construction is 'used in a variety of ways' and is thus a 'source of misunderstandings'.[82]
Hermann Boventer articulates his disapproval of the popular breezy quasi-scientific talk of an 'invented reality' as well as the concept of the 'invention' of reality.[83] The discomfort being articulated in this way has meanwhile come to be accepted as justified even by constructivist communication researchers. The very key concept of construction has remained unclarified for far too long; it seemed to suggest that one could rig up worldviews methodically and with specific goal-orientation and invent realities according to one's particular tastes. The popular book title 'The invented reality'[84] and other key slogans[85] have certainly generated unnecessary confusion in this connection. One may therefore agree with Siegfried J. Schmidt: it is necessary to stop exploiting popular metaphors for purposes of excitement and irritation because they have proved to be unproductive in the end.[86]

One can abandon the unquestionably misleading concept of invention without any substantial loss of insight as it renders the construction of reality arbitrary and intentional and as resulting from the creation of an autonomous mind.[87] The concept of construction should be reworked,

---

79 Cf. Glasersfeld (2002), p. 56.
80 Bentele (1993), p. 160.
81 Ibid., 161 (author's emphasis).
82 Neuberger (1996), p. 192.
83 Boventer (1992), p.161.
84 Watzlawick (1994).
85 Remember only Heinz von Foerster's dictum (1994, p. 40): 'The environment as we perceive it is our invention.'
86 Schmidt in conversation with Poerksen (2004f), p. 144.
87 Whenever Foerster speaks of 'invention', he is actually concerned with an ethical dimension, namely the responsibility of the individual pleading for a particular view of reality. Thus,

particularly in the analysis of journalism, into a conceptual set of instruments that could help to make individual steps and variants of construction processes visible. As will be discussed later with respect to ethical questions, these variants are to be placed between extreme values such as a construction of reality that takes place unconsciously and involuntarily, a potentially conscious reality formation, a conscious staging, and finally a conscious and targeted invention of reality. It will thus become possible to distinguish precisely between epistemological universal statements (example: One cannot *not* construct)[88] and trendy theses that must be corroborated empirically (example : we can observe an increasing tendency to stage media reality). The difference that is made perceptible in this way arises between the poles of an epistemological time-independent apriori and a gradualised concept, between the universal statement (following the pattern: 'always, inevitable...') and a trend diagnosis (following the pattern: 'evermore, increasing...').[89]

The Accusation of Arbitrariness and the Post-Modern 'Anything Goes'

The *charge of arbitrariness* rests on the equalisation of epistemological and ethical-moral relativism: the subject- and observer-dependence of perception is interpreted as the description and justification of arbitrariness. If all knowledge is made dependent on individual expediency, if the apprehension of the world can be realised largely at any individual's will, this kind of misguided interpretation of constructivism claims, then there can no longer be any reliable standards with which to judge the quality of media offers; the basis of journalistic work is destroyed epistemologically, as it were. Constructivism discards 'a concept of reality' that

> constitutes the foundation of journalistic work, a concept of reality that entails that reality exists for the most part independently of journalists, and that it is the task of journalists to capture that reality adequately and to represent it truthfully and as completely and comprehensibly as possible.[90]

Against such expostulations, two objections must be raised. For one, constructivist authors have forcefully defended the thesis—which will have to be dealt with extensively later—that it is the very observer-dependence of all understanding, which can serve as the justifying basis of an individual-related ethics of responsibility. This means nothing less than a turning of the tables, i.e. the direct assertion that it is the

---

invention really means: recognition of responsibility. Nevertheless, I think that the concept is not a happy choice in this connection because it suggests an argument of an epistemological nature (and not one related to an ethical stance). On this discussion, see Foerster/Poerksen, 2002, pp. 49f.

88   I owe this formulation to conversations with Stefan Weber.
89   See Weber (2001), p. 32, with great clarity.
90   Bentele, (1993), p.159.

realist concepts of knowledge that allow for the repudiation and delegation of responsibility, that make it possible to depersonalise one's perceptions and thus to extricate oneself clandestinely from the affair, to declare oneself an uninvolved observer. Only a constructivist position that acknowledges that we are ineluctably personally involved in all our knowledge products leads to a proper recognition of individual responsibility.

Furthermore, it must be doubted, as a matter of principle, that we need emphatic ideals of truth to prevent us from drifting off into arbitrariness and laisser-faire. 'Alone for pragmatic and psychological reasons', Siegfried J. Schmidt argues, for instance,

> there must always be some sort of evidence with whose help queries and misgivings can be confidently and thus successfully interrupted or arrested for a while. Uncontested certainties are quite sufficient here; we do not need objective truths that (can) actually only possess the status of such uncontested certainties, anyway.[91]

The Accusation that Constructivism Endangers the Practice of Journalism

The accusation of arbitrariness frequently goes hand in hand with the concern that especially the work of journalists would be put at risk by constructivist ideas: one is wary of *a particular threat to journalistic practice*. Hermann Boventer claims to observe a 'systematic de-moralising of the media and their practitioners'[92] as the result of epistemological indoctrination, and diagnoses 'disastrous effects'[93] on the practice of journalism if it should commit itself to the programme of constructivism. 'Inasmuch Radical Constructivism dismisses the postulate of journalistic objectivity', Ulrich Saxer writes in a similar vein,

> it damages an indispensable element of a democratic culture of communication and, moreover, the development of journalistic competence, in an important respect. It opens the floodgates for journalistic sloppiness in dealing with facts as well as for self-opinionated journalistic self-righteousness. It defends argumentatively the self-centredness of journalistic settings — which is declared to be inescapable — at the expense of the journalists' attention to their audiences, recognises journalistic manipulation as a normality and, moreover, even justifies theoretically the partially media-induced collective loss of reality in complex societies.[94]

The worry is that the concept of objectivity will finally be dissolved in the course of, and due to, an epistemological discussion — and that this disso-

---

91 Schmidt (2000), p. 61.
92 Boventer (1992), p. 164.
93 Ibid.
94 Saxer (1992), p. 182.

lution will then be understood as an invitation to forgery, manipulation, and lies.[95]

The logical pattern underlying all these concerns may be sketched out in the following way. According to constructivist doctrine, knowing subjects cannot say anything about an observer-independent reality. This doctrine will possibly in time come to be accepted by journalists and other professional communicators and inspire or encourage the attitude that the unrestrained arbitrary production of knowledge is the norm. In the resulting climate fakes, distortions, and manipulations will consequently become ordinary strategies of utterance, which can then no longer be disqualified on the grounds of professional ethics.[96] The first premise of such concerns is that epistemologies — of whatever kind — have the power of controlling everyday activities in a most direct and immediate manner.[97] The second premise implies that constructivists possess sufficient authority and influence to indoctrinate the practitioners and corrupt professional standards. The third premise, as already indicated, consists in the thesis that the abandonment of absolute truth necessarily legitimates arbitrariness and laisser-faire. But constructivists do not share this presupposition, either. On the contrary, they have been trying hard to provide a constructivist re-interpretation of the ideal of objectivity, to re-analyse practically-pragmatically the grand cognitive *ideal of truth* and to develop and introduce adequate substitute concepts. This discussion has made great progress in the meantime and has produced several new conceptual designs. They will be dealt with in detail later.[98]

The Accusation of Perspectival Foreshortening

In the critical discussion by professionals within the field of communication study, the further charge of *perspectival foreshortening* is raised, i.e. the charge that all matters are reduced to the perspective of the individual. In the wording of Ulrich Saxer: 'Constructivists extract themselves from *the situation of increasing uncertainty with regard to what is happening on the macro-level* by explicitly retreating to the individual and its cognition.'[99] Due to this kind of reductionism alone, constructivists are held to be inca-

---

95 Zschunke (2000), p. 103.
96 Acordingly, the interview forger Tom Kummer is, in the eyes of some critics of constructivism, a practising constructivist (see Ernst 2000, p. 65 and Hömberg 2002, p. 296) — a misunderstanding and a cheap offer of exculpation, which cannot but heartily please Kummer. The epistemological justification of fraud (Kummer knew what he was doing) is an expression of imprecise thinking because it mixes the level of the epistemological discussion illegitimately with the level of ordinary convention.
97 Cf. the distinction between a relationship of *stimulation* and a relationship of *derivation* described in the next section of the chapter.
98 See the chapter on raising ethical awareness.
99 Saxer (1993), pp. 65f. (author's emphasis).

pable of grasping the 'totality of a social phenomenon'[100] like public communication, which is defined macro-, meso- and micro-sociologically. The theoretical construction is, therefore — in terms of the chosen correspondence-theoretical metaphor — deficient as to its 'similarity of structure' and 'isomorphism'[101] with reference to its object of inquiry. The constructivist approach, therefore, necessarily remains blind to everything that goes beyond the narrowly delimited horizon of a microsociologically defined perspective; the occupational reality of the majority of media workers remains outside the field of vision. An accusation of this kind might perhaps apply to the prehistory and the early history of constructivist thought, which concentrated on the individual organism and the individual brain because of its primarily biological/natural-science orientation, but it overlooks the particularly fruitful later developments in journalism and communication studies. Since the beginning of the 1990es, the trend clearly points towards an integrative approach that no longer conceives of cognitive autonomy and social orientation as incompatible.

The conception of a 'sociocultural constructivism'[102] and the synthesis of systems-theoretical and constructivist considerations[103] represent just two examples of widely received research work from German-language communication studies, which makes the interface between individual and system its point of departure. Such work compensates for many a perspectival bias of the early phases of constructivist work. Broadening the field of vision, one can clearly see that the present theoretical work is definitely guided by ideas indicating an integration of different approaches; there is the tangible goal to resolve contradictions and to emancipate one's work systematically from the original, primarily biological-natural-science, conceptions.[104] There is the observable trend that might — ironically — be characterised as a *weakening of Being*[105] the de-ontologisation is radicalised in the direction of a mode of thinking, which is carried out without foundation and seeks its paradoxically specified justification in unjustifiability, and its stability in instability.

---

100 Saxer (2000), p. 89.
101 Ibid.
102 Schmidt (1994), p. 19, presents this conception and the associated change of paradigm in the following words: 'My plea for a more intensive occupation with questions of cultural studies is based on two arguments: the discourse of radical constructivism has so far been subject to a one-sided scientific orientation, it requires an expansion into cultural studies.'
103 Scholl/Weischenberg (1998).
104 See for instance also Weber 2000b, p. 455ff.
105 This formulation appears in another context in: Varela/Thompson/Rosch (1995), p. 311.

The Accusation of Solipsism

Constructivists have naturally been *accused of solipsism*: the world is supposed to be 'only a creation of self-referential systems', exclusively 'designed by observers',[106] only 'will and representation'.[107] The focal point addressed by the criticism is the 'solipsistic neglect of an observer-independent reality'.[108] Should such thinking gain ground in journalism, not only would forgery and manipulation be considered legitimate, but all criticism of the media, which is after all based on the comparison of (absolute) reality and media reality, would lose its foundation and the relaxing of professional standards would lead to calamitous consequences. 'On the practical-journalistic level of discussion', it is said,

> the constructivist approach makes it impossible to distinguish unambiguously between degrees and properties of reality content (and thus quality), between gutter-journalism and the serious journalism of quality papers. If all these are merely *constructions* of realities, if concepts like truth and objectivity are equally relinquished, if those constructions are nothing but communication offers that can only be judged by criteria like credibility (and not by whether they are actually offering true or false information), then all possibilities of proper criticism are eliminated, particularly the criticism of shoddy journalistic work.[109]

Constructivistically arguing communication researchers have countered this kind of attack by pointing out that it is not *the* comparison of realities as the basis of all media-critical efforts that becomes invalid but only the kind of craving for falsification that is explicitly or implicitly linked to a realist foundation, a craving that insists on being able to compare the distorted media reality with *'the (absolute) reality'*. This is to say that one cannot, for instance, use the data and realities of particular social systems (e.g. science, justice, health) in order to falsify a specific media reality in an absolute sense, or perhaps even verify it, because we are in every single case dealing with constructs and not with observer-independently given manifestations of an unconditionally valid reality. Naturally, constructivistically arguing communication researchers would admit that one can, of course, contrast different realities—and most certainly with specific critical intentions.[110] Media criticism *as such*, therefore, will not become superfluous or meaningless but merely one of its particular manifestations, namely the sort of realist media criticism that privileges particular observer perspectives, ontologises them and proclaims them to be eternal truths.

---

106 Saxer (1993), p. 70.
107 Saxer (2000), p. 89.
108 Saxer (1992), p. 179.
109 Bentele (1993), p. 163 (author's emphasis).
110 Weber (2002a), p. 80.

The Accusation of Self-Contradiction

The *accusation of making self-contradictory assertions* emerges in all the debates about constructivist issues, both within the field of communication studies and outside. One version is the following:

> Of course, from the point of view of the theory of knowledge, this theory cancels itself out; if human beings cannot know reality in itself, then Radical Constructivism cannot be empirically corroborated either.[111]

This kind of objection touches upon one of the fundamental problems of constructivist theory development, as will be shown in more precise detail presently. One can only tackle it successfully by rejecting the concept of ultimate validation, clarifying the status of empirical knowledge from a constructivist perspective, and maintaining comprehensive transparency with regard to the position that there can be no final proof and no observer-independent justification for constructivist theses. Biology and brain research can in no way claim to be the trailblazers for the verification of constructivist assumptions; they can make them plausible, they can illustrate them, they can supply relevant *indications*, but they cannot *prove* their truth in a categorical sense. Constructivism is in itself only a construction (among many others); it cannot be tested for its absolute truth but only for its utility, its viability. The most important thing is to develop effective procedures and assumptions, which will serve the purposes of particular observers. One must find out whether one manages to move on, whether one's theses and theories prove to be productive. Hans Rudi Fischer formulates succinctly with regard to the adequate architecture of constructivists theories, 'Scepticism that is consistent must remain free-floating, unreasonably justified or reasonably unjustified; if it does not it will lose its charm and turn into dogma.'[112]

5. Fundamental Problems of Constructivist Theory Development

The reservations and accusations described may essentially be reduced to three fundamental problems of constructivist theory formation, which can be grouped around questions and difficulties of self-application and the practical implementation of constructivist thoughts. These problems must be dealt with in a more exact fashion before the actual work of making them operational in the professional field can be attempted. The scheme of presentation will follow a simple pattern: I shall first explain the specific fundamental problem (1. the *problem of self-contradiction*, 2. the *problem of self-dogmatisation*, 3. the *problem of practice-relevance*) and then suggest pos-

---

111 Saxer (1992), p. 179.
112 Fischer (1993), p. 96.

The Problem of Self-Contradiction

The *problem of self-contradiction* has to do with a contradiction between one's own premises and the claims to validity that are put forward *explicitly* (in the form of direct statements and assertions of truth) or *implicitly* (e. g. in the form of a particular use of language). The basic constellation generating this problem may be circumscribed as follows. Whenever constructivistically arguing authors claim absolute truth for their assertion of the impossibility of attaining absolute truth, they turn themselves into meta-dogmatists and become entangled in a paradox that may be couched in the formula: If they are right they are wrong (and vice versa). For 'if there were unconditionally valid evidence for their theses, it would have to consist precisely in the very absolute truths that the realists have been looking for.'[113]

Already the use of a language permeated by impersonal (i.e.: apparently observer-unspecific) turns of phrase betrays a fundamental problem. Conventionally formulating researchers whose styles exclude stories and parables, creative metaphors and the depiction of personal thinking experiences and who, in particular, tangibly banish their personal selves from their texts, must inevitably appear to write in a language that at least strongly suggests claims to objectivity.[114] Such language, when used by constructivists and other sceptics, creates a paradox, which we might term a *rhetorical self-contradiction*. In a case of *logical* self-contradiction, statements are logically incompatible. ('The truth is that there is no ultimate truth.') The concept of the rhetorical self-contradiction, however, is meant to indicate that the chosen manner of expression, the diction, does not match the meaning of the assertion that one is making. One suggests authority and advances claims to finality and ultimate certainty, which one cannot at all justify if the original self-formulated premises are still adhered to. One insinuates, by virtue of the stylistic means employed, both the possibility of ultimate validation and objective description while, at the same time, disputing them on the content level by using a kind of diction, a jargon of irrevocability, that is incompatible with the fundamental

---

113 Schmidt in conversation with Poerksen (2004f), p. 144.
114 Kretzenbacher (1995, p. 34) considers the language of science to be characterised by three taboos (ego-taboo, metaphor-taboo, narration-taboo), all of which make the observer invisible: 'The ego-taboo suggests that knowledge exists independently of a human subject and that a scientific utterance can be transmitted independently of particular communication partners. The metaphor-taboo suggests that a fact of science can only be represented in one and only one quite specific way because it can only be perceived in one and only one way. And the narration-taboo suggests that, in the texts of science, the facts speak for themselves and do not require a human subject as a mediating instance.'

assumptions that were originally invoked. These original assumptions could actually be expected to inspire other, less constrained and especially observer-linked, modes of presentation and discourse.

However, paying particular attention to techniques of presentation and specifically chosen forms of language reveals something else, i.e. that the assertion of a self-contradiction frequently results from the terminological imprecision shared by opponents and supporters of constructivism alike. Mutual understanding and inter-professional communication are hampered enormously by the fact that terms like 'truth', 'reality', 'actuality' etc. are used in so many divergent ways. More drastically: terminological imprecision has generated a form of misinterpretation that may be called the *problem of referential confusion*. In the diagnosis of self-contradictions, statements referring to an (imaginary and observer-dependent) absolute reality/truth/actuality etc. are all too often confused with statements that are admittedly and expressly created within given frontiers of knowledge, i.e. that are meant to apply to the spheres of life-realities and experiential worlds.[115] Whenever constructivists assert in the course of a consistent argumentation that truth and reality are unknowable because observer-independent knowledge is impossible, then this means: *within the present discourse* one refers to a (absolute) reality/actuality/truth, i.e. one constructs per communicative means a *discourse of the other world* within the *discourse of the here and now*.[116] It does not mean, however, although the lack of precision in some constructivist discourse may all too often suggest it, that we can suddenly somehow reach out beyond our life-world and our own experiential reality and can feel capable of saying with ultimate certainty: knowledge of truth is impossible, must be impossible. This would indeed be, as we can now clearly affirm, self-contradictory speculation, pure metaphysics; the reality test of any assertion, from a constructivist perspective, will always and inevitably remain an internal test, situated in what is accessible only to ourselves alone: our own life-reality, our own experience.[117]

---

[115] Several authors have pointed out to me, however, that the concept of reference that I am using here is not compatible with the basic assumption of constructivist epistemology because theories of semantics are generally founded on realist epistemologies. The notion of reference, i.e. the act of referring to a portion of reality, applies according to that assumption only if that portion *actually* exists. And that means that the question of reference (and therefore of referential confusion) can be decided only if one has definitely clarified whether the objects and persons, the states of affairs and properties, actually exist and actually exist according to the given description. From a constructivist point of view, this concept of reference must be rejected. The object of reference must strictly be coupled with the referring observer. Cf. in another context e.g.: Hannappel/Melenk (1990), pp. 185ff.

[116] That dualisms like *reality* and *experiential reality* represent hidden realisms of the constructivist discourse, has been convincingly elucidated by Mitterer (2000).

[117] Cf. Luhmann (1994), p. 10.

The Problem of Self-Dogmatisation

The *problem of self-dogmatisation* arises when constructivism (or any other school of thought) becomes increasingly dominant and is eventually even promoted to serve as the ruling paradigm within the discourse of a professional field or discipline; it also arises whenever a philosophy with outsider status is turned into a fashion and is, in certain publications, even attributed the properties of a *weltanschauung* or a doctrine of salvation.[118] Such popularity is deeply problematical for a school of thought that by its very nature is opposed to all petrifaction of thinking because naturally even a relativistic epistemology may harden into new norms, fashionable creeds, and compelling dogmas.[119] Should this happen, then it cannot be changed because one cannot control how and in what ways particular thoughts are received and exploited. Still, and although such developments cannot be controlled and influenced, one can try as best one can to design and label one's theoretical framework in such a way as to prune the problem of self-dogmatisation as well as possible.[120] The intention here is therefore to designate the position advocated as *discursive constructivism* with six core characteristics:

- It is a variety of constructivism that endeavours to escape from dogmatic self-petrifaction through the radical self-application of its own premises. Discursive constructivism defends itself against any form of dogmatisation, even against the dogmatisation of constructivism by having recourse to specific disciplines (e.g. neurobiology). Discursively oriented constructivists may employ a diversity of perspectives as potentially viable inspirations. Their value is not decided by the degree of approximation to reality but by their individual and situation-specific viability.
- Discursive constructivism is a variety of constructivism whose (perhaps even primary) goal is the dissolution of mental rigidity and prejudice (and thus the creation of new possibilities and opportunities of thought). This attempt to explore a justification of this position will be called the *argument of antipodal legitimacy*. By this is meant that the discursive kind of constructivism ought to be understood primarily as a practice-relevant epistemology that attains its proper function within

---

118 As no personal polemic is intended here, I shall temporarily suspend the good old tradition of stating the precise reference.
119 For this very reason Krippendorff (1993, p. 19), amongst others, criticises the concept of constructivism itself; in his opinion, the term connotes — like any other '-ism' — some static and ultimate form of world contemplation.
120 Accordingly, I can understand Schmidt's ' re-writing of constructivism', published in 2003, as an attempt to deal with the problem of self-contradiction and self dogmatisation. Schmidt presents the comprehensive conception of a completely process-oriented philosophy that eliminates all the residual realism of constructivism (e.g. in the form of explicitly or implicitly ontologised dualisms) . His rewriting of constructivism could actually be considered as a particularly consistent form of its (self-) application.

specific constellations: it will be directed against certainties, against dogmatic claims to objectivity, against ideological fixations. It will serve as a corrective. One orients oneself systematically — by way of direct reaction — towards observable one-sidedness; one's own one-sidedness becomes legitimate whenever it reacts antipodally, as it were, to another kind of one-sidedness and thus, in the sense of a discursive dialectics, makes intellectual movement possible. Discursive constructivism does not aim at ultimate truth or unconditional consensus; it serves discourse itself, the continuation of dispute, debate and analysis, the refining capabilities of discrimination, the stimulation of thinking processes. As soon as the liquefaction of a static reality is accomplished, the strategies of discursive constructivism have fulfilled their task.[121]

- Discursive constructivism is an ordering hypothesis (never leaving the cognitive-mental aggregate state of the hypothetical), it is the manifestation of a moving search and will always maintain the character of a parasite: it preys, if you will, off the distinctions that are supplied by its counterpart. It is existentially dependent on such a counterpart whose intellectual rigidity it can correct by means of its own strategies in order to help new opportunities of perception to arise. In brief: the point is to observe something that someone else does not observe in order to alert that someone to blind spots.

- Such an attitude encourages the thorough appreciation of irritation and a kind of reflection that is *essayistic* in the precise sense of the word. Irritations must accordingly be understood as opportunities of learning and changing, must be accepted as means of stimulation that prevent forms of perception from becoming rigid by encouraging reflection and differential thinking.[122]

- Discursive constructivism is a variety of constructivism that becomes effective in and through direct encounters. As will become clear later on, it is a non-linear meta-theory of learning and teaching, which changes role models and self-images, transforms solutions into problems and answers into questions, that takes an experimental attitude towards the plethora of varying situations and that is constantly in need of design. In a formula: the point is to inspire and to irritate but not to dictate.

- Discursive constructivism does *not* involve an explicit plea for a particular worldview, for instance a specific kind of journalistic agenda, a particular conception of the most pressing objectives of the profession. Its primary concern and goal is not to prescribe contents (normatively) but much rather to reveal the multitude of opportunities of choice, the contradictions, paradoxes and aporias of the professional journalism,

---

[121] See in this connection also the stimulating essay by Stäheli about 'poststructuralist sociologies', which is driven by the question of how sociology can deal theoretically with what ' threatens to throw its conceptual schemata into disorder ' (Stäheli 2000, p. 9).

[122] See Bardmann (1991a), p. 7.

and thus to allow the individual journalists to make their own decisions. This means: discursive constructivism is a collection of tools for thought with whose help the niches for individual responsible action within the constraints of the system of journalism and media can be sought out and established. It is not a worldview filled with content.

The Problem of Practice-Relevance

Constructivism, one may state, is on the way to becoming *normal science*. The philosophical debate of fundamental questions is increasingly being replaced by attempts to develop concrete, discipline-specific adaptations and applications. To date, educational theory and didactic methodology, psychology and psychotherapy, management science and communication study seem to have profited most from constructivist considerations, or have actually accepted them and concretised them according to the demands and needs of their fields.[123] These are all disciplines and fields of application, which are in some way or other occupied with 'bringing about changes in human beings', i.e. with tackling the question of how to transform methodical attempts of external control into internal programmes of self-control that are then actually executed.[124] However, the *problem of practice-relevance* as such has not really been adequately discussed in any one of these disciplines. This is to say that nobody has addressed the question, and certainly not with proper attention to its foundations, of how the relationship between epistemology and everyday life, between theory and practice, between a (trans-disciplinary) school of thought and its discipline-specific concretisation and pragmatically viable adaptation, should be spelled out in detail. It seems indispensable, however, to accomplish some sufficient fundamental clarification of this problem before the actual work of concretisation and adaptation is undertaken, because only the adequate clarification of this problem can help decide what the basic potential for change is that one is prepared to ascribe to, and perhaps even confidently to expect from, constructivist declarations. With regard to this relationship between epistemology and everyday life, one might envision the construction of a kind of ideal-type typology of the circumstances that can be characterised more precisely with the aid of the conceptual pair description/prescription. Descriptive statements describe; prescriptive statements prescribe, i.e. they demand something that still appears to be unrealised, or as yet only incompletely.[125] My own thesis is that we must distinguish between relationships of *derivation, exclusion,* and *inspiration*. These are the possible conceptual models that capture the relationships

---

123   Scholl (2002) p. 12.
124   Foerster/Poerksen (2002, 65ff.) gives a survey of important impulses in these fields.
125   Weber (1999, p. 59ff.) presents his critical analysis of the variants of constructivist epistemology in media and communication studies in a comparable systematic way. I owe his systematic analysis decisive inspiring insights.

between epistemology and everyday life. I shall now characterise them more precisely in what follows.

- Pleading explicitly or implicitly for a *relationship of derivation* presupposes the following assumption: the epistemological insights (of constructivism) lead to immediate consequences with regard to everyday practical activity. An epistemology is bound to regulate any kind of practice. One can definitely state, therefore, what is propagated in some of the popularised accounts of constructivism. For instance: there is no ultimate truth (epistemological universal statement), consequently nothing is absolutely certain (life-practical consequence); we invent reality (epistemological universal statement), consequently everything is possible (life-practical consequence); absolute values do not exist (epistemological universal statement), consequently we must come to terms with total arbitrariness (life-practical consequence).[126] And so on.

- If one insists on conceptualising the relationship between epistemology and everyday life as a strictly linear-causally organised relationship of derivation, and thus chooses to solve the problem of practice-relevance in this rather extreme manner, one can do this — systematically expressed — with descriptive or prescriptive intention, or also conceivably with a combination of description and prescription. One can say that the relativity of all knowledge will inevitably *lead* to new insights and modes of action in everyday life (type 1, description). One can demand that the epistemological insight into the relativity of all knowledge *should lead* to new insights and modes of action (type 2, prescription). And one may, finally, deplore the fact that the insight into the relativity of all knowledge has *not yet sufficiently regulated* thinking and acting in everyday life, and that *this should now be undertaken with greater effort* (type 3, combination of description and prescription).

- The possibility of conceptualising the relationship between epistemology and everyday life that I have somewhat circuitously called the *relationship of exclusion*, constitutes an extreme position (similar to the relationship of derivation). One proceeds from a strict separation of epistemology and everyday activity. Supporters of this view assert the thesis that the two levels are not connected and must, therefore, be kept strictly apart. Constructivism is exclusively viewed as a theory of

---

[126] An exemplary formulation by a communication researcher, which implicitly supports the *relationship of derivation*, may nevertheless be cited here. 'The realisation of the closure of the cognitive apparatus', one may read in Merten (1993, p. 53), 'warrants the compelling inference that objectivity is nothing but an operative fiction.' And furthermore: 'As realities are inevitably constructed' (Merten 1993, p. 54), 'their authenticity is irrelevant: reality constructions cannot, therefore, be tested for their truth but only for their efficiency.' Assertions of this kind, which unite epistemological insight and life-practical consequences in such a direct and immediate manner, lend some justification to the accusations of arbitrariness as voiced by the critics of constructivism. Formulations of this kind are, to say the least, bound to be extremely misleading.

Premises and Postulates   47

the second-order observer, which allows for the reconstruction of reality constructions but has no relevance for everyday life practice of whatever kind in the sphere of first-order observation.[127] In this case the distinction between description/prescription does not really contribute very much to a further clarification. From the descriptive as well as the prescriptive perspective, it can only be stated that the epistemological reflection is of no significance for everyday activity and that it should not be permitted to gain significance for the world of everyday life.

- Between these two extremes lies a middle position that is advocated here and called a *relationship of stimulation*. It considers epistemological insights, models, conceptions and concepts, as *agents and instruments of inspiration and irritation* within some field of practice of whatever definition. These are in no way without effect but their actual impact or influence cannot be specified or spelled out in detail in every single instance. The premises and postulates focus attention, supply relevant distinctions, offer stimulation and inspiration, but do not permit the direct inference or even logical derivation of a given or desired kind of practice from them.[128] Thus, no unconditional, strictly defined causal relationship is presupposed. The connections are rather loose, more fragile, hazy, in no way compelling. The epistemological concepts and designs, which one would like to exploit profitably for one's practice and one's everyday activities, possess heuristic value. From this angle of vision, the assertions made by representatives of the *relationship of derivation* lose some of their (maybe exaggerated) stringency because epistemology and life-practice are not coupled in such an exclusive way. One is relieved of the need to prove direct and securely anchored correlations between theory and practice, between epistemology and everyday life, and between observations of the first and of the second order — something in all probability very difficult to achieve if at all. We are dealing here with requests for perceptions and searches, with incentives for observation,[129] which stem from the sphere of epistemological reflection and function as stimulating tools of orientation in the world of practical applica-

---

127 Bolz defends this position in a conversation with the author. See Poerksen (2002a), pp. 439ff.
128 Whenever constructivist postulates must be made operational in practice, another difficulty may arise that has often been observed in application-oriented projects (for a telling example see Winter 1999): it will here be called the *problem of the incantation of premises*. What is meant is that an author considers the clarification of the epistemological foundations of his project as the prime task of his activity — and that he does not or only in a very rudimentary form progress to a discipline-specific concretisation and actual application. And this implies, furthermore, in the sense of a self-critical interim-summary, that one must stop disputing and debating epistemological premises at some stage (as early as possible is usually best) — and that one should move forward and concentrate on working out the characteristics of the chosen domain of application under the guidance of the theory.
129 Cf., in another context and related to a constructivist ethics, Schmidt (2000), p. 65.

tions.[130] There is definitely no intention of defending the thesis that intellectual insight can and will necessarily unhinge and dislodge a conventionally established and valid pattern of action in a goal-directed manner.

- In this case, once more, three different kinds of patterns of argumentation and thinking are conceivable: One may assert that the relativity of all knowledge *inspires* (type 1, description) or *should inspire* (type 2, prescription) new insights and modes of action in everyday life. And the critical and perhaps plaintive comment would be that the insight into the relativity of all knowledge *has not yet sufficiently inspired* thought and action in everyday life, and that this *should now happen in greater measure* (type 3, combination of description and prescription). These patterns of thought and argumentation will be followed here — particularly when new conceptions of didactic procedures from a constructivist perspective have to be developed. Consequently, the ideal result of such an effort of thought appears defined; it is necessary to generate the new through the friction between abstraction and concretion, theory and practice, science and journalism, the observation of the second order and the observation of the first order: a practical theory, a kind of practice permeated by theory.

6. Recapitulation of the Argument

This chapter has specified in greater detail the foundation for the theory work in hand. Constructivism has been described more precisely in a threefold way: 1. as a transdisciplinary endeavour to solve the problem of knowledge in some way or other; 2. as an interdisciplinary discourse in which different activities and directions have developed; 3. as a set of ever-recurring figures of thought that lend structure and limits to constructivism, making it thus identifiable and recognisable. The pattern of description was designed according to a sort of contrastive principle: commonalities and differences, generally applicable questions and possible discipline-specific answers were described in turn. Then those accusations and points of criticism were described which have accompanied and, from time to time, determined the reception of constructivist theses in journalism and communication studies. The accusations were finally condensed into three fundamental problems of constructivist theory development — the problem of self-contradiction, the problem of self-dogmatisation, the problem of practice-relevance. The primary aim was always to assess the justification of these accusations and to work out possible ways and means of solving the fundamental problems, particularly in the form of newly coined concepts (rhetorical self-contradiction,

---

130 These requests for perceptions and searches are introduced here in an axiomatic way. They are — not necessarily — statements capable of proof but much rather rules of a game of consequence, as it were, whose effects are of particular interest. On this understanding of axioms, see Foerster/Bröcker (2002), p. 66.

the problem of referential confusion, discursive constructivism, a typology of the relationship between epistemology and ordinary life etc).

It was necessary to stress again and again that constructivism and journalism studies, epistemology and the concrete practice of education, should enter into a *relationship of stimulation*. This implies that constructivism is *not* simply a trivial programme for the generation of particular insights, modes of observation and learning effects, but that it is especially capable of achieving one thing: deepening the awareness for specific phenomena. Constructivism is a programme of inspiration and irritation, which can provide numerous stimulating offers for journalistic practice, for didactics and research work in journalism studies.

Surveying the relevant publications one may observe a *deeper critical awareness of scientific approaches and procedures* (a lessening of the naive faith in empirical data and the methods of scientific investigation), which can naturally be reflected and debated in the halls of a university. Furthermore, *deeper critical awareness of language* can be noticed (a determined effort to avoid emphatic assertions of truth and to question the implicit ontology of linguistic descriptions). Constructivist researchers in journalism and communication studies direct their attention to the specific properties of journalistic construction programmes, underline the increasing significance of media as generators of reality (*deepened awareness of the epistemology of the media*) and emphasise the observer-dependence of all perception. The fundamental disempowerment of claims to knowledge, and the highlighting of personal responsibility, have become essential inspirations for a *deepened ethical awareness*. Taken together, all these variants of deepened awareness represent the potential learning effects and possible learning objectives that might result from a constructivistically schooled scrutiny of the central contents of the field of journalism studies and the central competences of quality journalists. They will be described in the following chapters. The overall goal is to offer and spread materials, concepts and ideas, to delimit a field for reflection, to supply a framework of discursive debate and progressive analysis from which journalism studies and fledgling journalists may profit—in the sense of a more challenging training in thought and argumentation.

EDUCATIONAL OBJECTIVES

Chapter II

Deepening Critical Awareness of Science

1. The Inevitable Presumption: Indispensable Scepticism

History of an Experiment

In its issue no. 46/47, 1996, the American journal *Social Text*, a journal strongly supporting Cultural Studies, published an article whose appearance triggered an amusing scandal. The article was entitled 'Transgressing the boundaries: toward a transformative hermeneutics of quantum gravity'. Right at the beginning one could read:

> There are many natural scientists, and especially physicists, who continue to reject the notion that the disciplines concerned with social and cultural criticism can have anything to contribute, except perhaps peripherally, to their research. Still less are they receptive to the idea that the very foundations of their world view must be revised or rebuilt in the light of such criticism. Rather, they cling to the dogma imposed by the long post-Enlightenment hegemony over the Western intellectual outlook, which can be summarized briefly as follows: that there exists an external world, whose properties are independent of any individual human being and indeed of humanity as a whole; that these properties are encoded in "eternal" physical laws; and that human beings can obtain reliable, albeit imperfect and tentative, knowledge of these laws by hewing to the "objective" procedures and epistemological strictures prescribed by the (so-called) scientific method. But deep conceptual shifts within twentieth-century science have undermined this Cartesian-Newtonian metaphysics; revisionist studies in the history and philosophy of science have cast further doubt on its credibility; and, most recently, feminist and poststructuralist critiques have demystified the substantive content of mainstream Western scientific practice, revealing the ideology of domination concealed behind the façade of "objectivity".

The author concludes his essay with the complaint that to his day no 'emancipatory mathematics'[1] had yet been developed, and towards the end of his text formulates the following demand:

---

1   Sokal (2001a), p. 298.

> ... the fundamental goal of any emancipatory movement must be to demystify and democratize the production of scientific knowledge, to break down the artificial barriers that separate "scientists" from "the public". Realistically, this task must start with the younger generation, through a profound reform of the educational system. The teaching of science and mathematics must be purged of its authoritarian and elitist characteristics, and the content of these subjects enriched by incorporating the insights of the feminist, queer, multiculturalist and ecological critiques.[2]

The pages between the strange beginning and the passion-infused ending contain a whole lot of nonsense — presented, however, in a style that is in total conformity with scientific usage. The author of this product, the physicist Alan Sokal, brazenly dares to assert that the geometrical constant pi is a variable, that the theory of quantum fields corroborates the psychoanalytical insights of Jacques Lacan on the constitution of the neurotic subject, and that fuzzy logic fits leftist political theories much better than traditional classical logic. The editors of *Social Text* even let him get away with the claim that the bizarre new-age theory of the existence of morphogenetic fields (its originator is Rupert Sheldrake, a fairly marginalised figure in science) has been declared the guiding theory of quantum gravitation.[3]

As soon as the text had appeared, however, Alan Sokal raised his voice again. This time he offered a skilled debunking of himself, which the humiliated producers of the magazine now refused to print. Having received the article for publication they declared that the text did not meet 'the intellectual standards' of their magazine.[4] In the text that was then published elsewhere Sokal reveals that his essay on 'transformative hermeneutics of quantum gravity' was

> a mélange of truths, half-truths, quarter-truths, falsehoods, non sequiturs, and syntactically correct sentences that have no meaning whatsoever. (Sadly, there are only a handful of the latter: I tried hard to produce them, but I found that, save for rare bursts of inspiration, I just didn't have the knack.) I also employed some other strategies that are well-established (albeit sometimes inadvertently) in the genre: appeals to authority in lieu of logic; speculative theories passed off as established science; strained and even absurd analogies; rhetoric that sounds good but whose meaning is ambiguous; and confusion between the technical and everyday senses of English words.[5]

Places of Truth Production

The debate that followed in the United States of America and then also among European intellectuals revolved around the politicization and the

---

2   Ibid., pp. 294f.
3   See Boghossian (1997), p. 49.
4   Quoted in Sokal (2001b), p. 319.
5   Ibid., p. 319f.

truth status of science, the relativity or reality of knowledge, and the standards and conventions of publication in the specific environment of the humanities and cultural studies.[6] But as Alan Sokal and his academic colleague Jean Bricmont note in a book on these issues published after the affair, the debate also deals with the abuse of scientific terminology and the possibilities of intentional fraud as facilitated by the aura of exactitude and the prestige of the sciences.[7] The sciences are, in fact, viewed as places of truth production even by their critics: what a physicist has to say must be right or is, in any event, taken to be an especially ennobled kind of knowledge — and at least this seems to be what people believe. Until they are proved wrong by this very same physicist and exposed to the scornful laughter of the *scientific community*. One has, without doubt, been taken in by the 'effets par évocation d'un milieu'[8] and can now study their overwhelming effect: 'Quotations by experts are quotations by authorities.'[9]

Comparing — in a further step of the intellectual penetration of this pretty science parody — the cognitive situation of the *Social Text* editors with the cognitive situation of journalists, one may realise: they are essentially similar as far as the dilemma of forming a judgement is concerned, but they must definitely be assessed differently. Scientists — to put it simply — must certainly know their own field before passing judgement on the quality of a particular piece of research work. That they do not recognise a parody which touches upon their own specific competence is embarrassing; that they, when lacking the relevant competence, do not take the time to consult other experts is unprofessional; that they base their judgements about granting publication so obviously on prejudices and intellectual fashions merits criticism. Journalists cannot at all times be expected to possess the specialist expert knowledge and competence that is evidently required in a scientific environment; such a claim would be completely illusory and would not at all do justice to the professional constraint that journalists must generally be capable of commanding ad-hoc expert knowledge. Stated more forcefully, the implication is that the situation faced by the so artfully duped editors of that magazine is practically identical with the challenge potentially confronting *every* journalist. Journalists must assess sources that they cannot always evaluate on the basis of adequate expert knowledge; they must rely on data, methods and theories

6   It is important to underline here that not all conceivable aspects of that debate can be discussed in this context; Sokal must definitely be categorised as a vehement opponent of constructivism although one might argue that he has — surely against his will, and also certainly contrary to his effort to expose relativistic epistemologies as dangerous nonsense — by his very procedure staged a kind of experiment in social constructivism and the sociology of knowledge, which impressively confirms the defining power of prejudices, intellectual fashions and societal moods.
7   See generally Sokal/Bricmont (2001).
8   Bally quoted by Poerksen, U. (1988), p. 91.
9   Poerksen, U. (1988), p. 85.

whose origins and significance they simply cannot penetrate to the last detail in their hectic rhythms of production, the race for news, and the hunger for a scoop (the disclosure that creates a stir).[10] Journalists are necessarily dependent on the instant processing of enormous masses of text and have to rely on the statements of experts without being able to assess their reputation and the quality of their expert knowledge, because the time available for topicality-driven news coverage is always extremely scarce.

The inevitable presumption and, at the same time, equally inevitable necessity of judgement is made still more complicated by the fact that scientific knowledge has lost its epistemic un-ambiguousness in many quarters. It is no longer possible to weigh up clearly and unambiguously in every case what is valid and what is not. 'It is true that everyone is forced to dip into the pot of numbers', Ulrich Beck and Wolfgang Bonß write in their analysis of the use of social-science findings,

> but the combinations and conclusions tend to be different, particularly with regard to sensitive fields of interest. Science has so thoroughly investigated science as to render it incapable of decision; it has thus released a *new, indirect possibility of instrumentalisation* that defeats objectivity in the name of objectivity. Other definitions, indicators, methodological strategies, other institutional contexts, customers, other computer software, other data files etc.—and totally different "realities" emerge. Such a diversity of decisions can no longer be mastered by immanent, methodical-theoretical norms and controls [...].[11]

At the same time, scientific knowledge gains increasing relevance in *institutions* (i.e. in organised groups like unions, business and trade associations, political-administrative bodies), in *professions* (the trend of academisation is unbroken—in journalism, too), and *in ordinary life* as an ever-growing number of scientific concepts and patterns of interpretation penetrate human life-worlds.[12] 'Average couples describe the problems of their relationships or the education of their children like mini-psychologists', Ulrich Beck and Wolfgang Bonß formulate drastically,

> and football fans have long learnt to "explain" their "freaking out" at riots in a stadium by referring to "blocked aggression". On close examination, no social domain seems to be left that is not characterised by this change from traditional to scientific language games.[13]

At the same time, science—although not recognised any more as the source of indisputably acceptable truths in every instance and in every

---

10 See also Weischenberg's discussion (2001a, p. 150f.) of the topic 'journalism and time.'
11 Beck/Bonß (1989), p. 19 (authors' emphasis).
12 On this typology of the use of scientific knowledge see Beck/Bonß (1989, pp. 31ff.); on the scientification of everyday life see the critique of Poerksen, U. (1988).
13 Beck/Bonß (1989), pp. 32f.

environment—has turned into a 'life-defining power'[14] and transformed society; outstanding examples are e.g. the biosciences, robotics, the new communication technologies.

Non-Committal Commitment

Due to their peculiar cognitive and occupational situations, journalists are unavoidably forced into practising some kind of dilettantism with regard to questions of expert knowledge, a dilettantism that one may certainly lament but that one cannot simply remove by means of superior educational standards and demands. The ideal images of the exact scientist and the omniscient expert are definitely inappropriate model images for journalism. One cannot train a greater number of journalists—simply for reasons of time and money—with ever more precise expert knowledge in order to reduce factual mistakes and faulty interpretations, the uncritical acceptance of incorrect statements, and the occurrence of distorting exaggerations (i.e. mistakes that arise in the process of journalistic adaptation).[15] This idea, if taken to its extreme, would require, even for media with daily news coverage, the

> creation, institution and running of a broadly differentiated staff of specialists, expert journalists for the prevention of water pollution, for energy generation, social politics, law enforcement and penal systems, urban development, internal medicine, surgery, informatics, aviatics etc.[16]

The more promising way is

> to establish an adequately grounded and target-oriented *education of journalists* that provides not only the necessary techniques of transfer and research but helps to develop scientific thinking into a specific kind of operational competence. The journalistic methods and skills would be combined with an improved capability of reflection and thus reach beyond the job of professional reporting; it would also transcend the normal context of checking research, would employ modes of reflection for the critical analysis of interpretations and thus make use of a science-*adequate* method of the examination and testing of prejudices and hypotheses.[17]

The exploration of the instruments and methods of scientific practice should, however, be supplemented by the educational objective of developing a fundamental kind of healthy scepticism. It will result from a deepened critical awareness of science, in particular the epistemologically grounded examination of the methods and results of scientific investigation (see the subsequent discussion of the constructivist conception of sci-

---

14   Hennis quoted in Ruß-Mohl (1985), p. 266.
15   On this typology of journalistic mistakes see Haller (1987), pp. 308f.
16   Haller (1987), p. 312.
17   Ibid. (author's emphasis).

ence and scientific methodology and the constructivist examination of the results and products of scientific enquiry). Such scepticism relativises, as will be shown, scientific claims to truth in a fundamental way – and thus creates, one may expect, even in individual cases and in concrete situations, a climate of heightened attention and awareness for possible mistakes, for the instrumentalisation of data and statistics, for assumed expert status, and for the (possibly fraudulent) exploitation of pseudo-scientific authority. A kind of scepticism that is founded on epistemology and casts doubt on alleged ultimate certainties and scientific truths, and also the 'paradox of noncommittal commitment',[18] could help to develop a particular frame of mind in journalists who will then, in the ideal case, and even in the inevitably hectic daily job chaos, do their work less prone to mistakes, will no longer be all too easily pocketed for an apparently good cause, and will be able to develop powerful criteria for the efficient handling of uncertainty.

2. The Idea of Science: General Reflection I

The Guiding Difference of Constructivism

Whenever constructivists reflect the run-of-the-mill idea of science and their own unorthodox conception of science, they operate with a central opposition and three different strategies of representation. The central opposition – whatever its concrete formation and conceptual delineation – sets *observer-independent* and *observer-dependent* concepts of knowledge and science in opposition to each other. The strategies of representation work, first, with instruments of *critical analysis* (criticising concepts of science that assume a given, observer-independent reality and the possibility of apprehending it, i.e. that essentially argue from a realist point of view). They apply, secondly, methods of *contrasting* and *comparing* (contrasting variants of concepts of science, which either negate or accept the premise of observer-independence). And they aim, thirdly, at a *new formulation* of the current general idea of science – against the background of the fundamental insight that cognition can be understood to be strictly observer-relative, and that it actually must be understood in this way.

Setting up this central opposition and the three different strategies of representation as a systematic framework of its own, i.e. trying to observe constructivist observers in this way, a multitude of conceptual proposals and fundamental insights may be sorted and arranged in a synopsis. The target of critical assessments is always the realist idea of science asserting that a given, observer-independent, absolute, reality can gradually be approximated through the process of knowledge production, i.e the belief

---

[18] Bolz (2001, p. 173) with reference to Luhmann.

that an 'immaculate conception of truth',[19] as Niklas Luhmann put it sarcastically, is essentially possible. In contradistinction to realist positions, constructivist conceptions define scientific knowledge — naturally in connection with, and in productive continuation of, numerous proposals and designs by non-constructivist authors — as *cultural* (based upon and derived from societal-cultural pre-formations), as *temporal* (carrying a time-index and thus labelled as definitely provisional), as *historical* (embedded in the overall historical situation), and finally as *epistemologically relativised* (deprived of its claims to truth on the basis of scientific-biological research). This means: one constantly works on the observer-specific refraction of what is held to be certain.

Klaus Krippendorff — on the basis of a constructivist position — criticises figures of thought and rules of perception in scientific practice (e.g. abstraction, or the tendency to use objectifying language), which make for the exclusion of the observer and render the fact that they are also constructs invisible, as it were.[20] Heinz von Foerster declares, as already explained elsewhere, the central concern of classical realist science, i.e. the concept of objectivity, to be 'a subject's delusion that observing can be done without him'.[21] Humberto R. Maturana distinguishes two central attitudes (here, too, the opposition of observer-independence and observer-dependence forms the essential guiding difference), which he terms *objectivity in parentheses* and *objectivity without parentheses*. Both attitudes, or dispositions, fundamentally mark two different mindsets of researchers. Objectivity without parentheses implies that the observer-independent existence of objects is presupposed, and that these objects can at least potentially be known in their unique, original, true form. 'One lives' Humberto R. Maturana states, oblivious to the established and differently aligned understanding of the concept *transcendental*,[22] 'in the domain of mutually exclusive transcendental ontologies: each ontology supposedly grasps objective reality; what exists seems to be independent

---

19 Luhmann (1994b), p. 71.
20 See comprehensively Krippendorff (1995).
21 Foerster/Poerksen (2002), p. 148.
22 One may of course raise the question as to why the constructivist Maturana continues to use the traditional concepts of realism (objectivity and ontology). The answer reveals a peculiarity of the use of his conceptual creations that frequently appear so idiosyncratic but are nevertheless applied most consistently: his terminology starts out from the experiences of an individual observer without further specifications but simultaneously offers a different, a fresh view of these experiences. On the one hand, he wants to arouse the awareness and keep it awake that no observer-independent point of reference can be found for the validation of an observer's assumptions; on the other hand, however, it is *the very experience itself* that there *appear* to be observer-independent objects and a separate kind of 'Being', which is conceptually expressed and described at the same time. This principle of language use, therefore, seeks to achieve *simultaneously* ordinary, empirical-pragmatic connectibility *and* the mediation of new and as yet unfamiliar theoretical insights. For discussion see Maturana/Poerksen (2004), pp. 42f.

of one's personality and one's actions.'[23] The contrary attitude, *objectivity in parentheses,* consists in the fundamental acceptance of the observer-dependence of all knowledge:

> The distinction between objects and the experience of existence is, according to this path, not denied but the reference to objects is not the basis of explanations, it is the coherence of experiences with other experiences that constitutes the foundation of all explanation. In this view, the observer becomes the origin of all realities; all realities are created through the observer's operations of distinction. We have entered the domain of constitutive ontologies: all Being is constituted through the Doing of observers.[24]

According to this perspective, science in its entirety no longer appears as a

> domain of objective knowledge, but as a domain of subject-dependent knowledge defined by a methodology that specifies the properties of the knower. In other words, the validity of scientific knowledge rests on its methodology, which specifies the cultural unity of the observers, not in its being a reflection of an objective reality, which it is not.[25]

Stability and Contingency

In accordance with this line of argument it is only consistent that scientific research will no longer be said to deal with 'objects' but with 'problems'. 'Whereas talking about "objects" suggests subject-independence', the reasoning runs,

> talking about "problems" can only be envisioned as relational and as guided by the theory of differences: problems are system- and therefore observer-specific; they depend on previously made experiences, on available knowledge, on possibilities of action, interests, purposes, emotions, chosen values.[26]

Fundamentally, scientific work is no longer seen as the emphatic quest for truth and certainty but as an activity of 'social problem solving' that is tied to 'particular rules and demands'[27] and operates on different levels of observation. Those who experiment always necessarily also act as observers of the first order. Whoever observes as an observer of the first order, i.e. gets ready to decipher patterns of distinction under the guidance of theories and methods, carries out observations of the second order. Whoever — for instance in the role of an analytical philosopher of science — raises the question how he himself observes as an observer of the second order, and what distinctions of his own underlie his constructions of reality,

---

23 Maturana/Poerksen (2004), p. 42.
24 Ibid.
25 Maturana (1985), p. 309.
26 Schmidt (1998), p. 151.
27 Loosen (2005), p. 299.

operates accordingly as an observer of the third order: he practises latent observation in the mode of self-reflection.[28]

If scientific practice is considered to be the systematic purpose-bound attempt to solve problems, then theories can no longer be 'mirror images of an external reality' either [29] — irrespective of whether they are so-called supertheories, base theories, or the middle-range theories dominating the study of communication, which can be rendered empirical in a different and more direct way.[30] Theories are 'strategies to achieve particular goals' and 'strategies of problem solving'.[31] They 'systematise, as it were', a concise formulation runs,

> the experiences that the researchers have made with their experimental set-ups, they structure the experiential space of researchers and thus constitute their cultural unity and uniformity as the foundation of communicative intersubjectivity.[32]

Empirical knowledge, too — just as theory-guided research results — can therefore no longer be interpreted in the sense of an emphatic concept of truth.

This consequence of constructivist thought is double-edged. On the one hand, the result of an empirical survey frequently acquires the aura of factuality (outside constructivist circles), i.e. the image of a particular closeness to reality and truth: what has been shown empirically is considered to be secure and by comparison certain.[33] On the other hand, constructivists have often been accused of being slaves to empirical procedures and results in a downright simple, naive-positivistic way; they would positively not believe in truth but would show equally unconditional faith in the results of brain research. 'Empirical knowledge', Siegfried J. Schmidt emphasises with all due clarity,

> is nothing but knowledge of the world as we experience and formulate it. The experience that empirical knowledge can be shared intersubjectively does not indicate system- and cognition-independence but merely the degree of cognitive and communicative parallelism that results, first, from the way in which this kind of knowledge has been acquired [...], and, furthermore, from the experience that such knowledge can be demonstrated to all the persons that have been accordingly socialised, everywhere and at all times.[34]

---

28 See Schmidt (1998), p. 124.
29 Krippendorff (1993), p. 48.
30 The classical social-science definition of theories (a theory is a system of consistent statements from which empirically testable hypotheses can be derived) remains untouched by these general, epistemological-constructivist reflections. On the distinction between supertheories, base theories, and middle-range theories see Weber (2003a), pp. 18ff.
31 Schmidt (1998), p. 152.
32 Ibid.
33 See criticism in Nassehi/Saake (2002), p. 56.
34 Schmidt (1998), p. 44.

Whoever conducts empirical research on a constructivist basis, constructs logical, pragmatic and social stabilities, employs the procedures (= methods) tested and established within the *scientific community* to build up intersubjective consensus, and must in the end, in order not to contradict himself, at all cost avoid any kind of explicit or implicit ontologisation of the results of observation: what finally arises is potentially consensual, intersubjectively hardened knowledge, i.e. communicative stability.[35] Sibylle Moser, in her contribution on the contours of the constructivist understanding of science and research, summarises the possible forms of such stability in the following way:

> Logical stability corresponds to the consistency of conceptual systems as a specific form of cognitive *functionality* [...]; pragmatic stability corresponds to the *efficacy* of scientific frameworks of operation; social stability, finally, reveals itself in the discursive coordination of different *perspectives of interpretation* in scientific communication.[36]

The difference between the empirical and the theoretical, which is so frequently highlighted by scientists who do not argue from a constructivist perspective, is assigned a new functional place from a constructivist perspective. This difference remains meaningful from the point of view of research practice, but it loses in epistemological relevance as commonalities become more noticeable: we are dealing with different modes of the construction of scientific reality. The criterion of demarcation with regard to the degree of approximation of an imaginary pole of truth, which traditionally assigned the position of privilege to empirical procedure, no longer appears applicable. The centre of attention is now taken by the question of 'how the scientific observer constitutes his object through observation.'[37]

3. Methodology and Method: General Reflection II

Scientific practice implies: to tackle questions and problems of research methodology in a rule-bound, method-directed manner; to proceed methodically implies: to define objectives and problems of the investigation, to specify and demonstrate openly those procedures and instruments of problem solving which will be selected and employed for the solution of the given problem with maximum transparency. In journalism and communication studies, the instruments of problem solving consist in the qualitative, and especially the quantitative, methods of empirical social research.[38] Methodology is the study and teaching of methods, i.e. of the viable, tested and recognised ways of solving problems. In the

---

35 Cf. Schmidt (1998), pp. 195ff.
36 Moser (2004), pp. 20f (author's emphasis).
37 Nassehi/Saake (2002), p. 70.
38 For an introductory survey see Diekmann (2004).

constructivist view, a number of peculiar and specific epistemological problems arise that may be condensed into five questions. These questions will be dealt with in the following sections — once again in a kind of comprehensive survey of the points of view and possible lines of argument as might be encountered in the scientific world; no ready-made answers will be presented here, but merely imaginable dimensions of that fundamental sceptical attitude that has been addressed as the deepening of the critical awareness of science.

Quantitative and Qualitative

The first key question in the debate about methods is: What type of method — quantitative or qualitative — is suggested and recommended from a constructivist perspective? On the face of it, the answer appears clear and unambiguous: 'The quantitative paradigm', one may read in a new and rather crudely manufactured article on this debate,

> is based on positivism. Science is characterised by empirical research; all phenomena can be reduced to empirical indicators, which represent the truth. The ontological position of the quantitative paradigm is that there is only one truth, an objective reality that exists independent of human perception.[39]

Totally different and utterly contrary is the arsenal of qualitative methods, which — and this would still require proper examination — is given the rank and the completeness of a paradigm that cannot, at least according to the opinion of Thomas S. Kuhn, be combined with other paradigms.[40] One may therefore read:

> In contrast, the qualitative paradigm is based on interpretivism [...] and constructivism [...]. Ontologically speaking, there are multiple realities or multiple truths based on one's construction of reality. Reality is socially constructed [...] and so is constantly changing.[41]

This would mean that the methodology of qualitative methods is definitely in closer alignment with constructivist core assumptions, which deal with the subject — and observer-dependence and the relativity of all claims to knowledge and truth.[42] 'Whereas the quantified world of statistical social research', Armin Nassehi and Irmhild Saake, in an ironical-critical vein, add to such black and white images,

---

[39] Sale/Lohfeld/Brazil (2002), p. 44.
[40] See also Kelle/Erzberger (1999), p. 509.
[41] Sale/Lohfeld/Brazil (2002), p. 45.
[42] Here only those assumed differences between qualitative and quantitative methods will be quoted which are of epistemological relevance. Naturally, many other distinctions and opposites could be introduced for discussion (orientation by the single case versus orientation by general principles; idiographic versus nomothetic science; inductive versus deductive procedures; *Verstehen* versus *Erklären* etc. See for a survey Mayring (2003), p. 18.

ultimately sedates the observer by means of the simulated precision of the third post-decimal of the correlation coefficient, and thus makes the results independent of the concrete observer, the qualitative methodology of research blatantly demands a productive style of inquiry steeped in life experience and legitimated by the personality of the researcher. The further debate of methods will now take place within the self-defined space of plausibility between the two contrary poles of quantitative and qualitative methods of social research.[43]

Such contrapositions, however, do not necessarily meet with assent; and the dichotomy certainly does not define itself as 'plausible' at all — how could it? It has unquestionably been pointed out often enough with reference to qualitative procedures, either with descriptive, with critical, or with positive-endorsing intentions, that neither the instruments of investigation employed (e.g. an interview guide) nor the choice and the definition of the situation investigated, nor finally the apprehension of the objects under investigation are subject to comparable rigorous rules.[44] It is a humdrum kind of criticism that there are just no generally accepted 'criteria for the assessment of scientific quality'[45] as are available in much greater measure for standardised quantitative methods (content analysis, survey, observation, experiment). Nevertheless, the apparently discriminatory dichotomy between qualitative and quantitative procedures, which uses the admitted or programmatically negated dependence of knowledge on the subject of the scientific observer as the defining criterion of difference, is not at all universally accepted.[46] One would probably do better to distinguish between the *gradually variable visibility* of the scientist in the process of research because, if all knowledge is classified as observer-dependent anyway then the implication can only be that even the methodologically supported attempts to make the investigating subject invisible or to eliminate it altogether, must be doomed to failure. This means that the opposition *subject-dependent* versus *subject-independent* or *observer-dependent* versus *observer-independent* is a misguided choice, if we want to distinguish qualitative and quantitative procedures by subjecting them to an evaluation of some kind.[47] Every instrument of scientific problem-solving may be referred back to an active subject that chooses this particular instrument and then employs it individually with peculiar

---

[43] Nassehi/Saake (2002), p. 67.
[44] Loosen (2005). p. 300.
[45] Loosen/Scholl/Woelke (2002), p. 52.
[46] Loosen, Scholl and Woelke (2002, p. 53) do not consider the difference between qualitative and quantitative procedures to be really very serious; they rather see here 'different steps within a bipolar continuum.'
[47] It must of course be realised that not all qualitative social research is constructivistically oriented. Constructivist research is more inclined, according to Hug (2004, p. 130), to keep an open mind towards both variants.

variations; 'subject-dependence — also by way of scientific methods — fundamentally applies to all forms of observation.'[48]

Consequently, the essential contrast has to do with the extent to which intersubjective replicability is at all intentional, and to what extent such corresponding methodical rules are formulated and made explicit as may eventually become more or less consensual within the scientific community. It is, however, impossible to exclude the observer from the process of cognition, just because this is demanded by some programme fiat; even in strictly standardised processes of research the observer is the indispensable entity that cannot be eliminated. From a constructivist perspective there can be no place of complete neutrality, no sort of epistemological Switzerland. And this holds equally for the representatives of qualitative and quantitative methods.

Radical and Conservative Positions

The second key question of the debate about methods is whether methodologies and methods can be adopted at all without a scrupulous examination of their contexts of origin, which may be epistemologically tainted and possibly realistically connoted? The background to such a question is a 'problem of compatibility'[49] which has become the subject of intensive discussion in the meantime because empirical social research is widely dominated by the epistemology of critical rationalism. As is well known, this epistemology is rooted in the idea of the gradual approximation of truth in an endless process of the falsification of hypotheses, and must therefore be classified as a realist conception — although it considers ultimate verification to be impossible. Thus, we also face the question as to whether 'methods can be separated from their methodological and epistemological contexts of origin',[50] whether one could or even should understand them as cognitively indifferent working rules that are not really and distinctly affected by the epistemological position of the scientists employing them.

Looking through the still rather sparse literature on the topic, two contrary views emerge that will here be designated as *radical* or *conservative*.[51] A minority of researchers holds a *radical* position and considers methods of standardised empirical social research to be incompatible with constructivism.[52] This implies, at the same time, that either only a particular already available type of method (e.g. qualitative methods) is considered compatible with the epistemological premises, or that new adequate methods must be developed from within the constructivist discourse

---

48 Loosen/Scholl/Woelke (2002), p. 53.
49 Loosen (2004), p. 93.
50 Scholl (2004), p. 1.
51 See also Moser (2004), p. 12.
52 Cf. Loosen/Scholl/Woelke (2002), p. 52.

itself. Thomas Pfeffer, for instance, as the representative of a radical position within the debate about methods, voices a critical view:

> If it is attempted at all to combine constructivist theories with methods of empirical social research, the existing approaches generally restrict themselves to adapting methods that were developed in other theoretical frameworks so as to make them fit into the constructivist paradigm.[53]

One of his own proposals is the use of an interviewing procedure 'that has been developed authentically on the basis of constructivist concepts.'[54] What is meant is so-called circular questioning, a technique of interviewing widely practised by systemic-constructivist therapists, which can help to bring about the strategic change and purposeful relaxation of observer perspectives prevalent in the circle of clients. This technique is to be separated from its therapeutic context and to be applied in the social sciences, perhaps even elevated to the rank of an independent method — such is the proposal, such is the idea.[55]

The conservative position can be encountered much more frequently. It claims that 'nothing fundamental has to be changed about the methods that would not be compatible with the working rules derived from critical rationalism.'[56] There is thus, Siegfried J. Schmidt states bluntly, 'no total difference between a constructivist and a conventional methodology.'[57] What changes is the epistemological conception, the epistemological framework, within which research activity unfolds; what also changes is the interpretation of the results that can no longer be adjudicated emphatically for truth but must be considered as strictly contingent (not arbitrary!); what changes, finally, is the epistemological reflection, which may definitely affect concrete procedural steps and phases and the reality-constitutive potency of particular methods. As will be shown in the following, it does not make any difference whether the methods in question involve content analysis, surveys, observations or experiments.

Interpretation of Content Analysis

The third key question in the debates about methods is: How can the particular methods of empirical social research — content analysis, survey, observation and experiment — be interpreted constructivistically? Content analysis is undoubtedly regarded as the essential, the original method of communication studies. It examines media offers that are available as texts or in the form of visual products — i.e. as *permanent* communication documents, in any

---

53 Pfeffer (2004), p. 67.
54 Ibid.
55 See also Pfeffer's (2004) only moderately convincing illustration of this proposal.
56 Loosen (2004), p. 96.
57 Schmidt in conversation with Poerksen (2002f), p. 148.

event. The systematic character and the rule-orientation that governs the interpretation of the symbolic material distinguishes content analysis from the huge majority of hermeneutic procedures.[58] However, recalling the initial, the classical, definition of this essential method, makes immediately obvious that it deserves critical assessment from the constructivist point of view. Content analysis, the account runs, 'is a research technique for the objective, systematic, and quantitative description of the manifest content of communication'.[59] Several of these defining features have provoked the criticism of constructivistically oriented scientists. The apparently clean-cut distinction between the manifest and the latent contents of communication is deemed problematical from the point of view of communication theory, and it is considered counter-productive from the perspective of the pragmatics of research, because not only manifest content has to be made visible but latent dimensions of the meaning of a text must equally be teased out. 'By including the attribute 'manifest' in his definition', Klaus Krippendorff writes for instance,

> Berelson intended to ensure that the coding of content analysis data be reliable; this requirement literally excludes "reading between the lines", which is what experts do, often with remarkable intersubjective agreement [...]. My chief objection to Berelson's definition, and numerous derivatives of that definition, is related to his phrase "description of the manifest content of communication." It implies that content is contained in messages, waiting to be separated from its form and described.[60]

Obviously, the claim inherent in the quoted definition that the real, the objectively valid, meaning could be extracted reactivity-free from a text—a permanent, 'mute' and undistorted piece of communication—provoked objections. Klaus Merten has shown, for instance, that reactivity is definitely at work in content analysis, too, because the data that are gathered from the text result from the selective activity of the encoder.[61] This means: there is an interaction between the encoder and the object of analysis, which affects the research result because it produces, i.e. constructs, meaning—not least in connection with the specific situation and the particular given context. Texts therefore definitely possess no objectively given content that could be unambiguously recognised and expressed by all people of good will. From a constructivist perspective, texts are 'highly conventionalised multi-structured *stimuli* of cognitive operations [...], whose results (communicates) are conditioned not only by the text but also by the total state of the cognitive system in its concrete situation [...].'[62]

---

[58] Loosen (2005), pp. 301ff.
[59] Berelson/Lazarsfeld 1948, pp.5f.
[60] Krippendorff (2004), p. 20. (author's emphasis).
[61] See Loosen/Scholl/Woelke (2002), pp. 47ff. and Merten (1996), pp. 65ff.
[62] Schmidt (1994), p. 139. (author's emphasis).

Wiebke Loosen describes the formation of categories with which the analysis is carried out as a 'recursive process close to the material that may constantly irritate the process of operationalisation.'[63] The training of encoders, consequently, seeks to address the phenomenon of reactivity: it helps, ideally, to build up as much of a consensus as possible, it largely suppresses idiosyncratic interpretations, and it may help to create cognitive uni(formi)ty.[64] Still, there will always remain an observer-dependent rest of interpretation, which will not be excluded even by the most comprehensive training and the most advanced set of rules. '*Texts do not have single meanings* that could be "found", "identified", and "described" for what they are', Klaus Krippendorff sets out in his textbook. 'Just as texts can be read from numerous perspectives, so signs can have several designations and data can be subjected to various analyses.'[65]

Survey and Observation

Questioning people orally face-to-face or by telephone, or by means of writing, i.e. not analysing given texts with supposedly fixed content, makes the dominating role of the scientific observer immediately evident; it need not be explicitly exposed as in the case of content analysis. Quite obviously, reactivity cannot be avoided as a troubling factor even in the case of a *survey*, it is much rather of constitutive normality in the research process, irrespective of the extent to which survey situations and the relevant questions have been standardised, irrespective of whether an only minimally structured narrative interview, a partially structured guided interview, a problem-centred interview or a standardised survey with multiple-choice answers are used.[66] Reactivity can here be defined as the 'observation of being observed. [...] When one feels observed one behaves differently than when one is not observed.'[67] Depending on the definition of the situation and the role attribution of the interviewer, the interviewee will respond authentically or subject himself—for whatever reasons—to supposed expectations and societal and situative norms (this all-too-well-known phenomenon has been categorised as 'social desirability').[68]

The method of observation, realised for instance as the secret supervision of working processes in editorial offices, is not as obvious an interference with those under observation and leaves them to get on with their

---

63 Loosen (2004), p. 105.
64 Loosen/Scholl/Woelke (2002), p. 56.
65 Krippendorff (2004), p. 22 (author's emphasis).
66 Cf. Loosen (2005), pp. 303f.
67 Loosen/Scholl/Woelke (2002), pp. 45.
68 Ibid., pp. 45f.

activities whose causes and patterns are to be brought to awareness.[69] Observation does not (like a survey) serve the reconstruction of self- and other-observation, its purpose is the recording of behaviours that are then attributed meaning by the observer—a process of interpretation the contingency of which is made evident by the proverbial ambiguity of observational data. The validity of the results of observation is therefore comparatively unsafe.[70]

Experiment and Causality

The *experiment*, not ranked as a method in its own right in communication studies, is expected to minimise the ambiguity of cause-effect processes by its specific investigative design.[71] The essential components of an experiment are an experimental group with stimulus, an identical control group without stimulus, error control by randomisation, post-trial measurements by means of surveys, observations, or content analysis. Before analysing the presumed effect (e.g. the assumption of an increase in the readiness to use violence due to the reception of violent films), dependent, independent and intervening variables are identified, and interaction processes are temporally confined to the presentation of the stimulus and the final measurement of the different variables. This means: the complexity of social reality is purposefully reduced; causality is presupposed and tested by experiments. *Universal* determinism is asserted (every event has a well-defined cause), which could equally well—from a constructivist perspective—be considered as a *mental* mechanism of information processing,

> as a process that controls the perception and interpretation of temporally and spatially connected variables [...]. By linking certain phenomenal properties of two or more events and observing their differences one draws conclusions as to whether one event has caused another one.[72]

Causal explanations possess, it appears, a triadic structure, comprising the statement of a cause, the diagnosis of an effect, and the deciphering of a rule of transformation (a regularity or law of some sort) underlying the change and producing the form of effect that allows for the observation of differences, in the first place. Whoever observes in this way, deconstructs the concept of causality, and retreats, for a moment, from the consideration of the experiment in the canon of methods of social science research, is bound to notice: causality and the craving for certainty are closely

---

69 Even behaviours that appear totally authentic to a perfectly camouflaged observer cannot, for epistemological reasons, be judged to be closer to reality or truth in an all-embracing sense. Cf. on this Loosen/Scholl/Woelke (2002), p. 46.
70 Loosen/Scholl/Woelke (2002), p. 43.
71 On the following, see especially Loosen/Scholl/Woelke (2002), pp. 57ff.
72 Loosen/Scholl/Woelke (2002), p. 60.

related. Part of our everyday conceptions of a reliable, calculable and manipulable world is the idea that reality is governed by intelligible laws that we are able to decipher, that a cause will linearly produce an effect, and that we can relate a particular effect to a specific cause that may even be activated in non-natural ways. 'The preference of causal relations between variables' and this applies quite generally,

> is a problem for positions associated with systems theory and constructivism. The assumption there is that laws about causal relations can only be formulated for systems that cannot change in more than one way. To define this case as the standard case, however, is disallowed for domains of social life [...]. Relations between elements should essentially be seen as reciprocal. Reciprocity, in turn, leads to an increase in complexity.[73]

x	f	y
Input	Operation	Output
Independent variable	Function	Dependent variable
Cause	Law of nature	Effect
Minor premise	Major premise	Conclusion
Stimulus	Organism	Reaction
Motivation	Character	Deeds
Goal	System	Behaviour
...	...	...
.	.	.

Figure 1. The Notion of Causality has a Triadic Structure
(From: Foerster/Poerksen 2002, p. 57)

The Combination of Methods and the Constitution of Phenomena

The fourth key question of the debate about methods is: What insights may be expected from the combination of different methods? A combination of methods has repeatedly been recommended in order to raise the validity of findings, to approach and cover phenomenal domains step by step, as it were, so as to comprehend them with greater precision and depth. It has thus been proposed to integrate qualitative and quantitative procedures in a kind of traditional stage-model, to employ qualitative methods for the generation of hypotheses and quantitative methods for the testing of hypotheses, in order to create a more adequate picture with greater valid-

---

[73] Ibid., p. 59.

ity—an approach and a procedure that is described with the metaphor of *triangulation*.[74] This concept derives from navigation and surveying and there refers to the 'fixing of an unknown point by measuring from two known points'.[75] Assuming that the combination of qualitative and quantitative procedures, i.e. triangulation, increases the validity of findings, implies—at least implicitly—that both types of method 'may be different but are, in certain respects, methodologically of equal rank.'[76] This means: one fails to see the reality-constitutive impact of methods, which allows only a specific view of the phenomenon to be investigated or of the problem to be solved. What does a particular method, one must ask, help to see at all in comparison with another method? Is *the same phenomenon* captured by different methods? Are *different aspects* of the same phenomenon registered? Do these different aspects of the same phenomenal domain add up to a relatively complete picture or do they remain isolated, like the pieces of different puzzles, which cannot be connected or integrated into one whole? Does the employment of different methods lead to the constitution of different phenomena that are actually incomparable?

An epistemologically naive debate about the combination of methods may not appreciate the problem whether there are, at all, identical phenomena and problems that can be tackled with the one or the other method.[77] Such questions, Udo Kelle and Christian Erzberger note,

> are more than linguistic ploys because only if different methods explicitly deal with the same object can they be used for the mutual validation of their results; only in such a case different results may reliably indicate problems of validity. However, if different methods capture different aspects of the same object or even different objects, then obviously different results must be expected, but no conclusion as to the lacking validity of these results is permissible.[78]

One may add that triangulation—at least from the perspective of a methodologically interested constructivism—can never guarantee the quasi-cumulative validation in the sense of an emphatic idea of truth. Whether a more comprehensive description of one and the same phenomenal domain becomes possible is ultimately, to quote Heinz von Foerster, an undecidable question.[79] But there is no doubt that the use of different methods opens up new perspectives, new opportunities for thought and perception, which an observer may consider to be aspects of one and the same phenomenon.

---

74   Siehe Kelle/Erzberger (1999), pp. 511ff.
75   Ibid., p. 514.
76   Ibid.
77   See Hillebrandt/Hungerige (1997), p. 12.
78   Kelle/Erzberger (1999), p. 515.
79   On the distinction between decidable and undecidable questions and Forester's understanding of metaphysics, see Foerster/Poerksen (2002), pp. 152ff.

Requirements of Constructivist Research

The fifth key question of the debate about methods is: What are the consequences for constructivistically inspired research? Assessing the upshot of the debates, three important innovations may be spotted. They have to do with the description and the analysis of the *process of research* and of the concrete research contact that reveals the reactivity of all the methods mentioned. They refer to the *evaluation of the results* and finally also to diverse *demands of reflection* that may not be entailed by a constructivist observer-logic but that are still to some extent suggested by it — to formulate it quite carefully and somewhat defensively.[80] It must be noted: every research contact inevitably generates an 'interaction system: in surveys and observations between interviewer and interviewee or between observer and observed, in content analysis between encoder and text.'[81] The scientific observer, the personality of the researcher is, in these interactions, no ageless and genderless being whose impact could be kept separate from the research process. The acknowledgment of the subject-dependence of all knowledge, which is here related to specific scientific tasks, does not, however, imply the justification of arbitrariness or a plea for a methodological 'anything goes', but is meant to emphasise the need for careful reflection.

Perception is significantly conditioned by the epistemological paradigm (e.g. constructivism versus realism and critical rationalism), the specific formulation and the relevance of the problem (the context of discovery), the choice of the appropriate method (the context of justification), and the potential benefit of findings, which may influence problem focussing (context of exploitation). Such attention to the inevitable circularity between the observer, the act of observing, and that which is observed is, according to Niklas Luhmann, not at all problematical; the circle emerging in this way is not at all of a 'vicious' nature. 'All one has to do', he claims, 'is to keep track of the re-transformation of research results into research conditions and to give it sufficient time.'[82]

What generally suggests itself is, therefore, the disclosure of the chosen procedure (*requirement of transparency*), which obviously fits customary standards anyway, and is thus given additional justification here on the basis of constructivist epistemology. What seems required, furthermore, is the intensive analysis of the process of research, which turns this activity itself into an object of inquiry (*requirement of self-reflection*). Such self-observation, ideally, reveals blind spots, indicates what is unobservable in principle, raises to the level of awareness what is momentarily unobserved

---

80 Cf. also the already explained distinction between *relationship of stimulation* und *relationship of derivation*.
81 Loosen/Scholl/Woelke (2002), p. 40.
82 Luhmann (1994b), p. 9.

— and in this way underscores: Whatever is observed could always be observed differently (*awareness of contingency*).[83] From all this results, of course, a corresponding specific evaluation of research results. With regard to the problem of whether the results of scientific labour are

> true images representing the properties of the objects of inquiry (interviewees, observed agents, texts) or artefacts produced by the research contact itself, constructivism remains strictly agnostic. The responses of interviewees are messages, not contents of their minds, the observations of the observers are interpretations of the situation, not the actual behaviours of the persons observed, and the encodings of the content-analytical encoders are interpretations of the texts (in the sense of Siegfried J. Schmidt's "communicates"). In all these cases, we face indissoluble relations between the scientific observers and their objects, and not isolated properties (entities) of the object of observation, i.e. the interviewee, of agents observed, or of the text itself. Consequently, these relations cannot be referred back exclusively to the interviewer, the observer, the encoder, nor exclusively to the task executor, the observed agents, the text. Insisting on this relational perspective means to underline the relativity of the application of methodological rules, but certainly not their arbitrariness.[84]

The rest is, in total, the certainty of uncertainty.

4. Points of Reference for Knowledge: General Reflection III

Universe and Multiverse

The realist argumentation presupposes the observer-independent existence of objects that can essentially be apprehended in their intrinsic, i.e. their true form. It is the conception of a given, observer-independent reality that is coupled with the belief that definitive statements are possible. 'It is the reference to this reality that is held to make a statement objective and universally valid.'[85] The mandatory validity of statements is, one assumes, secured by the reference to something absolute; the point of reference of naive-realist concepts is *the* (absolute) reality, the universe in its ontic given-ness.

Humberto R. Maturana, as already mentioned, calls this position, this 'explanatory path', *objectivity without parentheses*. This explanatory path, he formulates drastically,

> is constitutively blind (or deaf) to the participation of the observer in the constitution of what he or she accepts as an explanation. [...] Accordingly, due to its manner of constitution, this explanatory path necessarily leads the observer to require a single domain of reality — a universe, a transcendental referent — as the ultimate source of valida-

---

[83] 'The searching look', Nassehi und Saake (2002, p. 70) write, 'will then not only see what is the case, but primarily what is *not* the case.' (Authors' emphasis.)
[84] Loosen/Scholl/Woelke (2002), pp. 40f.
[85] Maturana/Poerksen (2004), p. 39.

tion of the explanations that he or she accepts and, as a consequence, to the continuous attempt to explain all aspects of his or her praxis of living by reducing them to it. [...] Therefore, in this explanatory path, explanations entail the claim of a privileged access to an objective reality by the explaining observer, and in it the observers do not take responsibility for the mutual negation in their explanatory disagreements because this is the consequence of arguments whose validity does not depend on them. It is in this explanatory path that a claim of knowledge is a demand for obedience.[86]

If it is claimed, however, that no observer can have privileged access to the Absolute, then the assumed points of reference for knowledge (reality and actuality, an imaginary Absolute, Being, the universe etc.) must be judged differently, must also be designated differently. The purportedly unchangeable Being of the universe is transformed into a multiverse;[87] the one and only, obligatory, and absolutely valid, reality (understood to be the referential basis of all true assertions) is, from this perspective, transformed into a multitude of realities which appear to different observers (depending on relevant criteria of validity, and specific systems of reference for deciding about acceptability) as differentially valid, differentially legitimate, and differentially desirable.

The Normality of Plurality

A conception of this kind, if applied to the cognitive situation of the scientist, has at least three consequences:

- It becomes evident that assertions about reality made by different scientists, or perhaps by persons interviewed and observed in the course of an investigation, may always be assessed and evaluated from two different perspectives. One may subject such assertions to an *internal* check of validity and establish that they possess validity within the domain of reality of the scientists who uttered them, or that they must be judged to be false, illusory and untrue according to the very criteria of these scientists. However, one may also perform an *external* check of validity, i.e. use one's own criteria of validity as the basis of judgement and consequently diagnose what has been proposed on the basis of these criteria, e.g. scientifically accepted criteria, as being right or wrong. This means that this second procedure always additionally involves the degree of correspondence that obtains between two different domains of reality.[88]
- One is pressed, furthermore, to work with particular conceptual precision. Mentioning *the reality*, as the assumed reference base and the

---

[86] Maturana (1998), pp. 232f.
[87] Maturana/Poerksen (2004), pp. 38ff.
[88] See Maturana/Poerksen (2004), pp. 131f. and the two different ways of listening, which are of particular importance to didactics. They will be described in detail in the last portion of this book.

point of reference of all knowledge, is necessarily using nothing but an empty formula that needs exact specification, and the unreflective use of which is bound to provoke misunderstanding and unnecessary controversies. One might thus refer to an imaginary *absolute reality*, an exclusively observer-dependent object of knowledge, which might be intended to signal assumed privileges of perception. The empty formula would then support an emphatic claim to truth. It is conceivable that what is meant is the *proprietary reality* of a specific group or a particular profession ('the reality of journalism'). It is imaginable that scientists claim reality for their own findings that they explicitly declare, as required by the constructivist position, to have been produced within their *experiential reality*.

- The observer-dependence of scientific knowledge and the well-reflected distinction between internal and external checks of validity finally support the insight that the plurality of paradigms, theories, methodologies and methods, models and concepts is ineluctably part of ordinary scientific practice and part of normal cognitive activity. This makes clear: such a pluralism of realities does not constitute an unavoidable disadvantage, nor is it an indication of bad science simply because it still appears to be inhomogeneous and regrettably disordered. Whatever divergences and differences may be observed, they do not represent a transitory phase on the way to homogeneity and ultimate certainty but form the potentially productive normal case of a highly differentiated type of science. It is the multitude of viewpoints and procedures that permits the exhaustive exploitation of 'all the possibilities of problem-solving' and to reject and dissolve rationally 'all claims to singularity and monopolistic representation'.[89] In this sense, consequently, scientific thinking is committed to pluralism.

5. The Results of Scientific Enquiry: General Reflection IV

Explanation of Explanation

The central significance of the presupposition of the observer-dependence of all knowledge has been continually emphasised. It seems reasonable, therefore, to re-examine the central results of scientific enquiry against the backdrop of this premise, i. e. to redefine them as observer concepts. What does it mean, one may ask, to assert in a scientific community of discourse that one is able to prognosticate an event, to predict its occurrence, to have explained a phenomenon, discovered a fact, established intersubjective consensus, discovered a truth? In a constructivist view this means, in the words of Humberto R. Maturana:

> People making predictions speak of their expectations as observers. They believe to know all the factors influencing a system and assert

---

[89] Schmidt (1994), p. 46.

that certain states will result from other states that we can then observe.[90]

Whoever accepts an explanation as adequate and sufficient, through his acceptance terminates explanatory trials, phases of investigation and questioning; the formation of science enters a different condition of aggregation, if one so will.[91] 'An explanatory principle', Gregory Bateson writes, 'is a sort of conventional agreement between scientists to stop trying to explain things at a certain point.'[92] The state of affairs, the fact, accordingly figures as a 'type of experience that does not provoke disagreement'[93] and that, from the perspective of the sociology of knowledge, appears to be something manufactured, something fabricated, something constructed — occasionally in this context the etymology of the word 'fact' is called upon for support. The use of language has changed in order to signal the new understanding and the re-contextualisation of the concept; one no longer speaks of facts in an emphatic sense of truth; one speaks no longer of data (something given), but of *facts* (something made), no longer of data gathering but of fact production[94] — a proposal for conceptual refinement, which has, however, met with criticism even from amongst those scientists who think along constructivist principles.[95]

When intersubjective consensus has been achieved about what the facts are, when phenomena have been explained and problems of research have been solved, then this means simply — strictly in observer-relative terms — that one has reached a finishing point within scientific communication (a point that is, of course, always open to revision), a provisional termination, a state of affairs against which no serious objection is mani-

---

90 Maturana/Poerksen (2004), p. 79.
91 Cf. the instructive typology of Fleck (1993, pp. 146ff.). He separates a hypothetical *Zeitschriftenwissenschaft* [journal science] that is still diffident and insecure in its pronouncements, from a more decidedly summarising *Handbuchwissenschaft* [handbook science] that offers certainties, and finally a *populäre Wissenschaft* [popular science] that works with reductions and exaggerations.
92 Quoted in Foerster (1981), p. 35.
93 Weischenberg (1992), p. 173.
94 Schmidt (2002), p. 183.
95 Loosen, Scholl and Woelke (2002) have noted that empirical findings — in different phases of a research process — are always of both kinds: data (something given) and facts (something made). 'In the research contact itself', they write (2002, p. 38), 'gathering information by means of surveys, content analysis, observation or experiment, manufactures facts; processing (then) deals with given data that are only rarely problematised with respect to their character as constructs.' This criticism, however, results from a misunderstanding: Schmidt recurs to the epistemic-ontological status of facts; the authors refer to something else, i.e. to the different degrees and dimensions of awareness with regard to construction in the course of the research process and at its termination. Accordingly, both views are compatible without problem: epistemic-ontological facts will remain facts; they are inevitably something made; their cognitive categorisation does not at all affect their ontic status. In the process of research, however, the admission that one deals with something made, fabricated, constructed may gradually be weakened: what was first seen as a fact, may now appear to be something given, a collection of data.

festly raised at the moment.[96] To classify a statement as *true* means, in keeping with the present line of argument: to apply a strategy of discourse that classifies a statement or a result of research as 'temporarily uncontroversial'[97] and established beyond any doubt and any further calls for justification. 'As we cannot infinitely perpetuate our doubting for pragmatic reasons', Siegfried J. Schmidt writes,

> we must enable ourselves to interrupt the doubt-induced regress of justificatory operations in a potentially consensual way, and any such interruption must enjoy elevated social standing so as not to fall prey to an accusation of wilfulness. Both conditions are sufficiently fulfilled by the concept of "truth". Truth is *ascribed to* assertive statements and systems of such statements as long as *we* hold them to be true according to the state of the available knowledge, i.e. because of hitherto successful experiences. The kind of knowledge one can reliably introduce into progressive argumentation because no objections are manifestly raised against it, is recognised as true knowledge.[98]

Truth and Viability

The consequence is, however, that the concept of truth will still be used but with a meaning devoid of any connotation of an underlying theory of correspondence. Ernst von Glasersfeld, by contrast, has suggested to replace the concept of truth itself, and has introduced the concept of *viability* to diagnose the success or the failure of scientific problem solutions. 'Actions, concepts and conceptual operations', he defines, 'are viable whenever they fit the goals or descriptions for which we use them.'[99] The classical notion of truth in the sense of the *adaequatio intellectus et rei*, i.e. the correspondence between the cognizant spirit and matter or what is given, is here replaced by the concept of viability that explicitly refers to experiential reality. The question of ultimate justification is abandoned. What remains is a fairly unspectacular motive for knowledge: the goal is now to develop and present efficient procedures and assumptions that would match the particular purposes of an observer; only the (total) failure of our constructions would, according to the proposal of Ernst von Glasersfeld, prove a construction to be no longer viable because absolute reality would crush an arbitrary or definitely false imposition.[100] Establishing, however,

---

96 Schmidt (2000), p. 355.
97 Schmidt (1998), p. 154.
98 Schmidt (2003), p. 129 (author's emphasis).
99 Glasersfeld (1996), p. 43.
100 At this point, a contradiction arises in the argument. How is one to know that the failure of constructions must be taken to indicate a contact with absolute reality? How could this be established — without having access to this absolute reality, which is simultaneously declared to be impossible? Josef Mitterer (2001, pp. 123f.) critically notes: 'For the *success* of our constructions we are responsible ourselves — is nature, is reality responsible for their *failure*? Who determines whether constructions are viable or not? Reality or an*(other)* theory about

whether and when a scientific concept is viable depends on one's own values that cannot objectively be justified from a constructivist perspective. Viability, although derived as a concept from the theory of evolution, is a rather weak or soft criterion; it is, in addition, not really clear, to what it is actually meant to refer. To the explanatory power of theories, their capacity to solve problems? To the ethical or unethical goals that a scientist or a group of researchers may possibly pursue? It remains unclear, furthermore, how one can actually ascertain at a particular point in time that something proves to be useful or viable?[101] Establishing viability requires, it transpires, personal judgement and personal assessment, and it involves necessarily a subjective factor even though one's assumptions may at a later stage successfully achieve intersubjective plausibility and a consensus may be reached that quietens down the scientific dispute for a while.

6. Scientific Literacy

Criticism as the Drawing of Limits

The various points of view involved in the deepening of the critical awareness of science constitute a kind of practice ground for the training of the thinking and arguing of quality journalists, which quite deliberately cultivates well-grounded doubt and fundamental scepticism. Criticism here refers not only to evaluative or even exclusively negative assessments; this would be totally misleading because such an idea of criticism could hardly represent a significant educational objective. Criticism much rather stands here — in the tradition of a noteworthy definition from the history of philosophy — for the effort to 'illuminate, examine, draw limits.'[102] Such an 'illumination' of a central instance of truth in modern times — i.e. of science — from a constructivist perspective yields, in the ideal case, a growing alertness to the relative validity of all alleged certainties; there emerges — again ideally — a feeling for the difference between indispensable professional terminology and pseudo-scientific jargon, between authentic and merely assumed expert status.[103] Such 'examining' and

---

reality? Constructivism would become more stringent if it decides for the second option.' (Author's emphasis.)

101 Such diagnoses of viability that reach through the present into an unknown future would, strictly speaking, require some prophetic gift because certain current theories that may appear viable at this moment in time might possibly produce disastrous effects and side effects at a later date. And that could imply that if one did not want to perform as a prophet one would have to build a sort of time lag into the evaluation of theories. But then the connected question will immediately pose itself: when and with what time intervals can the diagnosis of viability be carried out with sufficient security?
102 Störig (1993, p. 396) referring to Kant's concept of criticism.
103 Such a distinction is at least suggested by the story of the science parody by Sokal presented at the beginning of the chapter.

'drawing of limits' reveals the reality-constitutive role of paradigms, theories and methods and shows that scientific knowledge rests on a wealth of presuppositions; it sharpens the sense for suspicious motives behind persuasively intended exchanges of professional opinions and professional reports, strengthens self-confidence in the handling of presumptions of objectivity and truth, and draws particular attention to the perils of inadmissible simplifications and prematurely proclaimed consequences for some kind of praxis. The well-reasoned shaking up of certainties and the clarification of the proprietary rationality of scientific operational procedures will certainly not facilitate journalistic activity, but it will be able to awaken and develop awareness of the opportunities and limits, the methods and structures of contemporary science. Constructivist didactics uses the concept of *'scientific literacy'*[104] in this context—thus indicating the independent, essentially sceptical but nevertheless knowledgeable and informed appreciation and re-enactment of the practice of scientific enquiry as well as the discipline-specific operations and procedures.[105]

Self-Reflexive Sceptisism

Even from a consistent constructivist perspective, the radical cultivation of doubt cannot be an ultimate Archimedean point, cannot form a paradoxically organised kind of finality, but must keep itself floating, must—if it takes the paradoxical structure of its own utterances seriously—remain enclosed in a situation of productive openness and non-suspendable uncertainty[106] that can only be brushed aside temporarily and for the duration of particular acts on the level of the observation of the first order. One can therefore claim to know, to formulate more precisely, that one will probably never know anything for certain, but one cannot assert this with unconditional certainty in the sense of something absolute. Ignorance will remain even when one asks oneself whether one might not at least make one's home in ignorance. Such a comprehensive and self-reflexive kind of scepticism is not at all a bad point of departure for journalists who must strive for exactitude, intellectual precision and depth of focus.

---

104 See Siebert (2003a), pp. 217f.
105 On this concept of *scientific literacy,* understood to mean a sort of fundamental education in terms of scientific thought and method, see Liebert (2005), pp. 245f.
106 See also Gloy (2004), p. 252.

Chapter III

Deepening Critical Awareness of Language

1. Linguistic Registers: The Sum Total of Choices

The Linguistic Interface

The linguistic universe that confronts journalists and that they have to handle is extremely rich in facets and differentiations. One can even sharpen this diagnosis: the linguistic universe as represented by the set of rules devised by systems linguistics exists as such neither for the journalists nor for any user of a language. The assumption that one merely deviates from the normal state of a kind of homogeneity postulated beforehand leads astray. Language, as demonstrated by linguistic pragmatics and socio-linguistics as the study of linguistic variation, is composed of the languages[1] of different groups, which may be observed and analysed from many different points of view.[2] Everyone active in journalism is confronted with this internal multilingualism as soon as they have to carry out research; they must delve into more or less strange varieties (= languages within language), which conjure up more or less strange realities in the imagination, require professional handling of several linguistic codes and enforce constant code shifting in a situation-adequate manner. Already as a researcher, i.e. in the early and elementary stages of communicative productivity, the active journalist has to move nimbly between linguistic territories: he conducts interviews with scientific experts, has to rush off to speak with the protagonists of some marginal

---

[1] Language means in this context: significant, supra-individually valid patterns of language usage.
[2] Nabrings (1981, pp. 36ff.), in her fundamental book on variational linguistics, distinguishes between the *diachronic* perspective (the study of varieties at different periods of time), the *diatopic* perspective (the study of spatially bound commonalities and differences, e.g. through the comparison of different dialects), the *diastratic* perspective (the study of varieties defined by class- and group-specific criteria), and the *diasituative* perspective (the study of varieties resulting from the communication situation).

group, possibly moves in circles of high-class culture as well as subcultures, reformulates the texts of others, collects group-specific quotations and shibboleths of the relevant kind of slang, which might be used, for example, in the construction of authenticity.[3] He uses articles from the archive, he edits and writes himself, and thereby lends the chosen linguistic variety his own formative characteristics, his more or less personal style.

It thus becomes evident: journalistic work necessarily happens at an interface of different communicative spheres, at a linguistic interface. It is at this interface that the speedy reception, the media-adequate transformation and the purposeful montage of utterly different varieties takes place, of varieties that may be attributed to diverse group-linguistic prototypes. To these varieties and the corresponding prototypes belong *specialist languages* (examples are the technical jargons of the sciences that have to be 'translated' after interviews with experts). Such specialist languages are—at least in the ideal case—primarily object-oriented; they serve the quick and precise communication about contents negotiated in a value-neutral way, and they help to make the communication between experts effectual and economical. Among the journalistically relevant varieties belong also so-called *sublanguages* that exhibit strong community-oriented components (for example the varieties created and used by young people and the private codes of couples of all sorts). These varieties are primarily spoken; their function is to bring together the members of a group and to exclude others. In the extreme case, such linguistic segregation can turn into wilful isolation by means of a kind of crypto-language communication (an example would be the language of prison inmates). Journalists delivering atmospheric reports about poverty and socially troubled areas, about criminality and subcultures, frequently use linguistic elements from relevant sublanguages (particular words, idiomatic phrases, extended quotations) in order to colour their descriptions and to underline and indicate their direct contact with the environmental conditions in question. The symptomatic function of language is quasi doubly coded here; what is said, allows—apparently—looking into the minds of the persons quoted and signals, at the same time, the closeness of the journalist to the object of his reporting.

Languages of trades and professions belong to a borderland between differentiated specialist languages and sublanguages: they oscillate between the primary functions of socially oriented and object-tied communication (a

---

[3] Recall the genre of social reportage that is—irrespective of whether it is presented in the printed media, on the radio, or in television—existentially dependent on recordings of original sounds.

well-researched example is the language of soldiers[4]). *Dialects* are varieties with regional peculiarities. Another prototype — also a frequently occurring variety in the everyday linguistic contacts of journalists — will here be introduced as *world view language* (examples are: ideological languages, languages of faiths, languages of programmes).[5] These are group languages with a double function and with a correspondingly organised two-track communication: they are used for purposes of internal stabilisation, for exerting external influence, consolidating the group and recruiting new members. They are spoken and written by political and ideological groups, sects and mission-intent communities of faith with a religious background, and they must be interpreted in relation to their underlying systems of belief and explanation.[6]

Features of Media Language

By contrast, the variety of journalism proper, *media language*,[7] is less clearly structured: it is unclear whether we are dealing here with the language of all the media or primarily the language of the *mass* media, whether we are dealing with the language of a particular media genre (e.g. printed media in comparison with radio, television or online media) or whether it is the language of a particular single medium, for instance a specific organ of publication, which is to be the focus of attention. Moreover, it is controversial whether only the language of journalism is meant or whether the language of advertising or the language of public relations must also be taken into account. In any event, the point of differentiation may be made with respect to other varieties; 'The language used in the media does not possess its own peculiar sounds like dialects, does not possess its own specific vocabulary like specialist languages, does not possess its own syntax, as

---

4   For one thing, the language of soldiers is the specialist language of the military; it is, furthermore, a sublanguage of soldiers, which primarily serves to secure the coherence of the group. See Möhn (1990), p. 1524.

5   This prototype is described by Poerksen (2005a, pp. 58ff.).

6   World view languages, therefore, claim a status of their own: they are not primarily regionally marked (like dialects), they are not primarily object-related (like specialist languages), they are not primarily community-related (like sublanguages), not primarily object- and community-related (like the languages of trades and professions), but in equal measure both internally and externally oriented. It is after all of the essence of political, ideological and a large number of religious groups to want to make an impact beyond the boundaries constituted by their own membership. It is a professed goal to seek and achieve general acceptance for the language used by the group. The effects upon the external world is quite obviously intended. A consequence of this general will to exert influence is that there are limits for the crypto-linguistic language usage of certain groups because a language that is hardly or not at all intelligible to non-members endangers or even prevents an effect or impact beyond the group. This means that the criteria of differentiation, *object-* and *community-orientation*, which have dominated previous linguistic analyses of group languages, must be supplemented by the criterion of *publicity-orientation* (understood as the extent of the attempts at persuasion directed at the world external to the group).

7   See Hennig (2005).

can even be found in some sublanguages.'[8] It is much rather an internally differentiated variant, a sub-variety, as it were, in the form of a selection from the standard language or community language, whose characteristics result essentially from a multi-layered catalogue of requirements:

- Media language must be intelligible[9], although intelligibility is obviously a requirement for any kind of communication. [10]
- Media language should be attractive above and beyond all groups because it is the instrument with which to communicate with a relatively anonymous mass of recipients who are differentially educated and differentially interested and who must be enticed by the relevant medium on the market of information and opinion (necessity of multiple targeting).
- Media language is, finally, subject to the conditions of an ever-escalating competition for attention, it is related to partner hypotheses of the first and the second degree[11], it derives its formative characteristics from a media genre, the concrete available medium, potentially also the editorial department, the chosen pattern of news reporting, and the currently preferred form of presentation.

With print journalism, this internal diversity becomes evident immediately when one visualises how markedly a magazine story, for instance, differs — even in its linguistic fine structure — from the report of a daily newspaper and the front-page story of a tabloid; the differences becoming apparent here have to do with a multiplicity of more or less optimal decisions about available selections.[12] One chooses particular forms of presentation and patterns of news reporting, decides about structuring models and strategies of topicalisation, works with a particular syntax, a specific sentence length, and a characteristic sentential rhythm, exploits rhetorical figures and embellishing attractors (metaphors, alliteration, variations of introduced formulas, slogans and catchwords etc.) in variable mixture. One purposefully uses strategies of presentation (personalisation, scenes,

---

8   Hennig (2005). p. 271.
9   A survey of the different concepts of intelligibility research, which cannot be examined here in detail, is given by Bucher (2005).
10 See Hennig (2005), p. 271.
11 Partner hypotheses of the first degree are hypotheses about the actual opposite number in the process of communication; partner hypotheses of the second degree deal with the partner hypotheses about the partner hypotheses of the opposite number. See Hannapel/Melenk (1990), p. 17.
12 The diversity of media-linguistic offers is further increased due to the fact that a number of very basic factors are of relevance here, which cannot each be dealt with in detail. Questions like the following arise, for instance: Who are the people that participate in medial communication? What kind of knowledge do they possess, what is their social status, what are the relations between them? What is primarily used: speech or writing? The very decision for the written format is already of the highest consequence, as writing and written text separate recollected experience from concrete persons and turn it into public memory. In speech, however, what is talked about remains tied to the special features of the speech situation and the capabilities of retaining and recalling of the actual interactants.

dramaturgical means of creating and managing suspense, etc.), chooses from different perspectives (e.g. first-person narration or distanced observation), and displays different variants of reader address.[13]

To formulate a provisional conclusion: whoever works as a journalist, must frequently adapt his linguistic registers in accordance with situative and medial conditions, must take these factors into account, must control a sort of *variety switching*,[14] must constantly check communication offers for suitability in order to make desired potential effects at least somewhat probable.[15] Deepening the critical awareness of language to the effect that, in the well-reflected handling of communication, *what*-questions will be systematically replaced by *how*-questions, thus rendering a central figure of thought of constructivism productive in practice, must accordingly appear to be a central educational objective for quality journalists. From such a perspective, one observes and analyses how a text is built, how an utterance is shaped, how an attempt at persuasion is constructed, and in this way trains structured viewing. One does not primarily focus on the problem of whether what is described is correct or even true in an emphatic sense. The essential point here is to move away from the realistically intended what-questions of the common recipient (*what* is said?) to the how-questions of a professional communicator (*how* is something said?).[16]

The following arguments are intended to illustrate this perspective that is, of course, recognisably in agreement with constructivism: the excursus, which presents the vocabulary of Neo-Nazi groups and is based on an earlier book by the present author, will make clear how language can be used as a means of reality construction. In a subsequent section of the chapter, the findings of this book will be further exemplified by material from public debates—the central sources and suppliers of journalists. The group-specific linguistic extreme turns out to be a case of variety-specific normality the study of which appears to be rewarding. What neo-Nazi

13 There are obvious facts about language, which are of most general validity and independent of any situative and medial variable: language is the instrument of intended change (appeal function), the instrument of representation (representation function), and the expression of an emotional condition or attitude (expression function). On this typology deriving from Karl Bühler see the summary by Schiewe (1998), pp. 13f.

14 This concept is taken from Möhn (1998), p. 171.

15 Statements about potential media effects of any kind, which are intended to claim factually occurring effects, will be avoided in this context. There will be no support for a language-based theory of manipulation that would moreover contradict constructivist premises (keyword: cognitive autonomy). Such a theory—if it is intended to make absolute claims and not as a provisional hypothesis or an intentionally overstated danger warning—possibly overestimates the power of language: the consequence is that recipients are declared to be the immature and incapable victims of seduction, and that they are in this way absolved of all responsibility for their actions. Language is attributed moral guilt instead of condemning the behaviour and the moral attitudes of its users.

16 On this genuinely constructivist perspective, also its application in the didactics of writing, see Eckoldt (2002).

groups want is, of course, and fortunately, not a general, not a wide-spread, and not a publicly advocated concern. Their kind of goal-directed use of language impressively reveals, however, that there are indeed universally applicable strategies of persuasion whose adequate appreciation is of great value to quality journalists, because such knowledge can help to immunise them against attempts of ideological-political instrumentalisation of any colour. The evidence demonstrates, in any event, what enormous energies, and frequently also what aggressivity, are mobilised to impose and enforce group-specific designations and descriptions — and thus to create and establish realities.

2. The Language of Neo-Nazis: An Extreme Example

Patterns of Devaluation

It is certain words that strike one immediately when first reading what Neo-Nazis write.[17] They irritate one's linguistic sensibility, scuff one's moral nerve fibres, and arouse one's outrage by their inhuman and debasing tendency. One notices words like *multi-criminal, spongers, parasites*. One reads of surging floods, of an *invasion* of immigrants, of a *mass murder of German prisoners of war*, a *raping of the past*, an ongoing *genocide*. In stereotyped monotony, one is told about *fraudulent asylum seekers* and *foreign-race* immigrants. There is the prediction of an imminent *death of the nation* and the danger of *being swamped by foreigners*. These words referring to imagined enemies are used as catchwords.[18] They are employed as concise pseudo-argumentative slogans in order to characterise the others as recognisable enemies. *Being swamped by foreigners* and *death of the nation* condense the historical development of migration into an ideological keyword, summarising time dimensions and historical lines: 'We Germans must', one may read, for instance, 'recognise the dangers of *being swamped by foreigners* and fight with everything we have against the threatening *death of the German nation*.' One fears to be overwhelmed by a looming majority of immigrating foreigners, fears the *death of the nation* as the result of *being swamped by foreigners*. The catchphrase *fraudulent asylum seekers*, just like the still current NS-expression *foreign-race*, serves to isolate the others from a community that is defined by special moral or racial-biological properties: the others are defamed as criminals or are to be

---

17 The sources of all the examples culled from a multitude of Neo-Nazi organs and quoted in the following pages or marked by italics, will not be related in detail here, because they would swell the general list of references beyond all reasonable measure. Readers interested in the precise assignment of particular expressions to magazines or perhaps even to individual persons, are requested to consult my book: 'Die Konstruktion von Feindbildern' (Poerksen 2005a).

18 The method of analysis applied to catchwords as well as the linguistic discussion of this category, a category that is somewhat unpleasant from the point of view of science, is described in Poerksen (2005a, p. 138ff.).

totally discredited because of alleged biological inferiority. The pattern of reality construction is always the same: the others are transformed into entities that do not deserve affection, respect or protection.

Now it would certainly not to be true to say that the Neo-Nazis who usually gather in fairly small circles in low numbers, have withdrawn themselves into the world of their ideology and have severed all contacts with the external world. They are trying very hard to respond to public evaluations and ascriptions and to official legal assessments of the thoughts and deeds of partners in spirit, they continue, furthermore, to battle against established public communication about National Socialism in order to devastate its effect — everything most probably in order to make their own campaigning efforts more successful, or perhaps even without much or any conscious awareness. This means: the topics of their agenda are to a considerable extent dictated from outside and essentially determined by publicly raised objections against which they rise up in arms.[19] Accordingly, they try to react to concepts that are part of general linguistic usage and that appear to them — in their own view, against the background of their own ideology — to be disadvantageous, annoying or malicious. These reactions usually consist in attempts to discredit the language of their opponents, to dismantle it so as to deprive it of its efficiency: a particular type of vocabulary is set against other publicly used words. On a flyer one can read, for instance, that *hate of foreigners* is a 'word of propaganda' used to criminalise the legitimate rejection of foreigners. And one now wants to react to this apparently highly unwelcome accusation of hostility towards foreigners with the buzz-phrase *deutschfeindlich* [enemy of German(y)]. In this way, a very specific and only group-internally corroborated kind of semantics is devised: the word *deutschfeindlich* is used to characterise attitudes and actions and by implication made to refer to any kind of siding and active involvement with foreigners. All those persons and parties that publicly voice the reproach of hostility towards foreigners or are actively engaged in helping foreigners are, consequently, lumped together under the catchword *Deutschenfeinde* [enemies of Germans]. One of the smallest parties, *Nationale Liste*, banned long ago, already warned of a so-called *Inländerfeindlichkeit* [hostility towards nationals] allegedly widespread in

---

19 What may be observed in this example of a coupling to the system of values of the opponent is a phenomenon that I would like to call *re-active linguistic productivity*. This concept is meant to indicate a causal connection that finds its expression in linguistic creativity and that can be sketched out in the following way: the more relevant an idea is in public perception and the greater the difference is between this idea and the views of the political-ideological group, the more this group will try to propagate specific tendentious words, competing expressions and specially formed neologisms, in order to bring about a correction of public perception. One can reasonably assume that the ideological group believes that their concern to demonstrate and finally establish the validity of their own interpretations is attacked and damaged by publicly distributed views. And it is this concern that induces the group to bring competing expressions into play: they are intended to serve the destruction of the reality of the opponents — and, at the same time, to support the construction of a new way and manner of seeing.

Germany, just like the *Nationaldemokratische Partei Deutschlands* (NPD) that is turning extremely radical at present. The label *Deutschenhetze [instigation to the hatred of Germans]* is intended to react to the accusation of the instigation to racial hatred that has repeatedly been raised against rightwing extremists. Thus, a concept is offered that covers exclusively instigation to the hatred of Germans and, at the same time, stigmatises the criticism of rightwing extremist and Neo-Nazi positions as impertinent agitation that should actually be classified and prosecuted as a criminal offence. Günther Deckert, former leader of the NPD, in the meantime sentenced for instigation to racial hatred by a court, once spread the following couplet in Frankfurt: 'Bubis raus aus dieser Stadt, wir haben Deine Deutschenhetze satt.'

Another method, finally, is reinterpretation, a method that illustrates once more that the Neo-Nazi publicists in this country are effectually tied to the value judgements of their opponents. Again the reaction is directed at a word in current public usage that is felt to be a nuisance because it irritates the rightwing world view and attracts verbal energy: in the texts of Neo-Nazi authors, *genocide* becomes the object of an attempted re-interpretation and thus a crystallisation point of the repression of history and a testimony of the offensive self-styling of one's own people as a victim. In the standard language, *genocide* is often used in connection with the crimes of the National Socialists. Neo-Nazi groups, however, separate this word from the conventionalised contexts of usage in the standard language and attempt to reclaim it exclusively for their own people, write exclusively about a purported 'genocide of the German people' or a 'genocide by the infiltration of foreigners'. One could, therefore, read in a magazine produced by and for young Neo-Nazis: 'Any kind of integration of ethnically foreign groups is clearly defined as genocide.' Or one might encounter the slogan: 'Integration is genocide!' These examples, when considered carefully, once again reveal a special system of semantics. *Genocide* appears in the Neo-Nazi and rightwing media as the result of immigration and integration. *Murder* means in this connection: annihilation of an ethnically conceived identity.

The Dismantling of Reality by the Occupation of Concepts

In order to grasp fully the ideological dimensions of this semantic refurbishing of the concept, one must clearly envisage that Neo-Nazis and other rightwing extremists dispute the fact of the National Socialist genocide; they either downright reject it or try at least to relativise it—frequently by having recourse to other crimes in the history of mankind or by submitting pseudo-scientific expert reports. The purpose of such propaganda efforts is to cleanse the NS-ideology of the stain of criminality in order to salvage the closely related patterns of thought of neo-Nazi right wing extremism as a tolerably legitimate, but in any case still useful attitude of the present time. They reverse the relationship between the murderers and their victims by styling their own people as the victim of a crime that has allegedly been committed by immigrants. *Genocide*, by virtue of this reinterpretation, turns into a word that signals and highlights purported crimes of the opponents, but not the crimes committed by their own group or by their partners in spirit. In a quite comparable way the concept *Holocaust* is used: one need only think of certain NPD-functionaries talking, for instance, of a *Bomben-Holocaust;* here too a pattern and a strategy is recognisable: the dismantling of reality by the attempted occupation of concepts.[20]

The accepted standard to be brought into play for the evaluation of such efforts of propaganda is simply *the historical truth*. According to the general self-assessment, this is the criterion of the analysis and representation of one's own history.[21] Truth is the possession of the group; beyond the bounds of one's own group the confrontation with lies or *the lie in itself* sets in.[22] One is keen, however — and this is a very telling neologism — to make the 'Auschwitz-truth' become finally accepted. The research activities of persons and groups sharing the same loyalties are considered to be activities of truth production; one claims the quality of ultimate certainty for one's own findings and assumptions, relies on eyewitness testimony by partners in spirit, by so-called experts who lack, however, all the features of expert status, do not possess the claimed professional qualifications or the required professional knowledge, and are financially dependent on their clients. In pseudo-scientifically arranged and presented reports one pleads for credibility, introduces the academic titles of individuals and the label *scientific* as signals of prestige, imitates forms of presentation the external formal trappings of which (the enumeration of sources, use of footnotes, coherent manner of quotation etc.) are expected to underpin the

---

20 The proper political-ideological commitment often remains strangely ambiguous, though. Self-descriptions and direct or indirect characterisations of points of view by means of greeting or parting formulas, which have been discredited fundamentally in public, are often furnished with an aura of doubt and basic indeterminacy. Some Neo-Nazis use allusions or vary their ideologically more than obvious and clear partisanship — and close their letters 'with forbidden greeting' or also with 'Heil und Sieg!', because the 'reverse of this age-old German form of greeting ' is still, as is added in a supplementary note, prohibited by law. The ideological language of the Neo-Nazis is given a crypto-linguistic component whenever *Heil Hitler* is coded by the number 88; each one of the two figures stands group-internally for the eighth letter of the alphabet.

21 It is a difficult question whether some of the Neo-Nazis who deny the Holocaust are really convinced of the validity of their campaign. Michael Schmidt recorded an interview with Thies Christophersen, the author of the brochure 'Die Auschwitz-Lüge', which makes fairly clear that he does not really believe his own assertions. Schmidt, M. (1993), pp. 341-43.

22 Occasionally, probably in order to avoid prosecution, the word *Lüge* in conjunction with the definite article is advertised and propagated as an ideology-language synonym for *Auschwitz-* and *Gaskammer-Lüge*. One recognisably vacillates between the desire to be semantically unambiguous and to formulate in a legally incontestable way.

exactitude of the contents. One refers to the—purported—statements of renowned and recognised institutions and builds up veritable cartels of citation and corroboration in one's own media landscape, which generate the image of a hard and fast reality through constant repetition and suggest, through continual mutual quotation, that there is a diversity of sources and an enormous quantity of documents to support one's own assertions.[23]

Word Formation and World Perception

One may now ask oneself why some of these words and new expressions (*Bomben-Holocaust, Auschwitz-Wahrheit*) are actually formed. The answer is: they are linguistic manifestations of an ideologically influenced process of enquiry; they are formed because one thinks that the conventionally accepted designations are incorrect, that they are misleading, that they do not represent a perceived reality adequately. One wants to put public perception right with the means of word formation, one wants to express and formulate what ought to be perceived. Often particular neologisms[24] are created for the sole purpose of taking action against other variants of designations and conventionally established words, in order to set up a sort of competition of designations. In this way, a battle of words and a quarrel about alternatives of designation, which are differently oriented, arises in a kind of borderland between group language and common standard language. the concept of a multicultural society are rejected by right wing extremists. When Heiner Geißler 1988 introduced the concept of a multicultural society into the debate he intended this newly created expression to mean that the fact that Germany had become a country of immigration had simply to be acknowledged. What he wanted to designate had the character of a concrete utopia, of a realistic vision, that required critical debate. Right-wing extremists now react to this concept of a *multicultural society* that had for a long time been positively interpreted in the public sphere, with extreme irritation and diverse newly created expressions. With the word blend *Multikultopia* an author wants to communicate that he considers the concept of a multicultural society as utopian. Utopias are worthless. They are nothing but airy, unnatural, creations of the imagination, far removed from ordinary life and reality. The neologism *multicriminal* contains the assertion that the multicultural society is primarily characterised by the large number of crimes committed by foreigners. This new invention, however, shows a certain measure of creative linguistic refinement. *Multicultural* and *multicriminal* are partly identical and formed according to an analogical pattern. A slight variation on the plane of expression is intended to express the alleged true meaning of the

---

23 On the methods of holocaust deniers cf. the comprehensive contribution by Virchow (1996).
24 A summary of the relevant literature on neologism can be found in Poerksen (2005a), pp. 185ff.

concept, to disambiguate it—adequately in terms of the ideology. *Multi-Kulti-Mafia* is formed in order to express an assertion related to a conspiracy theory: it suggests that the concept of a multicultural society is part of a sophisticated system of conspiratorial plans designed, as a flyer proclaims, to create disorder and unrest among the population. *Mafia* as an element of word formation is always particularly suitable and most happily used whenever something is not to be explained but to be obscured and mystified. Such linguistic forms seem to give feelings of fear-driven rejection adequate linguistic expression.

Autodynamics of Linguistic Imagery

Repeatedly one hits upon words in the texts of right wing extremists and Neo-Nazis, which may be described as metaphors.[25] They deal, for instance, with a *Volkskörper* that seems in danger: the *Volkskörper* is one's own and it is put in jeopardy by enemies, it is equally the subject and object of ideological activity and worry. The abstract, unfeelable and invisible entity of the people is made concrete by this metaphor. The people is turned into a biological organism of a kind that may suffer damage in its entirety. The deviation from an imaginary ideal state of the body is then, if one sticks with the logic of this imagery, the disease. And the elimination of the disease appears to be the advised therapeutic procedure, the health-inducing order of the day. In the flyer of a neo-Nazi group one can read the sentence: 'We must simply take it upon ourselves to burn out the cancerous metastases, the plague spots and pus-filled blisters from our German people's body'. *Cancerous metastases,* plague *spots,* and *pus-filled blisters* are disease metaphors that are used to characterise objectionable persons (targets are: judges, prosecutors, journalists). The favoured therapy is a brutal one: the demand is to *burn out* the disease's focal areas. No postulate of gradation is in force or introduced that could serve as a guideline for the appropriate therapeutic effort. The application of lighter medication and measures at the beginning of treatment is not considered. And the operating agent in the treatment of the people's body is not to be a doctor, whatever the legitimation (not a dictator, not a deputy of the people), who could perform the operation. The surgeon of the state—Benito Mussolini[26] saw himself in this role—is not available, if one so will. The people itself is declared to be the chosen therapist; it has to become active itself: *we must take it upon ourselves to burn out*—that is the order.

The entire sentence ('We must simply take it upon ourselves to burn out the cancerous metastases, the plague spots and pus-filled blisters from our German people's body.') shows the closely structured relations within the

---

25 On the concept of metaphor and the paradigms of the theory of metaphor cf. Poerksen (2005a), pp. 212ff.
26 On Mussolini's metaphors see Rigotti (1987).

image-giving domain, the metaphorical elements *body*, *disease* and *therapy*. From the body one proceeds to the event of the disease and then arrives — apparently quite plausibly — at the need for therapy. There is an obvious connection and a chain-like arrangement of metaphors from different image-supplying fields. And this connection may be reconstructed via the implications of the metaphor: an image supplier (here: the body) is transferred to an image-receiver (here: the people). The metaphor of the *Volkskörper*, the people's body, emerges. The implication of the image-supplier (a body may fall ill) opens up the possibility to spin out the metaphor and to move in an apparently conclusive way to a new image-supplying field (here: disease). Persons perceived as opponents are described as diseases (*cancerous metastases, plague spots, pus-filled blisters*). The image-supplying field of disease entails (more conspicuously than the field of the body) the idea of therapy: in this way one has moved again back to the image-supplying field of medical therapy, again in an apparently conclusive way, which then expresses itself metaphorically in the command to *burn out* the disease. One can quasi start with the metaphor of the people's body, i.e with a metaphorical supposition whose contingency becomes invisible. This supposition is (supposedly) a suitable basis for the following metaphors; and thus one constructs the appearance of convincing necessity.[27]

Time and again, citizens of other countries are labelled *parasites*. Parasites exist, in the language of biology, at the expense of hosts and, as a rule, cause damage to other living beings. If a people is described in a more general way as a living being (and not specifically as a body), then another metaphorical thread may be reconstructed. The dangers that are envisioned can then be turned metaphorically not only into diseases but also into parasites that attack this living being: the enemy remains the destructive element, the releaser and the cause of profound injury. Neo-Nazis describe the German people as the *host people* that is exploited by foreigners. They would 'soak themselves like parasites with the blood of the German people.' This is a more than obvious identification with the language of the National Socialists. Adolf Hitler called the Jews 'parasites in the bodies of other people', which would 'suck them dry'. It is this metaphorical precedent that allows for the elaboration of the appeals implicitly carried by the parasite-metaphor: in the ideologically prepared context, this word must, by its allusion to the murdering of the Jews, be understood as a

---

[27] I suggest calling this phenomenon of the associations between different image-supplying fields, which has already been registered and treated in the relevant academic literature, a *chain of implications* or an *implicational chain*. By such an implicational chain I shall understand the associations between metaphors from different image-supplying fields, which can be reconstructed via the implications contained within them. The quoted sentence can be described as the result of such an implicational chain generating a certain apparent plausibility of the utterance in question.

threat of annihilation — at least in the German-language area. The description of a human being as a parasite, as a low and unpleasant animal, makes the murdering of this human being, in the sense of this metaphor and its implications, appear as an act of mere vermin killing; the parasite metaphor is intended to generate revulsion, and to lower the threshold of the inhibition to destroy.

The Construction of Dichotomous Realities

Metaphors of war and fighting — an equally central element of a particular metaphorical tradition — are especially suitable for black and white pictures, as they unavoidably always evoke the image of clear delimited fronts, and also posit, in every case, the distinction between friend and enemy as well as the existence of polar positions. The enemy as the aggressor: one describes immigrant foreigners in right wing texts as *invaders* or as *invading troops*; one states: the *foreigner mafia* conquers Germany. One claims to foresee an *invasion of foreigners* in Europe and speaks of a *theatre of war of the destruction of the German people*. A *battle against the infiltration of foreigners* is being fought. A fight for the defence is called for. *Defence action* must be taken, operations of *resistance*. The perspective expressed is dichotomous. On the one hand: the offensive metaphors highlight the violent actions of the enemy that has intruded into the metaphorically created horizon as an aggressor. On the other hand: the defensive metaphors describe one's own actions as operations of resistance and construct metaphorically a sort of situation of self-defence. One only defends oneself; the aggressors are the others, the enemies.

What gradually emerges is an ideologically stable parallel community, a world without grey colours, without nuances, a world of crude simplicities, where the children of the light and the spawns of darkness are neatly separated from each other. The opponent and the objects of the use of force are the liars, the wielders of power, the guilty, the evil, the criminals. One's own community — the collectively defined We — normally sees itself as the endangered victim, inferior and maltreated, stirred by the love for truth, acting solely in self-defence, incorporating the essential good. Language is thus used here in such a pitiless and brutally action-bent manner that no room is left for even the slightest doubt about the diagnoses rendered, that there can be no differentiating assessment, no time for deliberating and waiting, examining and probing. It is all just — one must put it so drastically — words and turds, calling and killing.

3. Generalisation of the Findings: The Linguistic World View

The Competition of Designations and the Daily Labour of Journalism

It has become evident that every act of designation is preceded by a conscious or unconscious decision about proper selection. The words, sentences and slogans used for this purpose express what *is* perceived and what *should* be perceived. They are terms of interpretation and tendentious words, which may even constitute — if they are considered within the total context of antagonistic interpretations — ideology-specific variants of designation as well as competing expressions. They must reproduce one's own opinion and point of view, and they are directed against other perspectives becoming manifest in variants of designation. However, such quarrelling about words and interpretations of reality is not a special phenomenon and observable only in small circles of extremists but proves to be a constitutive normal case of public language use, i.e. also an essential element of daily journalistic practice.

Learning Effects of a Deepened Critical Awareness of Language

The central findings — essential elements of a deepened critical awareness of language on a constructivist basis — will now be summarised here by means of a survey.

- Language signals, generally stated, what individuals or groups experience as reality, how they describe this reality, how they order it, and how they utilise it by differential evaluation. This implies accepting that speakers actually hold the views that manifest themselves in their use of language, even if one may personally reject these views — for whatever reasons. 'The fact', Hans Jürgen Heringer formulates concisely, 'that the speaker holds views different from mine, and my belief that these views are false, does not at all entail that the speaker is dissimulating.'[28]
- The proper understanding of linguistic communication, the deciphering of misunderstandings, and the cognitively profitable observation of differences in interpretation, are all stymied if the position of linguistic realism is taken and additionally mixed with partisanship deriving essentially from the following figure of thought: 'There is a clearly recognisable political truth. This truth manifests itself in language. We are able to recognise truth. Therefore, our language is the language of truth. The political opponent/enemy is not able to recognise truth or denies truth. Therefore, their language is the language of untruth, of deceit and of lies.'[29]

---

28 Heringer (1990), p. 50.
29 Qoted in Klein (1998), p. 188.

- The proper understanding of linguistic communication is facilitated and may be noticeably improved in the long run, if a constructivist view of language is adopted, which operates according to the following premises, amongst others: language is not a passive medium of mirroring an observer-independently given reality; it is not meaningful to presuppose essentially 'correct' designations, to assert that direct links exist between an extra-linguistic reality and (particular) linguistic forms, or to assume universally valid meanings for words, which would then commit everyone to reject specialised systems of semantics as erroneous and, in case of doubt, force them to enter into a direct, seemingly symmetrical dispute about what is allegedly prescribed by reality.

- The primary requirement, however, should be the training of the second-order observation of linguistically mediated realities, in order to reveal contrasting options, to demonstrate opportunities of thought manifesting themselves in different varieties and resulting from a comparison of different semantic systems. The particular attention devoted to different standards of the perception of reality will also prove that there are three constellations of group communication, which may essentially be distinguished and which will be categorised in a concise ideal-type format as *group-internal*, *group-relating* and *group-external*.[30] With regard to the question of a relative homogeneous world view, the use of language will be called *group-internal* if the system of reference underlying the interpretation of reality by the participant persons is identical in its essential features, if the participants are committed to shared specific values and also share a linguistic code. A *group-relating* use of a variety is based on the fact that the participants commonly presuppose at least comparable standards of reality interpretation. The *group-external* use of language, finally, concerns those with whom no given knowledge can be shared, and who do not belong to a similar group as members. They may be potential opponents, hold different views, but they may also be indifferent recipients. This kind of typology provides explanations for problems in communication that frequently result from the use of a group language that is not adequate to given situations; the group language in question may indeed be used between groups or outside groups but will then obviously not be understood.[31]

- A constructivist conception of language will help to register the constellation of varieties employed, to recognise competing designations with special sensitivity to the plurality of interpretative approaches, to

---

30 This triple is derived from the typology of the *internal*, *interactive*, and *external*, uses of professional or specialist languages, widely current in the study of linguistic variation. See also Möhn/Pelka (1984), p. 26.

31 A common example in this connection is, for instance, the group-external use of medical terminology to patients who lack the necessary medical knowledge.

elicit and establish competitions of designation[32] through comparing conventional, context-related, and private, semantic systems. It lends plausibility to the resolution to discard the idea of observer-independent, quasi objectively existant states of affairs that can be apprehended by language. 'Whenever the points of view and the representations diverge strongly', Hans Jürgen Heringer writes, 'it is reasonable only in a limited sense to speak of one and the same state of affairs. The differences of view are perhaps so considerable that sameness does not exist. Sameness will exist only in that the participants understand that they would like to speak about the same state of affairs, that they have a sort of common communicative point of departure or point of fixation, which alone will allow them to enter into any discussion or dispute.'[33]

- The goals and the views of reality, which are represented by individual agents or groups, are specific; the linguistic strategies, however, are universal.[34] One can develop catchwords and counter-catchwords from normal words, create neologisms and novel turns of phrase; one may use text-internally concatenated and mutually adjusted metaphors; one may re-interpret and re-evaluate concepts of opponents, purposefully exploit lexical ambiguities, leave the 'intended meaning suspended in ambiguity';[35] one may deliberately employ attractive key terms and highly charged expressions (e.g. *truth, freedom, human dignity, democracy*) without enlightening the group of addressees as to potentially differing interpretations.[36] One defames by association and subsumes opponent standpoints under as negative a global category as possible; correspondingly, one pleads for one's own cause with positively connoted flagwords,[37] constructs dichotomous conditions and sharp contrasts, and hardens one's own conceptions of reality by frequent repetition; one produces graphic demonstrations by means of strong visual expressions, and instigates word battles in the borderline areas between the different varieties that are understood to transport inevitably different views of what is commonly and vaguely called *the reality*.

- Whoever successfully manages to establish their designations and descriptions of reality, whoever manages to make their interpretative terms appear to be the only legitimate interpretations and to universalise the group-linguistically negotiated system of semantics, will establish their view of the world—will in this way create the reality

---

32 This is to mean: the differential interpretation of a potentially controversial concept by various language users. See Klein (1998), p. 192.
33 Heringer (1990), pp. 50f.
34 On such linguistic strategies, see the essential and as yet unsurpassed book by Dieckmann (1964).
35 Dieckmann (1964), p. 154.
36 On this kind of manipulative exploitation of so-called *ideological polysemy*, see Bachem (1979), p. 56.
37 On the terminological distinction between flagwords and enemy-words see Hermanns (1982).

that will become the standard point of orientation for themselves and everybody else.[38]

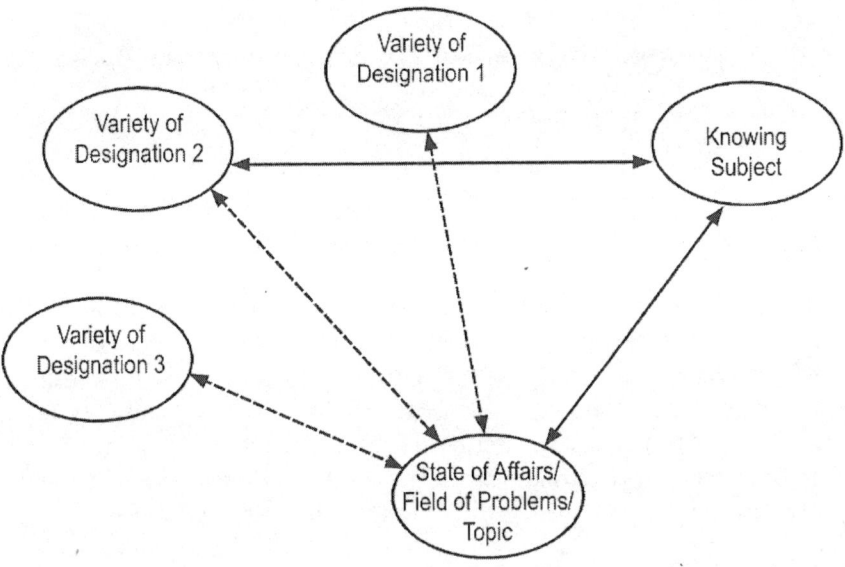

Figure 2

The use of language by an individual in a multiverse of interpretations of reality: a knowing subject, multiply formed by culture and nature, refers to a state of affairs/a field of problems/a topic, to which no observer-independent existence can be attributed from a constructivist perspective. The connection between linguistic form and state of affairs/field of problems/topic is not determined by nature. The description of the selected state of affairs is coupled directly with the knowing subject, is a symptom of their mode of observation and an expression of the specific variety chosen. This interpretation of reality through language takes place in a framework of other interpretations of reality that may simply have to be assigned to other varieties and other observers and are generally used in different constellations: with persons who essentially share one's own interpretations (group-internal use); with persons who only partially share them (group-relating use); or with persons who adhere to a completely different picture of the world (group-external use). These varieties of designation do not refer to one and the same state of affairs but represent products of interpretation, which are correlated by observers with a potentially identical, potentially similar, or totally different state of affairs; thus, the targeting precision of the reference to reality—the condition of the possibility of a difference of opinion—already proves to be the subject of controversies.

By way of a further interim summary this means: on the way to a constructivistically founded mode of reflection as well as a set of instruments for observation, which has been called the deepening of the critical

---

38 See also Heringer (1990), p. 48.

awareness of language, a number of elements must be attended to, i.e. the observer — (traditionally: the knowing subject), the observed (traditionally: the object of knowledge), and the linguistic, variety-specific formulation of all observation.

4. Against Linguistic Realism: Constructivist Considerations

The Principle of Linguistic Relativity

In the very first chapter of a fundamental book by the psychologist Ernst von Glasersfeld, the originator of radical constructivism, we hit upon the statement: 'Problems with the notion of reality cropped up early in my life because I grew up with more than one language.'[39] What then follows is an autobiographical sketch interspersed with reflections on the philosophy of language and the theory of knowledge. Growing up as the child of a family of diplomats, Ernst von Glasersfeld learnt German, English and Italian in the environments of his childhood, and French at a boarding school in Switzerland. After studying mathematics at Zurich and Vienna, he was skiing instructor in Australia, farmer in Ireland, journalist and translator in Italy, finally professor of cognitive psychology in the USA — domiciled proverbially in ever different, and ever new, worlds, and never subjected to the monopoly of interpretation by only one exclusive, apparently ultimate view of the world. Very early, he says, it had thus become clear to him, 'that to get into another language required something beyond merely learning a different vocabulary and a different grammar. It required another way of seeing, feeling, and ultimately another way of conceptualising experience.'[40] On the complex process of language acquisition we can read:

> The child realises already at the beginning of its life that it can achieve incredibly much by means of the sounds it utters, that these sounds are an extremely effective tool. But it also realises that it is very difficult to learn how to use this tool. At the beginning of one's life one is not given a plan that explains all the meanings, but one is dependent on learning them from situations and by trying out language by using it. The application of every single word is accompanied by mistaken inferences; one cobbles one's own word meanings together only step by step and in a very long-drawn-out process. And the meaning that one associates with a sound or a sequence of letters finally results from the experience that one makes in interactive situations with other speakers. When I live among Italians, I get to know a particular way of looking at the world and dividing it up. And when I am sharing experiences with English people, at the same time, then I very quickly realise that there are marked differences between these two languages. The Italians and English speakers may each believe that their own language grasps the world in an exact manner. To me who lives between these languages

---

39 Glasersfeld (1996), p. 24.
40 Ibid., p. 25.

and worlds, it is merely possible to accept the non-transcendable subjectivity of word meanings and to state the characteristic differences in their views of reality. And from this experience of my life results the interest in what is called reality.[41]

What is formulated and illustrated[42] here by examples of the different use of prepositions in different languages and the conceptual relations generated by them, and furthermore by examples of the use of particular verbs, is part of the basic knowledge of linguistics and goes under the title of *Sapir-Whorf-hypothesis*[43] — an assumption in the philosophy of language which is approvingly mentioned by the constructivist Ernst von Glasersfeld.[44] The assumption is that the grammatical and lexical structures of a native language[45] specify the cognitive potential of its speakers and consequently affect, through complex processes of influence, the behaviours and the organisation of the societal lives of these speakers in their entirety.

Topics of the Constructivist Reflection of Language

Whether one considers the assumption of linguistic determinism plausible or not, the ideas put forward by Ernst von Glasersfeld may nevertheless be taken to be symptoms and expressions of a typical mode of observation, i.e. of a particular world view: they represent — as can be confirmed by many examples from the constructivist literature — a profound interest of the constructivist cue-providers in the philosophy of language and the criticism of language, which involves different core topics:

- First of all, a position has to be chosen for dealing with the core problem of the philosophy of language, i.e. establishing the adequate

---

41 Glasersfeld (2002), pp. 61f.
42 Ibid., pp. 62f.
43 The hypothesis claims, as already explained, that different languages convey different ways of viewing reality to their speakers. To verify this assumption, Whorf (1963) investigated the language of the Hopi Indians, amongst others, and compared it with other languages.
44 Mitterer (1993, p. 33ff.) has, by contrast, formulated the epistemological criticism of this hypothesis that it can hardly be considered compatible with a consistently argued kind of constructivism: one still assumes, after all, that only *one* reality exists as the point of reference of the diagnosis of linguistic differences; and it is this single reality that is, according to the assumption, only interpreted differently by different languages. On a relativisation of the Sapir-Whorf-hypothesis from the perspective of linguistics, cf. Gipper (1972).
45 This means furthermore: the Sapir-Whorf-hypothesis is positioned on a particular level, i.e. the level of native languages and linguistically defined nations. Systematic attempts of a group-related reformulation of this *principle of linguistic relativity* and the corresponding linguistic and cognitive determinism in connection with concrete varieties do not exist as far as I can see. Conclusions of this kind seem warranted, however: on a group-level — and in dependence on the inter-group mobility of speakers — the assumed cognitive constraints will certainly not be effective with total force. They merge with interfering group-languages that possibly transport different world views and thus loosen the compulsory modes of perception of the other variety without, however, opening up the view towards the *one* reality that Whorf obviously presupposed. The assumed determinism is, therefore, one may surmise, re-configured and re-constellated, but not suspended.

relationship between language and (absolute) reality and an observer-independently given external world, and ascertaining that the topicalisation of this relationship makes sense at all from the perspective of a consistently argued and conclusively elaborated kind of constructivism. Whenever, for instance, Humberto R. Maturana speaks of language, and speaking about language simultaneously illustrates an autological structure,[46] then he does not refer to a system of signs, which is used for purposes of communication or even for the transfer of information. He is not concerned with the meaning of concepts (semantics), the structure of words and sentences (lexicology and syntax), the purposeful usage and the situation-bound application of concepts, words and sentences (pragmatics), but with the transcendental condition of all reflection and all potentially epistemological statement and assertion: 'We must be quite clear about the fact that the very idea of something given and existing, and the very reference to some reality or some sort of truth, unavoidably involves language. Whatever we are able to say about that truth or reality is dependent on the availability of language. What is supposedly independent of us becomes describable only when language is available, emerges only through an act of distinction by means of language.'[47] This means: language is no prison from which one could escape either by means of sophisticated attempts to break through its walls or by the considered rejection of language-bound incarceration, language is much rather a form of existence, a mode of co-existence, about the other world of which one may certainly speak, but to which one cannot simultaneously add the dimension of that other world. Even the fundamental problem of the philosophy of language, i.e. negotiating the relation between the intrinsically linguistic and the extra-linguistic, consists in the observer-specific effort of correlation, which can only be enacted within the cognitive system. Consequently, the 'operative apprehension of non-linguistic realities by means of language ' and the 'striking impact of the external world on language'[48] belong to the domain of metaphysical speculation. To formulate it briefly and concisely with Richard Rorty: 'The world does not speak; only *we* speak.'[49]

- Moreover, the *knowledge-forming influences* of language have been spelt out extensively from a constructivist perspective. One comes across the assumption of a general linguistic determinism in the constructivist literature (as for instance the Sapir-Whorf-hypothesis that was introduced and discussed earlier on), but one also meets with explicit statements pointing out the consequential cognitive costs of

---

[46] In the very moment that one speaks about language, language is generated; the concept requires itself in order to be defined.
[47] Maturana/Poerksen (2004), p. 29.
[48] Luhmann, quoted in Winter (1999), p. 153.
[49] Rorty, quoted in Winter (1999), p. 153.

particular linguistic forms and expressions. Heinz von Foerster, quite in keeping with such considerations, has evaluated linguistic nominalisation, i.e. turning verbs into nouns, as an epistemological kind of partisanship, as the more or less conscious advocating of an ontological point of view: actions and processes would be turned into things, apparently substance-like entities; one would transform movement into stasis, ontogenesis into ontology.[50] And Siegfried J. Schmidt, in a book chapter on 'language, writing, thing and truth'[51] assesses orality and literacy as two different variants of cognition with their own specific demands and possibilities. Oral cultures are, he concludes, 'moulded by the ephemeral character of speech and the constraints of oral communication (e.g. limited range, co-presence of speakers and hearers in the same situation).'[52] Writing, by contrast, would allow 'the production of a line of continuity of thought that would exist in texts, independently of individual minds and communications, and could thus be utilised again and again. Knowledge becomes storable outside human minds, retrievable, consultable. In view of growing archives, however, remembering and forgetting become a problem, and conceptions of knowledge and information as material objects are encouraged. Writing effects a separation between the knower and the known (science) and creates the condition of the possibility of ideas of objectivity and de-personalised truth. It promotes introspection and the individualisation of the lonely writer and reader.'[53]

- Realist theories of language and meaning have been subjected to penetrating criticism. The concept of reference of classical semantics, which is based on the premises of a realist epistemology[54], has been rejected from the point of view of a constructivistically designed semantics, which consistently places all reference to sections of reality into the universes of linguistic activity and conventional agreements on the basis of given knowledge. Semantic reference, according to Siegfried J. Schmidt, is 'a linguistic operation related to communication and common-sense knowledge, not to an observer-independent reality.'[55] The combination of sound-image and meaning is unavoidably something that individuals carry out actively, and in which they partake to an extent that need not involve or require consensus. The meanings of an element of language are, therefore, not identical in a verifiable sense. 'In my view, it is impossible to expect that a person's utterance activates precisely the same thoughts and conceptual net-

---

50 Cf. Segal (1988), pp. 65ff.
51 Schmidt (1998), pp. 93ff.
52 Ibid., p. 94.
53 Ibid., pp. 95f.
54 Reference obtains, according to the presupposed epistemological assumption, if the object of reference actually exists.
55 Schmidt (2000), pp. 27f.

works that the person originally associated with it.[56] The situation, however, is this: 'The receiver of a piece of language, be it a word, a sentence, or a text, faces a task of interpretation. A piece of language directs the receiver to build up a conceptual structure, but there is no direct transmission of the meaning the speaker or writer intended.'[57] If one wants to check the quality of a particular act of understanding, one can only go by what one has said oneself — and by what the other has said or done, which is naturally mixed with individual and subjective experiences of one's own; the cognitive system of the opposite number is totally inaccessible to analysis. The *impression of understanding* arises because the other does not say or do anything that would indicate any interpretation of what has been said, which one might consider to be false or misleading.[58]

- One pleads finally for a change in the use of language on the basis of constructivist premises because of the inevitable fundamental question: How can one speak or write in a way that will make the thesis of the observer-dependence of all cognition visible at any moment of speaking? How can one show that all our descriptions of the world are not the descriptions of an external world but the descriptions of an observer who, when arguing as a realist, takes these descriptions to be descriptions of the external world? Siegfried J. Schmidt decides for the explicit topical foregrounding of the problem of language in order to evade the objection of a rhetorical self-contradiction and writes: "I would like to request the reader to substitute tacitly all assertions of existence and activity (A is …, B does…) in the following text with formulations like 'I describe A as…', 'in my theoretical proposal the supposition is that B … does'."[59] Ranulph Glanville programmatically connects *second order cybernetics,* which is closely related to constructivism, with the use of active verbs, a style of writing in the first person, and the admission that any kind of observation possesses an autobiographical dimension.[60] And Heinz von Foerster, in this context, contrasts the *existential operator* (the mode of asserting existence according to the pattern 'there is…') and the *self-referential operator* (the mode of observer-relative judgments according to the pattern 'I think that…').[61] He provides, as it were, the epistemologically justified rehabilitation of first-person speech and writing.[62]

---

56 Glasersfeld in conversation with Poerksen (2004h), p. 40.
57 Glasersfeld (1996), p. 230.
58 See Glasersfeld in conversation with Poerksen (2004h), p. 40.
59 Schmidt (2000), p. 22.
60 Glanville (2004), p. 4.
61 Foerster, in conversation with Poerksen (2004g), pp. 6ff.
62 The founder of the movement *General Semantics*, Alfred Korzybski, tried to develop a different form of language in order to make clear to his readers: the word is not the thing; nobody can say everything about an event; everything changes. Out of this certainly most honourable search for a new form emerged, one might be tempted to say maliciously, a bureaucracy for relativistic thinkers. Korzybski suggested adding the number of the year in small print to every

5. Linguistic Realism in Journalism: A Proposal for a Systematic Approach

Objectivity and Orientation

Truth and *reality*, *fact* and *objectivity* are, as can easily be shown, key concepts of the self- and other-observation of journalism. According to the first edition of an introduction to journalism that has become widely known, an item of news — to be understood here as a form of presentation, not as the raw material of journalistic editorial procedures — is 'the objective communication of a generally interesting and newsworthy topic or state of affairs in a particular formal setup',[63] Serious journalism, a publicist writes, occupies itself with reality and strives to approximate truth.[64] 'Facts, actuality, reality — these are the points of orientation of the endeavour for objectivity',[65] one can read in a practice-oriented textbook that reflects the norms of the profession. This is certainly a clearly formulated assumption that would meet with consensus within the trade, but it is epistemologically problematical and thus must stimulate and inspire conceptual differentiation.

Accordingly, reality is the *point of reference* of presentations, the pole of orientation for observers. Reality is or should be central to journalism; and reality possesses — depending on the concrete pattern of expression — a descriptive and a prescriptive dimension. One may state that journalism represents reality; one may demand or complain that this does not happen. Or one may mix prescriptive and descriptive statements, which can then be reduced to the following formula: journalists can indeed represent reality, but they do this in an insufficient and inadequate manner; the quality of representation must be improved in the future, the degree of correspondence between representation and reality must be raised in the direction of the final, structurally point-to-point-isomorphic medial representation of reality.[66] Hence, the approximation of the truth marks the *cognitive process* and indicates *the method of enquiry* in a general sense. The

---

name in order to express clearly that human beings and things change in the course of time. He further recommended to index every ambiguous word with a figure in order to make clear which of the specific meanings (1, 2 or 3 etc.) was being referred to at the moment of speaking. On the discussion of this curious proposal, which once more suggests and pursues an un-ambiguousness of meanings that is unattainable, see Poerksen (2004f, pp. 151f.) in conversation with Schmidt.

63 La Roche, quoted in Zschunke (2000), pp. 102f.
64 Weck (2002), p. 58.
65 Zschunke (2000), p. 118.
66 The guiding difference *descriptive/prescriptive* is proposed by Weber (1999a, p. 60) to mark different epistemological positions.

concept of truth stands for the *result* of objective, reality-related representation, the ultimate goal of observation.[67]

Discrediting Reality and Avowing Truth

This conceptual distinction will enable us, in a further step of systematic re-organisation, to subject the current vocabulary of journalistic self- and other-observation to critical analysis and reflection, and to dissect it roughly by its goal-orientations: the different varieties of *truth avowal* must be distinguished from patterns of statement that are used to *discredit assumptions of reality*. Both variants can be used descriptively and/or prescriptively.[68]

- The discrediting of methods of enquiry in journalism[69] is practised, for instance, with the following words and word groups: *lack of distance/independence, excessive closeness, subjectivity, partisanship, lack of neutrality, lack of reality reference, lack of direct connection with events, lack of adequate relation between text/item of news/medial presentation and reality*. Processes of enquiry may be discredited with expressions like the following: *distort, falsify, obscure, conceal, estrange/alienate, stage/dramatise, lie, deceive, disfigure, stray from the truth, pass reality by, move away from the truth, obstruct access to reality, have no counterpart in reality, lead astray, manipulate, spread prejudices, exaggerate, overstate/blow up, represent only a small section of reality*. Results of enquiry may be fundamentally depreciated by describing them as *lies, falsification, fiction, mistake, distortion* and *perversion, staging/dramatisation/show* and *accusation/insinuation without foundation, incorrect assertion, emotionally charged news reporting, mixing news and opinion*. Possible diagnoses will state, depending on the social temperature of the media-critical controversy, a *distorted perception* and a *disturbed relationship with reality*; the insinuations pointing in the direction of characterising an antagonist as pathological are more than obvious.

- Truth avowals relating to methods and processes of enquiry are expressed by the following vocables: *depict, reconstruct precisely, describe objectively, prove, verify, present in a matter-of-fact way, know, reveal, disclose, uncover, unmask, convict, unveil, look behind the scenes, approximate reality/objectivity/truth, render in an unadulterated way, render the pure naked news/information, possess maximal proximity to reality.*

---

67 On this proposal of terminological precision see, as already noted elsewhere, Weischenberg (2001a), p. 16.

68 The following reflections owe decisive stimulation and many examples to the work of Mitterer (2000a and 2000b as well as 2001), particularly his criticism of dualistic philosophy and argumentation.

69 Numerous exemplary expressions and turns of phrase have been collected by Mitterer (see especially 2000a and 2001); linguistic examples used to discredit assumptions about reality or relating to forms of truth avowal in journalism can be found in the discussion of the journalistic ideal of objectivity presented by Zschunke (2000, pp. 101ff.). On the corresponding linguistic strategies, see also Weber (2000a), pp. 28f.

Typical formulations of solidifying reality are: unprejudiced consideration proves...; it is completely clear that...; a neutral observer must state...; as is well known...; careful examination of the truth contents yields...; every expert can confirm...; it is uncontroversial...; serious sources confirm...; unbiased research confirms. Avowals of truth by which results of enquiry are to be assessed and linguistically certified can be found in the core vocabulary of realism: *in reality, factually, undoubtedly, realistic, sure, certain, reality/actuality, evident fact, fact, final proof, truth.*

Avowals of truth as well as formulas used to discredit assumptions of reality work with the concept of the 'right distance' and the 'idea of objective distance'[70] upon which corresponding diagnoses are based.[71] 'According to this idea', Josef Mitterer writes, 'judgements that are made from a certain distance, namely the right distance, are considered to be more reliable than judgements that are not based on the same kind of distance. This distance may be of a temporal, spatial or an emotional nature.'[72] The truth avowals and the assumptions of an objective distance are usually offered in de-personalised form,[73] the discrediting of other statements, however, is referred to a specific observer: 'One's own view is de-personalised, because it is this view for which the claim to truth is made. [...] The deviant view, on the contrary, against which the objection of falsehood is advanced, is personalised.'[74] The observer retreats to the point of irrecognisability (*it becomes apparent that...; one may state with certainty...*) behind his observations, he turns into a mere mouthpiece of the experience of Being. By contrast, the assertion that a statement is untrue, frequently uses the strategy of personalisation. Here the total burden of untruth is chained to the subject (the opponent *erroneously believes..., holds the wrong view..., falsely assumes...*).[75]

---

70 Mitterer (2000b), p. 243.
71 The problem of the right distance in journalism is succinctly formulated by Krainer (2001, p. 162), who writes: 'Journalists must (be able to) keep close to, and well away from, an event. The closer they are the greater the danger of involvement that may cause perspectival blindness—the greater the distance the more difficult the acquisition of relevant sources of information. To be able to criticise holders of power, journalists must keep a critical distance from them, to be able to acquire relevant (additional) information, they must cultivate a certain relationship of closeness to those in power.'
72 Mitterer (2000b), p. 243.
73 From a constructivist point of view, the question of the right distance can naturally not be clarified with ultimate certainty because diagnoses of this kind presuppose at least partial knowledge of the Absolute—how else would it be possible to assess the closeness or the distance in relation to an unconditional kind of truth? The distinction between event and medial processing and representation must, by consequence, also be considered to be a posited and not an ontic difference.
74 Mitterer (2001), p. 91.
75 Cf. Mitterer (2001, p. 91) and also the above-introduced distinction Foerster's between an *existential* and a *self-referential operator,* which also recurs to the strategies of assertion described here—depersonalisation and personalisation of assertions.

6. Understanding and Improving

Considering the collected findings in their totality shows that the constructivistically founded programme of deepening critical awareness of language pursues and serves four objectives:

- It is, first, intended to enable students to decipher communication problems in their daily journalistic work, to relate them to a use of language that is possibly inadequate for the communication situation, that does not match the constraints and demands to which the journalists are exposed and subjected. Well-reflected language criticism is not of the kind that cultivates a pedantic obsession with the popular sport of hounding words and expressions from other languages or nurses the worries of schoolteachers in connection with spelling reforms — thus mixing linguistic and social criticism with the defamation of disliked persons in a more or less justifiable way.[76] Well-reflected language criticism is, as a rule, always criticism of the adequate use of language in relation to speech situations and the constraints of the medium involved. Adequate critical awareness of language is, therefore, inevitably context-bound, orients itself by concrete language usage, persistently indicates the normality of misunderstanding, the improbability of successful communication, and all the many conditioning factors that permeate every act of linguistic communication.[77]

- Deepening the critical awareness of language on a constructivist basis is intended, secondly, to draw attention to the manifold linguistic strategies that can be employed for purposes of persuasion and manipulation, whenever events and assessments, controversies and debates of public (and thus always also: journalistic) interest are concerned. Understanding these mechanisms in the ubiquitous processes of persuading and convincing, and observing the corresponding strategies at work, is useful because it will help to limit illegitimate attempts to exert influence, at least in the ideal case.

- Thirdly, optimising one's own communicative and media competence through the mode of second order observation is a further item on the list of desirable objectives. Analytical competence and the intensive occupation with the *how*-questions of a professional communicator make up the decisive first stage of acquiring communicative competence whose regular accompanying features they will (have to) be later on.

---

[76] On the history and the varieties of language criticism in a more specific sense, cf. Schiewe (1998).

[77] What is necessary is that the communicating individuals control a language, know the rules of the situation (situational knowledge), possess lexical, syntactic and genre-specific knowledge (linguistic knowledge), can appreciate particular terms and states of affairs, and are able to place the event in question in the appropriate slot of the news reporting process (encyclopaedic and episodic knowledge). And finally, they must, of course, be motivated to produce an utterance and — depending on the mode of interaction — produce appropriate follow-up utterances.

- And it is, fourthly, the explicit concern of the project to point out more or less hidden realisms and ontological contaminations[78] that pervade linguistic varieties and the languages of the media.

This process of deepening the critical awareness of language makes evident what one can do with language, i.e. generate descriptions that cannot be compared with an absolute reality but certainly with other descriptions. The object of a description — supposedly positioned in an imaginary other world of language to which one refers when using linguistic symbols — is dissolved into descriptions that continue themselves, that can be counteracted, corrected or simply terminated by new descriptions. Descriptions from now on are based on descriptions so far. 'To talk about an object', Josef Mitterer writes, 'means to continue the discourse so far in a discourse from now on. To describe an object means to continue the description so far /an object/ and thus transform the object into a new object of further descriptions.'[79] No single description, consequently, possesses the dignity of a particular closeness to its object in the sense of emphatic truth. No description can be separated from the object of the description, can be peeled out of its linguistic garments, as it were, and be assessed in its pure, naked form. All descriptions drift in time, are deepened for the most diverse reasons, break off at some stage, start afresh, continue an already available description, but are and will remain unavoidably and at any moment just one thing: finally provisional.

---

78 Ontologically contaminated forms of assertion describe, as I would like to define it, particular entities and phenomena as given independently of an observer. They entail the presupposition of a special privilege of knowledge for the speaker: it is the speaker who diagnoses closeness to truth or criticises deviation from reality.

79 Mitterer (2001), p. 107 (author's emphasis).

Chapter IV

Deepening Awareness of Media-Epistemology

1. The Programme of Media-Epistemology: Sketch of an Idea

Contours of a Concept

Media-epistemology, Siegfried J. Schmidt notes, cannot 'really be considered to have become an accepted term'[1]. His programmatic article containing this remark was published in the year 1999; however, the diagnosis of deficient conceptual contours has in the meantime lost nothing of its topical significance. The concept of media-epistemology has emerged from within the context of media-philosophy, which seems to become more firmly established day by day.[2] It is constituted through the delimitation from media-*ontology*,[3] is discussed in connection with the philosophy of pragmatism[4] and in close association with constructivism,[5] and can also be correlated with core assertions of the systems-theoretical modelling of the mass media.[6] Media-epistemological investigations show a certain substantial affinity to the current debate about *medialisation*.[7] And finally, the

---

[1] Schmidt (1999), p. 120.
[2] On media-philosophy, see for foundations: Hartmann (2000), Sandbothe (2001), Münker/Roesler/Sandbothe (2003), and for a systematic presentation of topics of reflection also Sandbothe/Nagl (2005).
[3] Cf. the proposal by Weber (2003e, p. 174), who quite clearly distances himself, though, from the traditional philosophical understanding of the concept when he writes: 'By ontology I here understand the set of all universal statements about the (relatively time-independent) essence of all knowledge, by epistemology the set of all trend-statements about temporarily dynamic and, therefore, changeable processes of cognition.' Media-epistemology would, by consequence, be the epistemologically grounded and empirically interested observation of trends in the domain of the media.
[4] See the conception of a pragmatic media-philosophy by Sandbothe (2001).
[5] Schmidt (1999) and Weber (2003e).
[6] Just think of Luhmann's (2004) fundamental book with the title: 'Die Realität der Massenmedien'.
[7] Observers of processes of medialisation confirm the increasing amalgamation of medial realities with societal and political spheres. The process of medialisation, according to

growing importance of the Internet and the explosive boosting of net-based communication have recognisably strengthened the attraction power of this concept; after all, the constructability of perceptions and realities in virtual spaces has become a tangible experience for everyone and so has media-epistemology as the daily practice of designing and producing images and structures of new worlds. 'Media-epistemology, as a variant of epistemology in the epoch of the Internet, of systems theory and constructivism', to quote Siegfried J. Schmidt once again, 'begins with the recognition of difference, of dissension and plurality, in particular of a plurality of different cognitive systems and of a plurality of different realities and orders of values.'[8]

If deepened media-epistemological awareness is projected as an educational objective for quality journalists, then one has to face the fundamental problem of how to plan and organise an introduction to an area of research that does not yet exist in clearly contoured and fully matured form. However, to make the proposed educational objective more precise, it cannot be sufficient to report the state of research, to rearrange what is available and to condense it according to the specific interests of studying and teaching. It is much rather necessary to proceed from one's own suppositions and to answer a number of core questions in order to be able to illustrate the programme of a media-epistemology in further chapter sections by means of such exemplary analyses as are, or could be, of importance to the practice of journalism.

The Position of Media-Epistemology

The first basic question that must be answered in the course of the gradual staking out of the area of investigation concerns what systematic position ought to be assigned to media-epistemology. Media-epistemology could be classified as a special case of epistemology, or as a case of its application; systematically speaking, it would then belong to philosophy, perhaps also to media philosophy, although the status of the latter as a genuine discipline is still questionable and controversial.[9] This consider-

---

suggestions by Schulz, is characterised by four types of phenomena. Among them are: the extension of media offers (*extension*), the replacement of medial activities by non-medial activities (*substitution*), the mixing and disassociation of medial and non-medial activities (*amalgamation*) and, finally, the orientation of (political) agents and their organisations by the logic of the media (*accomodation*). The debate is certainly paradigmatic in its claim that media are significant for the formation of society, culture, identity, and daily interaction; still controversial are, however—depending on authors and definitions of the concept of medialisation—the degree and the intensity of such determination. Cf. Donges (2005), p. 324 and Schulz (2003a), pp. 4ff.

8   Schmidt (1999), p. 119.
9   Cf. the contribution by Seel (2003, pp. 10ff.), who declares media-philosophy to be a transitory albeit important fashion: it changes, the argument runs, the perspective of philosophy, but cannot claim the status of a discipline proper and should not be granted that status in the future.

ation appears evident if one remembers that epistemology as a special and central domain of philosophy has always, in its classical European constitution, occupied itself with the relationship between, and the specific constellation of, subject (the observer) and object (the observed).[10] Epistemological conceptions always treat that which influences, forms, limits or enables perceptions, i.e. whatever may be effectively happening between subject and object, between self and world, and in whatever ways that possibly require and deserve closer scrutiny.

This basic constellation of epistemological distinctions and questions is spelled out quite differently by various authors: systems theorists like Niklas Luhmann replace the concept of subject by the concept of system and deal with epistemological questions of foundation — for example — by having recourse to the formative influence of the mass media; these fundamental questions are reformulated on the bases of an operative constructivism and second order cybernetics, they are then transposed and translated into another form of theory.[11] Constructivists like Siegfried J. Schmidt understand reality as the (temporarily) stable results of processes that emerge from a self-supporting domain of effects consisting of four instances (cognition, communication, media, and culture); cognition and communication are, according to this assumption, structurally coupled by means of media offers, and this happens by means of culture that is here understood as a programme of interpretation of dichotomously organised models of reality that are topicalised in media offers.[12] The pragmatist Mike Sandbothe — inspired by Richard Rorty — connects media-philosophical theory work with the concern to support and improve democratic core virtues (equal opportunities, fairness, tolerance etc.); his goal is to replace self-centred academic philosophising by concentrating on knowledge with practical application.[13] A *theoreticist* conception of media-philosophy (reflection as an end in itself, as an intellectual glass bead game) is taken under fire and a 'pragmatic service function'[14] of media-philosophy is demanded. At the end of his book, Mike Sandbothe proposes the concept of an *experimental media-epistemology*: 'Its concern is', we can read, 'to investigate technical distribution media as instruments that, due to their influence on semiotic media of communication and spatio-temporal media of perception, can contribute to a transformation of

10 Other epistemological concepts and approaches, which do not involve the strict separation of subject and object, can only be mentioned here. See for an exemplary discussion, Varela in conversation with Poerksen (2004i).
11 See in particular Luhmann's (2004, pp. 16ff.) explanation of his understanding of constructivism.
12 On this model, see e.g. Schmidt (1999, pp. 122ff.) and Weber (2000a), pp. 41f.
13 A summary of the central arguments and claims is provided by Margreiter (2003, pp. 164ff.) and Sandbothe himself (2003, pp. 185ff.).
14 Sandbothe (2001), p. 13.

our everyday understanding of reality.'[15] Theorists inspired by post-modern thinking, like Frank Hartmann, promulgate the (new) indistinguishability of reality and simulation with a slightly euphoric undertone and make out an irreversible mixture of discourses,[16] in which improvisation and association replace systematic argumentation. This methodical anti-method culminates with Frank Hartmann in the formula that will hardly admit a science-conforming interpretation: 'It's all jazz.'[17]

But still, despite all their differences, the quoted examples from relevant work make the fundamental problem of media-epistemology quite clear, a problem that may be condensed into the following question: How do media construct reality, and how and because of what investigative approaches, concepts, discourses etc. can the reality of their construction of realities the observed?[18] The options available in the domain of potential basic theories show that the more specific positioning in some discourse must be decided about in a well-reasoned way. In the present context, the proposal is supported that media-epistemology be understood as a component of constructivism and be conceived as a constructivistically grounded epistemology that occupies itself with the production of media realities. The consequence: the focal problem is not *distortion* in an emphatic sense of truth,[19] because that would 'presuppose an ontological, a given, objectively accessible, and construction-free apprehensible reality, basically the old cosmos of essences.'[20] The goal, or perhaps better, the distant goal is, in a formulation by Siegfried J. Schmidt, the *rewriting of relevant epistemological* questions for media societies.[21]

Relevance of Media-Epistemology

The second fundamental question is: Why is such a proposal, i.e. to involve and perhaps even harass fledgling quality journalists with media-epistemological questions, made at all? The answer is to be found in the widely accepted insight that socialisation today is largely and increasingly socialisation through media, that the logic of the media exerts

---

15 Ibid., p. 236.
16 See Hartmann (2000), p. 329.
17 Ibid.
18 On this key question see also Luhmann (2004), p. 20.
19 This also implies that a certain form of the lamentation of loss, which is propagated by critical or post-modern media theorists, is no longer possible. They speak or write of *de-realisation* and the *de-realisation of the world*, of the *disappearance of reality*, of the *loss of true reality* etc. (some examples can be found in: Weber, S. (1995), p. 110). The problem with diagnoses of this kind is their epistemological naivety: whoever argues in this way propagates at least implicitly a clandestine realism. Talking about the disappearance of reality presupposes the knowledge of *the* reality as the pole for comparison and experience, for purely logical reasons, whose evanescence is then deplored.
20 Luhmann (2004), p. 20.
21 See Schmidt (1999), p. 121.

growing structure-forming influence, and that the possibility of personal and private control of authenticity and primary experience for a media public enmeshed in a worldwide communication space of gigantic dimensions is, for practical-pragmatic reasons, more or less non-existent. Media today possess monopolistic powers over realities, at least in the sphere of secondary experience, which are constantly gaining in importance as to quantity (increased utilisation of media) and quality (increasing perfection of illusory effects).[22] 'If the media have become the primary generators of reality', Stefan Weber formulates in precise terms, 'then constructivism could lead their practitioners to an appropriate understanding and appreciation of the fact that the realities created by the media and the journalists are *important, fundamental* and *elementary.*'[23] This means: media-epistemology as a potential objective in the education of journalists encompasses the profound knowledge of rules and the understanding of medial and journalistic programmes of construction; and it serves the overall goal to making the involvement of the media in prevailing views of the world comprehensible, and thus to awaken sensibility for the relevance of professional practice.

Topics of Media-Epistemology

The third fundamental question is: What media and what media genres[24] are investigated by media-epistemology? Niklas Luhmann, in his systems-theoretical conception, declares the mass media to be the appropriate object of enquiry, and states in the very first sentence: 'What we know about our society, and even about the world in which we live, we know through the mass media';[25] the overstatement is probably due to his concept of world.[26] Mike Sandbothe focuses on the Internet. Siegfried J. Schmidt and Frank Hartmann favour a broader pull: all media and media genres are made the legitimate object of synchronic and diachronic media-epistemological investigation and media-philosophical reflection. Accordingly, Siegfried J. Schmidt, in his conception of media epistemology, includes considerations of the history of printing, radio, film and tele-

---

22 See in this connection, and with a critical view of constructivism: Neuberger (1996), p. 198, and with approval: Schmidt (1993), p. 115, and Weber (1999a), p. 27.
23 Weber (1999a), p. 27 (author's emphasis).
24 On a comprehensive understanding of the concept of media genre cf. Haas (2005).
25 Luhmann (2004), p. 9.
26 The sentence could be interpreted in such a way as to suggest that the mass media are stylised as absolute filters or screens, which quite obviously does not correspond with experiential reality: there are other media and sources of knowledge that cannot meaningfully be called mass media, and that constellate and influence what one knows about society and the world. Nevertheless it is true to say: what exists (and that is indeed a great lot) beyond the immediate, the purely private and exclusively individual horizon of experience, becomes accessible and knowable more or less only through the mass media. On the discussion of this sentence cf. also the conversation between Poerksen (2002b, p. 443f.) and Bolz, and Baecker/Bolz/Hagen (2004), pp. 109ff.

vision, the Internet and, more fundamentally, the history of the media as the history of the reorganisation and militarisation of perception.[27] There is much to be said for such a broad kind of access; the research field of media-epistemology, based on a common epistemological perspective, remains open to interdisciplinary cooperation and topical innovation, which is particularly important in an age of extremely dynamic media evolution.

Forms of Statement and Assertion of Media-Epistemology

There is finally the general question: What is actually by assertions to the effect that media influence, form, and even primarily constitute conceptions of reality? What sort of statement or assertion is made in this way? Is it a question of *at all times*? In this case, the media-epistemological programme would be inseparably connected with epistemological universal statements[28] — and the search for a key statement of media-epistemology could come up with the following formulation, for example: *There is no other world beyond the media*.[29] Only with the help of and by media, the argument of the representatives of this position runs, can we organise the world according to our purposes, can we access experiences, develop perceptual schemas, and reduce complexity. Revelling in pithy and sharp expression and the rhetorical effects of radical theses, Norbert Bolz formulates, for instance: 'There is no aspect of reality that is not pre-structured by media — and that implies that medial reality and lived reality are identical.'[30] In contradistinction to the epistemological universal statement, a trend hypothesis examines processes from a diachronic perspective and, for instance, permits diagnoses like the following: in *growing measure* (keyword: *evermore-ism*), media today impose reality experiences and prove themselves to be formative instances.

Independently of the chosen form of statement and assertion, this ideal-type contrastive opposition is useful in a decisive respect. It forces one to formulate precisely what is meant and to specify the concept of medium that implicitly or explicitly underlies the specific diagnoses.[31] It is certainly possible to take both points of view in a constructivist framework of argumentation; it is not necessary to decide for a particular form of statement or assertion.[32] One may, for instance, consider language as a

---

27 See Schmidt (1999), pp. 139ff.
28 On the distinction between epistemological universal statements and empirically verifiable trend hypotheses see Weber (1999a), p. 54.
29 See Bolz (1993), p. 180.
30 Bolz in conversation with Poerksen (2002a), p. 439.
31 On the dimensions of the media concept (media as *middle, means, mediation* and *mediated*) see Weber (2001), pp. 24ff.
32 On these questions of adequate forms of statement and assertion cf. the fundamental discussion by Weber (1999a, p. 54 und 2003e, pp. 173f.), who pleads for a much stricter

Deepening Awareness of Media-Epistemology   115

non-transcendable medium (epistemological universal statement), and one may simultaneously exploit the more or less frequent use of particular forms of language *usage* as the basis of media-epistemological trend hypotheses (motto: the excessive use of particular catchwords is an indication of...). It would be nonsensical, however, to subject epistemological universal statements to empirical investigation: in such a case, one would assert pre-formation and unconditionally valid impact, something that one intends to investigate and document in its gradual manifestation and practical-concrete intensity, in the first place. It would imply that one presupposes what has yet to be shown.

Media-epistemology here designates, one may summarise, a constructivistically anchored area of research in which all kinds of media are examined as to their reality-constitutive formative power, and where one's findings, in dependence on the underlying conception of media, are formulated either in epistemological universal statements and/or as empirically intended trend hypotheses. The corroboration of the assumption that the investigation of the media-epistemological key questions - How do media and journalists create reality? How can the reality of their construction of reality be observed? — should be of use in the education of journalists, has not yet been achieved. In order to illustrate the usefulness and the specific viability of this assumption for the profession, I shall proceed in the following way. It will first be explained that theories of newsworthiness can be shown to be elements of media-epistemological research. In the course of my account, certain interpretations widespread in the field (Walter Lippmann as an early constructivist etc.) will be revised. The general approach will consist in re-examining some selected studies from the history of the investigation of newsworthiness in the light of a consistent constructivist analysis. It is important to underline that this is only *one* possible object for the demonstration of media-epistemological reflection. There will be no detailed discussion of gatekeeper research, of news bias research, nor of the framing concept that — after appropriate constructivist reformulation — could also be integrated into the topics catalogue of media-epistemology.[33] A discussion of the theory of media genres will then follow because it may be seen as a case of the application of media-epistemology. Finally, I shall show that the constructivist theory of distinction may be used as a set of instruments for observation and interpretation in media epistemology. The chapter will end with a few notes on the relevance of media-epistemological insights to the practice of journalism, i.e. to the craft of professional communication. It may be emphasised

---

separation. In his view, universal statements are empirically empty and ultimately meaningless; in my own view, however, they are surely not amenable to empirical investigation but they may nevertheless be stimulating and inspiring in investigations because they focus attention.

33   On these approaches, see the surveys by Frerich (2005) and Ruhrmann (2005).

once more at this point: the following sections are merely intended to serve as illustrations of the very wide-ranging concept of media-epistemology.

2. Event and Message: Programmes of Construction I

Basic Epistemologies of the Investigation of News Values

From a constructivist and media-epistemological perspective, the scientific treatment of the categories *event* and *news message*, which has found its systematic place in the investigation of news values, is most revealing. One may there, first of all, find a broadly researched programme of construction[34] in a catalogue of news factors that is observed by journalists. This means that the investigation of news values supplies convincing and rich material for illustration; with its help, one can exemplify how journalists constitute media reality through professional design. It thus becomes explicable — for example — why a Scottish newspaper made the sinking of the Titanic known under the headline: 'Aberdeen Man lost at Sea',[35] i.e. why it attributed absolute status to the criterion of the geographical proximity of the medium of publication and the hometown of the missing person.

Furthermore, the scientific reconstruction of this construction programme can be observed in a constructivist manner; one will thus be able to discover that different basic epistemologies have been at work in the investigation of news values since its beginnings, and that they have lent structure to the design of news messages. This perspective is not only intended to reconstruct the construction programme but also to observe the scientific reconstruction of the journalistic construction process, and it may therefore be doubly revealing: it does not only say something about journalists but also about the scientists who observe them, whether they are constructivists or non-constructivists. The analyses here undertaken, however, will be only exemplary ones; comprehensive research reports and extensive surveys have been available for a long time.[36] The primary and important goal here is to present media-epistemological core problems with the help of some of the key works of news value research — and to point out their constructivist resolution.[37]

One may define the beginning of the research of news values with the appearance of the classic work *Public Opinion* by Walter Lippmann, published for the first time in the year 1922. In it, one may read sentences like the following:

---

[34] This concept is the fruit of conversations with Siegfried Weischenberg.
[35] Quoted in Weischenberg (1995), p. 152.
[36] See for example Frerichs (2000), Ruhrmann (2005), Schulz (1990), and Staab (1990).
[37] The works quoted in the following will therefore only be summarised most selectively.

> For the most part we do not first see, and then define, we define first and then see. In the great blooming, buzzing confusion of the outer world we pick out what our culture has already defined for us, and we tend to perceive that which we have picked out in the form stereotyped for us by our culture.[38]

The world does not appear to the observer in its original undistorted and true shape, but it is filtered and broken up by a culturally taught repertoire of stereotypes.[39] This repertoire wields particularly uninhibited power if primary experience is impossible, i.e. if one depends on mediation. But even eyewitnesses cannot be wholly trusted. Even

> the eyewitness does not bring back a naive picture of the scene. For experience seems to show that he himself brings something to the scene, which later he takes away from it, that oftener than not what he imagines to be the account of an event is really a transfiguration of it. Few facts in consciousness seem to be merely given. Most facts in consciousness seem to be partly made. A report is the joint product of the knower and known, in which the role of the observer is always selective and usually creative.[40]

Although many core sentences in the book *Public Opinion* appear as if they had been taken from an introduction to constructivism, and although the author is frequently appropriated for constructivism without reserve,[41] a more intensive appraisal of his book makes plain that the epistemological position of Walter Lippmann must be seen as ambivalent. It obviously corresponds to an ideal of enlightened pedagogy that incorporates thoroughly realistic features. On the one hand, the constructive character of all perception is stressed. On the other, there is the clear supposition that news messages represent the 'body of truth'[42] under certain conditions. On the one hand, the ubiquitous presence of stereotypes is highlighted, which regulates even the primary experience of eyewitnesses. On the other, there is the repeatedly outlined plan of an epistemological educational program, which is designed as a cure of dogmatisms but is also expected to help (and right at this point the self-contradiction becomes manifest) 'to bring our public opinions into grip with the environment. That is the way the enormous censoring, stereotyping, and dramatizing apparatus can be liquidated.'[43] The awareness that human beings are prone to error, and 'subjectivism' practised in the

---

38 Lippmann (1929), p. 81.
39 See ibid., p. 85f.
40 Ibid., p. 79f.
41 See for example Burkart (1999), p. 66, who actually takes the perspective of a critic of constructivism.
42 Lippmann (1929), p. 335.
43 Ibid., p. 407.

right kind of way, could actually both serve 'as a stimulating introduction to the study of truth.'[44]

Be that as it may, however, Walter Lippmann finally transfers his general insights into the organisation of perception to the press and the practical activity of reporters and news editors. They also select according to a grid of stereotypes — under the pressure of time and therefore often with the speed of lightning — from the pre-selected set of messages from suburban reporters the suitable items of news, which are then received by the readers again more or less selectively. And this selection from what has already been selected, which ends with new selection processes on the part of recipients, is not accidental but oriented by the 'news value'[45] that is transported by an event or attributed to it. Among such aspects of an event and such attributions of relevance that decide about the news value, belong according to Walter Lippmann: the extraordinary character of the event, the connection with established topics, the temporal limitation and simple structure of the event, the potential consequences for the population, the involvement of influential and famous persons, the spatial distance between the place of the event and the medial area of distribution.[46]

The Criticism of Reality Distortion

It is this catalogue of features that has been further elaborated and modified in the research traditions dealing with news values in North America and finally also in Europe.[47] Central considerations have been contributed by Einar Östgaard. He has condensed the various news factors into three central complexes of factors.[48] They are: simplification, identification, and sensationalism.

- *Simplification* means that media prefer simple items of news to items with complex structures; and pieces of news with more complex structures will be simplified for actual publication. This means: we have here both a principle of news selection and a principle of news design.
- The possibility of *identification* arises, the assumption is, through spatial, temporal and cultural proximity. What has just happened, what is culturally familiar and geographically not too far away, stands a better chance of publication; powerful and famous persons and the general possibility of personalising an event or a happening, offer opportunities of identification and arrest the attention of the public.
- *Sensationalism* designates the inclination to publish dramatic and emotionally upsetting events, crises and wars, conflicts and catastrophes,

---

44 Lippmann (1929), p. 409.
45 Quoted in Staab (1990), p. 41.
46 Ibid.
47 Ibid., pp. 42ff.
48 See Schulz (1990), p. 13f. and Ruhrmann (2005), p. 317.

gossip and rumour etc,—which has led to the all-too-well-known complaints about the negativism of news casting.[49]

Of media-epistemological interest, however, is not only the journalistic construction programme condensed into complexes of factors here by Einar Östgaard, of equal interest are the hypotheses of media impact that he has formulated. News media, he states for instance, would cement the status quo, represent a much more conflict-laden world than is actually the case, and would accentuate the use of force as a means of overcoming conflicts.[50] It is assumed that the reality of news casting does not conform to actual reality, that the rules and selection processes transform what is actually happening, misrepresent it and thus induce a potentially distorted perception of the world.

A similar argument is advanced by Johan Galtung and Mari Homboe Ruge. In an article that has become a classic, they assemble twelve news factors, which are then differentiated systematically.[51] They consider the majority of these factors to be anthropologically constant; some of them (4 to 12), by contrast, are considered to be culture-determined; consequently, they exercise their effect as selection rules with varying intensity, and in dependence on the cultural environment. According to the assumption of the authors, the following types of events are preferred in the choice of news items:

1) Self-contained events of relatively short duration, which take place in synchrony with the frequency of the media, stand a greater chance of publication (news factor: frequency).

2) An event must overcome a certain threshold of attention and set itself apart from other events: the nastier, the bigger, the stronger—the greater the attention (threshold factor).

3) The fundamental point is: 'The clearer, simpler, the more consistent an event, the greater its news value. It is the quasi one-dimensional item of news with a comparatively low variety of meanings that is basically preferable.'[52] (News factor: unambiguity).

4) Events are the more accessible to media, the more familiar the public is with them—and the more directly they can be expected to affect the everyday situation of the public in question (news factor: familiarity).

5) The better an event matches the expectations and wishes, which one can reasonably suppose the public to entertain, the greater the probability of publication. To put it bluntly: one is offered to read, see and

---

49 See Weischenberg (1995), p. 156.
50 See Schulz (1990), p. 15.
51 On the discussion of Galtung/Ruge, cf. for example Schulz (1990), pp. 15ff. and Schmidt/Zurstiege (2000), pp. 133ff.
52 Schulz (1990), p. 16.

hear what one would like to read, see or hear. 'In the sense mentioned here', Johan Galtung and Mari Holboe Ruge state concisely, '"news" are actually "olds"'.[53] (The authors call this particular news factor: consonance).

6) Surprising events are basically most accessible to the media; however, they must be capable of adjustment to familiar schemas of expectation and meaning (news factor: surprise).[54]

7) When an event has been defined as an item of news and thus as worthy of publication, then it will continue to be published; this is true even in the case that its news value drops to the level of comparable but medially still un-noticed happenings (news factor: continuity).

8) Events that vary the pre-dominant practice of news reporting by introducing new angles, may achieve particular attention (news factor: variation).

9) and 10) The recognisable relationship between an event and elite nations and elite people increases medial attention - at least, as the authors note, in 'the north-western corner of the world'[55] (news factor: relationship with elite nations and elite people).

11) Especially attractive medially are events that lend themselves to personalisation (news factor: personalisation).

12) Negative events like wars, catastrophes, accidents etc. possess greater news value than positive happenings (news factor: negativism).[56]

The authors finally formulate far-reaching hypotheses about the concurrence and interaction of all these particular factors[57] and examine and test some of their assumptions by performing a content-analytical investigation of newscasts about a number of crises.

Comparison of Realities

For media-epistemological reflection, two other pieces of work are helpful and revealing, first of all the methodologically founded criticism by Karl Erik Rosengren and the discussion of the epistemological premises of the theory of news values by Winfried Schulz. Karl Erik Rosengren's criticism of the study by Johan Galtung and Mari Homboe Ruge is concerned with the fact that, although the study purports to deal with aspects of events, it examines the existence of these aspects only with regard to the way they

---

53 Quoted in Schmidt/Zurstiege (2000), p. 136.
54 See also Schulz (1990), p. 17.
55 Quoted in ibid., p. 18.
56 On all these hypotheses (selection hypothesis, distortion hypothesis, repetition hypothesis, additivity hypothesis, and complementarity hypothesis), see Schulz (1990), pp. 19f. and Schmidt/Zurstiege (2000), pp. 137f.
57 See Staab (1990), pp. 62f.

are reported in the media.⁵⁸ If questions of the adequacy of news reporting or questions of the distortion of reality are to be investigated, he insists, then it is necessary to compare so-called intra-media data (the news reporting by the media) systematically with extra-media data. The concrete implication is that the reporting of an event must be checked by adducing sources apparently closer to reality, and which are not part of the domain of the media (such sources are for instance: statistics, official sources, archives etc.), and by then performing a proper analysis and comparison so as to be able to state in the end whether the medial representation has been verified or falsified. The consequence for the practice of research would be, as Joachim Friedrich Staab notes, that only those events can become the legitimate subject of news-value research about which actual inter-media and extra-media data relating to their relevant aspects are available. However, this obtains only in exceptional cases.⁵⁹ One may add from a constructivist perspective that the comparison in question does not involve absolute reality and medial representation, but different variably designed and processed versions of reality, i.e. different constructions. And no type or no presentation form of such constructions (e.g. statistics) must clandestinely be ontologised.

Winfried Schulz begins his (knowledge-) theoretical re-orientation of news value research with the criticism of the ontologising comparison of media reality and factual reality.⁶⁰ Criticising previous approaches, he states that Karl Erik Rosengren certainly did not intend to compare *the factual reality* (meaning probably: the unconditionally valid, ultimately true reality) with its medial representation but 'only reports from different sources [...] (these sources themselves may apply different selection rules, but they must be interpreted only in the sense of difference, not as "correct" or "false").'⁶¹ His justified criticism of epistemological naivety leads him, however, to produce a number of exaggerated conclusions. Winfried Schulz arrives at the result, 'that the attempt to compare items of news with 'what really happened' is impossible, in principle',⁶² because 'what "really" happened, what the "correct" picture of reality is, is ultimately a metaphysical question.'⁶³ The obvious point here is that the author speaks of an absolute reality whose incomprehensibility he asserts because someone else (in this case: Karl Erik Rosengren) apparently postulates its comprehensibility and seems to assume that absolute reality can be identified with statistical and official data. The exaggerated radical conclusions by

---

58 On Rosengren, cf. extended discussion in Staab (1990), pp. 75ff.
59 See Staab (1990), p. 107.
60 See Schulz (1990), pp. 25ff.
61 Ibid., p. 25.
62 Ibid., p. 26.
63 Ibid., p. 27.

Winfried Schulz actually result from an unclear separation of absolute and relative spheres, something that has already been described in this book as the *problem of referential confusion*. The over-reacting rejection of any reality comparison by Winfried Schulz fails to attain the level of social consensus, lacks the dimension of intersubjective plausibility.[64] More drastically: one may naturally check whether given figures are correct or whether they are not; such a procedure does not at all and in no way touch upon the metaphysical speculation of whether particular given figures correspond with the absolute reality of what is given. And if it did, if the absolute reality could indeed be accessed by some quoted figure or other — what kind of super-observer would be capable of checking it?

Fully convincing, however, even from a constructivist perspective, is the fundamentally new orientation of news-value research proposed and demanded by Winfried Schulz. The core problem is accordingly no longer the topic of truth but the question as to what characteristics the reality constructed by the news media actually has, and what the criteria of selection and interpretation are.[65] In the course of his study, he distinguishes clearly between the concepts *news factor* (= journalistic hypothesis of reality, which to the recipients appears to be a characteristic of the event) and *news value* (construction for the sake of justifying decisions of selection, attribution of publication relevance),[66] and arranges and combines the diverse news factors into six factorial dimensions in order to improve their operationalisation.[67] It is most revealing and of particular importance for all further media-epistemological debates that it remains inconclusive and open in the end whether a news factor is a feature of the event, or whether this feature is only attributed to the event by an act of interpretation, whether it is inscribed in the so-called event and into a more or less amorphous world.

The Event as Journalism's Centre of Meaning

What is actually an event, one may well ask, having been trained in the constructivist logic of observation. One answer is: events are the centre of meaning of professionally practised journalism;[68] they are observer-specific constructs, therefore inescapably self-descriptions through the attri-

---

64 In later work this assumption is, however, varied and de-radicalised. Cf. the contrasting opposition of a 'Ptolemaic' and a 'Copernican' conception of the mass media (Schulz 1989) and the positive reference to critical rationalism. In a recent, popularised, presentation (Schulz 2003b, p. 38) he laments — in the diction of a realist — that the 'orientation by news factors' is the reason 'that we are often given a distorted picture of reality [...].'
65 Schulz (1990), p. 28.
66 The distinction between news factor and news value has in the meantime become fully established in German-language research. See Maier (2003), p. 30.
67 See Schulz (1990), pp. 29ff.
68 See Weischenberg (2001a), p. 287.

Deepening Awareness of Media-Epistemology

bution of relevance and focusing. One defines beginning and end, one punctuates causally, one highlights aspects that one holds to be particularly important. 'In all this', Joachim Staab notes,

> the progression of some happening may be divided into variable units according to the goals and interests of enquiry. One can illustrate this by an example: one may dissect the event "aeroplane crash" into ever smaller event units, into ever more specific event units—e.g. the stopping of the engines, the hitting the ground, the dying of individual passengers etc., but one may also integrate this event into ever more comprehensive sequences of events and processes, which actually define it in its entirety in the first place—e.g. deficient security checks as the causes of the crash, possible construction faults of the type of aeroplane, reports by experts etc. The delimitation and the expansion of events may, in theory, be continued indefinitely, and an infinite regression may result in two opposite directions.[69]

What is described here is closely connected with one side of the construction of events, i.e. the practical and pragmatic side: journalists who have become witnesses of an incident or who are confronted with reports and messages must make decisions. And they do this, as described, on the basis of news factors, which they consider to be intrinsic properties of events. Whenever one observes how scientific and journalistic observers observe the constitution of events, different and diverse criteria of distinction and typology emerge.

- One can classify events as *announced* (e.g. anniversaries, parliamentary sessions), *unexpected* (e.g. natural catastrophes, crimes) and *enduring* (e.g. a protracted civil war, a political debate about principles).[70] Basic criteria of setting up a typology are the degree of expectedness of, and the familiarity with, the event.
- Events may be distinguished according to assumptions about their relationship with (an absolute) reality: thus Günther Bentele asserts—on the basis of a realist epistemology—that the majority of the events about which the media report is, in an ontological sense, independent of the journalists involved.[71] Stefan Weber—based on constructivist thought—somewhat confusingly speaks of *constructed events* that are invented and planned by the media themselves in order to enable the media to report on them.[72] Be that as it may: it is definitely the epistemological position that implicitly supplies the premises for the choice of the appropriate typology of events.
- Different typologies of events hover between media criticism and a more or less clearly formulated epistemology. Norbert Bolz makes the diagnosis that it is becoming increasingly difficult 'to distinguish

---

69 Staab (1990), pp. 103f.
70 See Frerichs (2000), p. 122.
71 See Bentele (1993), p. 167.
72 See Weber (1999a), p. 38.

between war and war games, between events and staged performances, between the real thing and its simulation.[73] Daniel Dayan and Elihu Katz analyse *media events*.[74] Daniel Boorstin has proposed the concept of the *pseudo-event* in order to attract attention to media-oriented stage management.[75] Hans Mathias Kepplinger distinguishes systematically between *genuine events* (events that take place without any media involved, for example, accidents or earthquakes), *mediatised events* (events that change their character due to media observation, for example, party conferences), and *staged events* (events that are organised exclusively for being reported, for example, press conferences).[76] The basis of division in all these cases is a characteristic mixture of media criticism and epistemology.

- Events may finally be distinguished by the form of the causal relationship into which they appear to be embedded.[77] It is often assumed, explicitly or implicitly, that journalists react to events, and that their reactions generate a model of selection: an event possesses, the corresponding assumption is, more or less objectively definable properties and is therefore selected for reporting. The cause of reporting lies in the past; according to a transformation rule (here: through the routine choice by journalists) an effect is created in the future in the form of the specifically designed contributions which are then published. The basic form of causality is the *causa efficiens*.[78] Hans Matthias Kepplinger has supplemented this view with a finality model and introduced the concept of *instrumental actualisation*.[79] Here the choice of an event turns into the cause of its intended impact; the event is not only the impact but also itself the cause of an intention and the means to attain the goal of a specific impact. This means in concrete terms, for instance, that journalists select particular events simply because they can be utilised to accentuate and actualise specific aspects of events and to focus on topical elements in order to arrive at their own particular goals and purposes.[80] An intended effect in the future triggers actions in the present. The archetypal image of this finality model, which shows a certain closeness to the concept of *causa finalis* but is really a combination of both concepts of causality, is definitely the campaign, the kind of reporting and news casting with self-defined goals: one reacts — and accentuates with a clearly given goal-orientation in sight.

---

[73] Bolz (1993), p. 125.
[74] See Dayan/Katz (1994).
[75] See Schulz (2004), p. 9.
[76] See Kepplinger (1989), p. 13.
[77] See ibid., p. 9.
[78] See Foerster/Poerksen (2002), p. 50.
[79] See Staab (1990), p. 96.
[80] See ibid., p. 96f.

Deepening Awareness of Media-Epistemology 125

Directions of Thought

By way of a generalising summary one can conclude that the observation of the construction of events will always reveal something about observers and their perspectives—to paraphrase Heinz von Foerster: 'Tell me what you consider an event and I shall tell you who you are!'[81] From the point of view of a constructivist media-epistemology there can be no *event in itself* and no ontic *solid body of news*, no observer-independent phenomenon whose properties could be rendered by journalistic forms of presentation.[82] The ways of perceiving the relationship between event and news reflect different directions of thought[83] and such traditional concepts as presuppose a linear transfer of information, consider difficulties in communication as problems of transport, and frequently turn information into an object.[84] Realists commonly posit the event as the primary cause that will make its impact upon predominantly passive journalists. Constructivist tend to reverse this logic of thought. Journalists accordingly construct events, journalists are the primary source of influence, journalists actively attack a more or less amorphous field that is usually in a roundabout way called reality.[85] What is perceived as a real event will, in conjunction with other events, in the end yield the social reality that forms the framework and the foundation of journalistic decisions of selection.[86] To reduce the significance of all this to a formula: the reality of news casting is the reality of those who produce this reality—be it through the professional routines of journalism, be it via the forms of thought and the methodological routines of scientific discourse that equally constitutes a reality, or by its own proper reality through the reconstruction of constructions.

3. Schemas and Genres: Programmes of Construction II

The Dominance of Form

To start with an example: In his widely known book with the title 'Exercices de style', Raymond Queneau relates an extremely boring and uninteresting occurrence.[87] It has to do with *Autobus S*. An observer on the bus line S notices that a passenger standing in the bus's aisle is repeatedly jostled by other passengers getting on or off at several stations and re-acts

---

81 See Foerster/Poerksen (2002), p. 153.
82 See Frerichs (2000), p. 177.
83 See Weber (1996), pp. 145ff.
84 See Krippendorff (1994), p. 86, pp. 91f. and pp. 97f.; Frerichs (2000), p. 123 and p. 125.
85 Cf. in this connection also the criticism by Weber (1995, p. 126 and 1996, pp. 146f.) applied to the concept of selection as a central para*dogma* of journalism study.
86 See Ruhrmann (1994), p. 240 and Weischenberg (1995), pp. 178f.
87 See Queneau (1990).

with protests and angry words. Later on the same passenger is seen standing on a square in Paris next to a companion who tells him that he should have 'another button' sewn on his 'overcoat'.[88] This is the perfectly trivial story that Raymond Queneau tells in his book — in 99 different variants and variations! That is precisely his stroke of genius. What happens or much rather what does not happen is offered to the reader in the guise of a short story and a telegram, as a police report, as an incensed letter or as a Japanese haiku, as a sonnet or a blurb. From time to time Queneau abandons traditional forms, uses exclamations, jumbles the consonants in a text, then returns again to the customary genres.

Whoever reads these 99 tales will notice: the content as it emerges through different schemas of presentation, different patterns of reporting, is always a different kind of content, always a new kind of content. What is not only recognisable in these exercises in style but can be actually experienced is the content-shaping effect of forms of presentation, genres, and patterns of reporting.[89] Forms of presentation, genres and patterns of reporting are — as the example demonstrates — forms of creating order. They erect a frame for the presentation, they direct the access to so-called reality, they analyse and structure this reality, and they are, therefore, a proper topic of media-epistemological investigation. The very fact that this story has such an unimportant and infinitely irrelevant kind of substance makes the dominance of its form so conspicuous, exposes the epistemic effect of the chosen pattern of reporting. What did in fact happen on Autobus S? One cannot clearly remember after the 99 different retellings — but the confusion generated by Raymond Queneau is most stimulating. A number of theses may be extracted from these 'exercises' that are useful and productive for a media-epistemologically founded analysis of forms of presentation, patterns of reporting and genres.[90] These theses and reflections refer to the *systematic localisation* of the topic of genre, the *cognition-theoretical debate* of forms of presentation and patterns of reporting, and the *practical-pragmatic question* of what the significance of the knowledge of genres, usually implicit knowledge, might be for journalists and their public.

Epistemology of Genres

As the experiment by Raymond Queneau suggests, the forms of presentation, the genres and the patterns of reporting (apart from a plethora of other factors of influence), can be shown to generate media reality, may be understood as programmes of construction and as the expression and

---

88 Ibid., p. 7.
89 Poerksen, U. (1997), pp. 40f.
90 No comprehensive survey of the highly differentiated research on kinds and genres, forms of presentation, textual kinds, and patterns of reporting is intended here.

manifestation of a *hidden epistemology*, as Gregory Bateson used to say. Theories of media genres would then be, according to Siegfried J. Schmidt, a 'special branch of media-epistemology',[91] which considers genres of whatever kind as a scanning grid in the apprehension of reality. They articulate the functioning of the basic rules of the game of ordering the world, 'they incorporate perspectives on the world, reflect attitudes towards phenomena of reality, of the world, however strongly refracted.'[92]

The question to be posed would then be how forms of presentation, patterns of reporting and genres become cognitively and communicatively effective construction programmes for journalists.[93] An answer based on constructivism is given by Siegfried J. Schmidt and Siegfried Weischenberg.[94] Their approach is fundamentally function-oriented, they are not primarily interested in definitions and typological classifications but in understanding 'how genres observably function.'[95] Their concept of genre is a middle-range concept[96] in comparison with extremely small-formatted or extremely large-formatted concepts, which ultimately identify genres with forms of presentation or understand media genres in an extremely general way as culturally specific, socially solidified, solutions of communicative problems.[97] The authors speak of schemas, in particular media schemas.[98] These schemas become consolidated or rigidified through repeated application, commonly shared experiences; they are only partially conscious, they combine cognitive and affective elements, and they cause the constitution of expectations, and of expectations of expectations.[99] They reduce complexity, allow for quick reaction, organise

---

[91] Schmidt (2001), p. 412.
[92] Steinmetz, quoted in Schmidt/Weischenberg (1994), p. 221.
[93] Schmidt (1994, p. 168) understands cognition and communication as a guiding difference that leads him to the distinction between concepts of genre (cognitive level) and designations of genre (communicative level). This guiding difference is neglected here, however, because I fail to see its analytical potential in this particular case of application. Nor will Schmidt's proposal (see for instance 1994, p. 190 and 2001, p. 414) be taken up, i.e. to distinguish designations of genres and schemas of media genres from the so-called macro-schemas of journalism (patterns of reporting).
[94] See Schmidt/Weischenberg (1994).
[95] Schmidt (1994), p. 165.
[96] Over and above all that, one can distinguish genres with differential capability of integration and abstraction (the novel in comparison with the leading article), one can adduce formal-structural or topical aspects (the sonnet in comparison with the travel guide). Finally, even the unambiguity or ambiguity of textual functions may be used as a criterion of distinction (the direction for use in comparison with the novella). See Schmidt (1994), pp. 167f.
[97] See Haas (2005, p. 226) and Saxer (1999b, p. 117). The latter sees journalistic textual kinds 'primarily as *problem-solving structures of media organisations*' (author's emphasis).
[98] On different schemas and different types of schema organisation (scripts, frames) see Schmidt (1994), pp. 170ff.
[99] See Schmidt/Weischenberg (1994), p. 213 and Schmidt (1994), pp. 171f.

'singularities into totalities',[100] and make possible the extremely swift condensation of perceptions into a complete overall impression. Genres are, if one follows this specific application and development of the theory by Jean Piaget,[101] 'cognitive and communicative schemas for the purpose of the construction and intersubjective establishment of models of reality. Genres are, as it were, programmes for the intersubjective construction of meaning and its recursive (self-) confirmation.'[102]

This further implies that the designations of genres regulate what counts as real in the domain of professionally structured communication — and what must eventually be assigned to the sphere of fiction, that they represent a foil and a grid to diagnose and to describe in detail[103] processes of hybridisation, of the mixing of genres, and of the syncretism of textual kinds.[104] They facilitate the presentation of media offers in the form of genre rubrics. In the sphere of the audiovisual media, they structure to a certain degree the planning of programmes, the allocation of broadcasting slots, they influence the storing in archives of what has been broadcast. Such media schemas or media genres generally differ in their overall strategy of reference to reality (modality of reference), the topicalised domain of reality (communicative semantics), and in the concrete representation and mediation of all media offers (aesthetics and stylistics).[105] They oscillate between conventional standards and the more or less strongly utilised playing spaces of individual arrangements and adjustments.[106]

The Creation of Expectations

The characterisations of genres, patterns of reporting, and forms of presentation, function — in the view of the public, too — as shorthand codes

---

100 Schmidt (1994), p. 169.
101 However, it is somewhat controversial, as Frerichs (2000, p. 89) notes, what kind of epistemological position is held by Piaget himself. Frerichs considers him to be a realist — in opposition to a large number of constructivists — because Piaget assumes that ever more complex schemas will make it possible to improve the knowledge of the world.
102 Schmidt/Weischenberg (1994), p. 216.
103 As examples of such mixtures and de-differentiations, one can quote forms of hybrid journalism like *infotainment, edutainment, emotainment, confrontainment, advertainment* and *computainment*. See Weischenberg (2001b), p. 69.
104 This concept is from Saxer (1999b), p. 131.
105 See Schmidt (1994), pp. 179f.
106 On the basis of these considerations, the concepts of *patterns of reporting* and *form of presentation* may be defined in the following way: *pattern of reporting* (like information journalism, precision journalism, investigative journalism, New Journalism etc.) constitute comprehensive strategies of referring to reality as well as of topicalisation. *Forms of presentation* (like report, feature, reportage, and commentary etc.) are different possibilities of designing and presenting particular media statements and assertions. They are historically-grown and strongly conventionalised forms of journalistic texts, which are arranged in a hierarchy and possess three fundamental functions (information, evaluation, entertainment). On the patterns of reporting and forms of presentation, see the comprehensive discussion by Weischenberg (1995), pp. 111ff. and (2001a), pp. 41ff.

and ciphers for expectable communicative processes. Opening a volume of Japanese haikus, reading a book of interviews by a journalist, buying a newspaper or a magazine and then studying the published portrait of some celebrity—all this is carried out after completed media socialisation and on the basis of knowledge that frequently remains implicit and will only be articulated in the case of irritation or disappointment. It is the place of publication that supplies orientation, it is the meta-textual characteristics of factual information or fiction, (popular) science, non-fiction or novel, which lend contours to a whole bundle of expectations.

It is evident, furthermore, that genres, forms of presentation and patterns of reporting provide useful patterns of orientation, which meet the journalistic requirement 'to produce quickly and in great mass unique objects'[107] by means of the standardisation of surprise and shock; they support and guide the categorisation of media offers, and structure expectations. The suggestions, therefore, to soften the established conventional canon of forms of journalism (for instance with reference to a constructivist position) do not seem particularly convincing—to give up, for example, the strict separation of news message and opinion, of neutral information and straightforward value judgement.[108] The argument is: as everything is evaluation or opinion of some sort or other, anyway, it is simply impossible to detach what is non-opinion unmistakably, and therefore the distinction in question had better be abandoned altogether. Such a demand overlooks, however, that these distinctions are viable in the sphere of media genres, although they are obviously not unconditionally valid or static in an ontological sense. They provide orientation, enable quick placement, and especially allow for the assessment of the credibility of a media offer. From such a perspective of usefulness, the discussion of the relevance of categories like opinion and information, news and opinion, and ultimately also fiction and fact, finally ends in the clearly economic justification of the morality of journalistic work, which Norbert Bolz has condensed into the formula: *'Cheating does not pay.'*[109] The obvious upshot is—and simply for the reasons of the trustworthiness of sources and also the marketability of media offers—'the ultimately economic enforcement of a journalistic ethics and a minimum of seriousness within the mass media.'[110]

Commands of genres are—from the point of view of the author, in the view of the journalist—essentially commands of perception; they focus journalistic attention already in the process of research. It may be worthwhile to recall for a moment what Helge Timmerberg, one of the

---

107 Saxer (1999b), p. 118.
108 See Weber, S. (1995), p. 245.
109 Bolz in conversation with Poerksen (2002a), p. 448 (author's emphasis).
110 Ibid.

best-known journalists in the German-language area,[111] has written about the so-called 'briefing' by editors:

> Briefing — an ugly word. Some editor has thought up some pretty project and the reporter is expected to execute it. This may be a normal thing but it has nothing to do with life. An example? Let us say, you are travelling to Africa. You are supposed to report on AIDS. And the briefing goes in the direction of horror story. Corpses in the streets. Stench from sheds, pestilence, horror, death, panic. And then you are indeed confronted with death, but not with horror, with pestilence but not with panic, and there are not at all as many corpses as planned. In brief: life does not cooperate with your briefing. What will you do then? The orthodox journalist will most probably not even realise this kind of contradiction any more. Because he or she doesn't know anything else.[112]

And this means, furthermore: certain topics in combination with the selection rules of journalism will stimulate the interest in particular things. Who regularly publishes as a journalist and is used to choosing specific patterns of reporting and forms of presentation, will immediately have a clear view of the genre-inherent commands of perception: all of a sudden one begins searching for quotations (presentation form: report), all of a sudden one becomes sensitive to the gestures and facial expressions of a particular person (presentation form: portrayal), suddenly a dramaturgical idea gains weight (presentation form: reportage) which is developed further through additional research. Helge Timmerberg calls such 'visualising of stories', which precedes actual research, and the specific training of the journalistic view, 'briefing'; it does not always require an editor, however, to explain to a reporter on location what he wants. The socialisation as a journalist will make briefing an unconsciously operating mechanism of reality construction: the openly declared manipulation and precise specifications of the tendency of a planned report tends to be the exception. As a rule, journalists learn what they have to write in a sort of 'osmotic' process in the environment of their editorial office.[113]

It may thus be stated that genres, patterns of reporting and forms of presentation are of central importance: they make contingency invisible, and they make contingency controllable in all the stages of the handling of media offers (production, distribution, reception, processing).[114] They function in daily practice as mechanisms that limit and reduce to manageable proportions the multitude of possible perceptions of the world, the points of view, the approaches and procedures etc. They orient the individual journalist in the process of research and the negotiation of media offers; they help the public of the media to generate at the speed of light-

---

111 Timmerberg is a protagonist of New Journalism.
112 Timmerberg (1988), p. 19.
113 See Blöbaum (2000), pp. 73ff.
114 See Saxer (1999b), p. 124f. and Schmidt (1987), p. 168.

ning patterns of expectation that facilitate reception, which are turned into objects of reflection only in the case of their disappointment. The assertion that everything can always be presented in a different way, that the world will always appear differently in the corset of ever-changing forms of presentation, is the core thesis of the linguistic experiment by Raymond Queneau that was presented at the beginning of this section. It is also the starting point and the terminating point of a media-epistemological treatment of this topic.

4. Media-Epistemology as a Theory Of Distinctions: Programmes of Construction III

Thinking in Differences

Media-epistemological analyses, as defined in the present context, are an element of the constructivist discourse and invariably display a double perspective: they reconstruct medial programs of construction, but consider these reconstructions as constructs themselves, which can be reconstructed in a newly initiated process of observation (of a higher order). A set of instruments of the reconstruction of constructions, which includes the possibility of self-reflection, is incorporated in the constructivist understanding of the operation of observing. Observing, according to this assumption, may be understood as the introduction and further processing of distinctions and designations; distinctions are observer-relative, they refer back to the one making these distinctions. Connecting such a relativism of distinctions[115] with the program of media-epistemology would have to yield, the assumption is, a set of instruments of description that may be used in manifold ways: one can use it to extract trends and tendencies, to systematise diagnoses and theory offers[116] relevant to the domain of the media, and to formulate scenarios for the future. From this perspective, the programme of media-epistemology may be conceived of as an applied theory of distinction. It rests on the premises and procedures described in what follows.

The first and foremost task must be to establish the relevant distinctions. They determine the spectrum of all the possible or all the already defined

---

115 On this concept, see Hansen (1996), p. 69.
116 Possible guiding distinctions of the general observation of theories are, for instance: *descriptive-analytical* versus *prescriptive-normative*, *affirmative* versus *critical*, *optimistic* versus *pessimistic*, *purely theory-immanent* versus *(potentially) empirical*, *realist* versus *constructivist*, *agent-oriented* versus *system-oriented*. The discussion of theories is further inspired by distinctions between *subject* and *system*, *technology* and *content*, *text* and *context*, *selection* and *construction*, *effect* and *use*, etc. Guiding differences and central dualisms of specific basic theories are, for instance: *langue* and *parole* (structuralism), *signifiant* and *signifié* (semiotics), *sex* and *gender* (feminism), *system* and *environment* (systems theory), *observer* and *reality*, (constructivism), *production* and *reception* (Cultural Studies), *state* and *market* (media-economic theory). Cf. Weber (2003d), pp. 327ff.

positions, and they delimit the domain of what is given and what appears conceivable. Taken together, they reveal the contours of digital worlds of communication, i.e. make discernible the outlines of a rapidly changing world, but not any divisions immutably implanted in the life-world.[117] It is thus made apparent, for instance, that the treatment of the Internet and the consequences of web communication in a phase of highly dynamic media evolution is shaped drastically by a multitude of competing descriptions. There is talk of a different kind of politics and education, of changes in teaching and training, of a transformation of the media trade as a whole, of a new order for the economy, of a different kind of marketing, and of an administration of justice adapted to the global conditions of communication. There is no lack of predictions drawn up on a grand scale: 'The attitude to knowledge, labour, the forms of employment, money, democracy, the city, will all be re-invented', we can, for instance, read in the writings of Pierre Lévy.[118] In brief: people see a new kind of culture and society appearing on the horizon.

Thinking along the lines of the theory of distinctions, suggests sorting and arranging the multitude of themes and assertions by means of guiding differences. The following distinctions which have been characterised and justified elsewhere at greater length[119] may, for instance, be considered of central importance: *affirmation/criticism, topical/non-topical, analogue /digital, education/e-learning, data/information, remembering/forgetting, fact/fiction, legislation/self-regulation, heterarchy/hierarchy, information offer/ information overload, classical politics/electronic democracy, complementarity/competition, mass communication/individual communication, media reality/world perception, humanity/technology, online/offline, , private/public,* and so on.

One may now ask where these distinctions come from. Are they not just arbitrary creations by a scientific observer? Questions of this kind can only be dealt with by the—necessarily self-critical—statement that the distinctions as they are characterised more precisely do not possess any ontological correlate but are most definitely observer-dependent. They are distinctions that cannot be ascribed truth-values in an emphatic sense. The reconstruction too, it must be underlined again, is of course nothing but a construction.

Such a mere listing of guiding differences obviously does not tell us what they mean; they must be processed further, i.e. interlinked and inter-

---

117 The considerations presented here owe their essential inspiration to Schmidt (2002) and attempt to apply his specific conception of culture (culture as a programme of interpretation, consisting of networks of distinctions and divisions) to a more narrowly circumscribed topic. For reasons of simplicity, however, I shall not include here a detailed discussion of Schmidt's elaboration of a logic of distinctions.
118 Lévy (1996), p. 70.
119 See Poerksen (2002b). In this article, the dislocations and adjustments of differences are illustrated by numerous examples..

preted — according to author and approach — in order to attain the concrete gestalt of a position and an interpretation.[120] From the interpretation of the central distinctions and the specific mode of their further processing as well as correlation, result the particular discourse, the decided opinion, the personal view, predictions, or invocations. One may call this the semanticisation of guiding differences; they are endowed with meaning, loaded by interpretation.

Typology of Distinctions

It must be remembered, furthermore, that there are fundamentally different types of distinctions. In the wide field of net communication one may, for instance, encounter:

1) Distinctions that distinguish something from something indeterminate (e.g. *topical/non-topical*);
2) Distinctions that distinguish something determinate from something determinate (e.g. *mass communication/individual communication*);[121]
3) Distinctions whose relevance and scope — with regard to the totality of societal communication — is comparatively limited (e.g. *education/e-learning*);
4) Distinctions whose relevance and scope — with regard to the totality of societal communication — is more wide-ranging (e.g. *fact/fiction*);
5) Distinctions one side of which or both sides of which are — within certain groupings — positively or negatively connoted (e.g. *legislation/self-regulation*).

The core idea of these considerations is that such a set of instruments for description represents a sufficiently complex model of media-epistemological observation that is capable of further refinement and elaboration and may be expanded any time by new differences of alleged relevance in order to bring into focus a variety of scenarios (derived from the theory of distinction).[122] For, generally speaking, such a method of meta-observation permits us to achieve at least three objectives:

- *The description of a thematic area.* For instance, one may consider the findings on net communication as sets of relevant guiding differences. This mode of examination, conditioned by the constructivist concept of observing, which has up to now been generally applied to the study of large-scale unities (i.e. functional systems like science, politics, journalism), is now employed in order to bring about a description that is

---

120 Cf. Schmidt in conversation with Poerksen (2004f), pp.170 f.
121 Problems of the symmetry and asymmetry of distinctions and the corresponding terminological differentiations, which are not taken up here, are dealt with in Winter (1999), pp. 92 ff.
122 I should like to stress explicitly that other authors might very well propose a different collection of guiding differences.

as detailed as possible. It no longer seeks the unique, universally valid code but operates on the presupposition of a plethora of possible differences that may delimit a thematic area.[123]

- *The reconstruction of particular positions.* The views of different authors may be reconstructed as interpretations of interconnected distinctions; different views and assumptions manifest themselves as dissimilar semanticisations and combinations of networks of distinctions.
- *The characterisation of changes.* Finally, more or less comprehensive discourse changes may be characterised by means of the philosophy of distinctions.

Scenarios of the Theory of Distinctions

The observable processes of the dislocation and the adjustment of discourses may be assigned to a number of scenarios of the theory of distinctions in an ideal-type manner:

- *Scenario I: the recombination and refinement of distinctions.* Guiding differences may generally be reformulated, recombined, supplemented, and refined. They are not static and ontologically fixed shapes but patterns emerging from the changing discourses of science and the public.
- *Scenario II: replacement or disappearance of distinctions.* They may gradually be replaced by new ones or be discarded altogether because they are — for whatever reasons — believed to be useless, 'unrealistic', sub-complex etc. at a certain point in time and in particular discourse formations. This means that the use of specific guiding differences is constantly subjected to discursive scrutiny, and that specific distinctions are observed and tested for their usefulness (naturally on the basis of other or perhaps even the very same distinctions).[124]
- *Scenario III: gain or loss of relevance.* Guiding differences may gain in relevance or lose in clarity and diagnostic sharpness by virtue of differential grading in the diverse enclaves demarcated by communication. Here empirical investigations and predictive considerations must attempt to establish processes of boundary changes in the field of current and future media communication.
- *Scenario IV: empirically observable loss and recovery of relevance in normative discourses.* It is also conceivable that guiding differences combined with normative demands will re-surface because of a reinforcement of the categories. Distinctions that may empirically have lost all rele-

---

[123] Knorr-Cetina, in a critique of Luhmann's systems theory, has advanced the thesis that the orientation by a code is not tenable empirically; she claims that the 'multiplicity of codes' (Knorr-Cetina 1992, p. 413) that is observable, for example, in the science system, may just as well be encountered in other systems.

[124] Even the application of a distinction to itself is conceivable. Such a recursive application of a distinction to itself is discussed by systems theory under the keyword 're-entry.' Cf. Winter (1999), pp. 107ff.

vance will then be preserved in normatively anchored discourses and repositioned as defences against observable harmful developments.

The overall goal must be, to summarise approach and procedure, to collect the central distinctions, to learn to understand the social structures of journalism and the media as the results of operations of distinction, to interpret the structure and the dynamics of those fields of research, which are of relevance to media-epistemology in their dependence on, and connection with, operations of distinction.[125] The guiding questions of this labour of interpretation are, why particular distinctions and designations have established themselves, what makes these distinctions and designations visible or what makes them invisible, how and for what reasons complete frameworks of distinctions rearrange themselves in new constellations. Epistemic practice and theoretical insights of a media-epistemology so conceived are quite obviously based on the first commandment of a constructivist philosophy of difference: 'Draw a distinction!'[126]

5. The Practice-Relevance of Media-Epistemology

A number of conclusions of practical relevance may be derived from the programme of media-epistemology—despite its being anchored in the theoretical field of discourse. For one, the analysis of programmes of construction can be utilised to examine the very basic question of whether a possible topic is really a topic for the media. The meta-rule of selection for the discovery of journalistic topics is: *It is necessary to search for the exceptional, the extraordinary, the striking and the unknown, which may be connected with what is known and what is amenable to experience.* The personalisation of factual questions, the combination of experiential reality close to everyday life with abstract content, the concentration on conflicts, the staging of surprises, of interruptions and variations, are all techniques of communication that help to make one's own offers of topics more attractive, to present them according to the logic of the mass media.[127] This means: the program of media-epistemology supplies results that may be utilised for the checking of topics and ultimately also strategically for purposes of attracting attention.

On the other hand, the programme of media-epistemology fundamentally deepens the awareness of (journalistic) rules and principles of construction as they typify this profession, whether they concern characteristics of the construction of events, rules of the selection of news items and the processing of news messages, features of genres, patterns of reporting and forms of presentation, or specific clusters of distinctions and

---

125 See Bardmann (1997), p. 17.
126 See Foerster (2002), pp. 34ff.
127 See Gerhards (2002), p. 133.

pre-dominant guiding differences, which structure the observation of the media. This insight into the proprietary laws of journalism and the media in their totality may be formulated as a central principle of the practice of communication. The meta-rule of potentially successful communication is, consequently, as follows: *It is necessary to reflect one's own goals and nevertheless orient oneself by one's counterparts and one's audiences.*[128] It is this alignment with the construction programmes of the others and the simultaneous concentration on one's own purposes which will improve the chances — depending on the circumstances — of achieving comparably adequate and calculable effects although exact, linear-causally organised external control must be considered impossible due to the operative closure of the other (or generally: the system). The reason for the potential effectiveness of this meta-rule is that observing it always entails attending to the fact that external stimulation is recognised as internally relevant information; it is the other who will impose the criteria whose satisfaction may then impress.[129] The barrier of operative closure may obviously be crossed or overcome if the proprietary logic of the other is minted for one's own programme of construction. The insight into such connections is extremely useful and productive for quality journalism, but also for every professional communicator because it encourages and helps to present communicative and media offers in as goal-oriented a way as possible.

---

[128] On the question if and under what circumstances an instructive interaction might be possible at all, and if the understanding of the proprietary logic of human individuals might be abused for purposes of manipulation, see Maturana/Poerksen (2004), pp. 68ff.

[129] On these reflections and the concept of context control see Willke (1987), p. 334 and pp. 351ff.

Chapter V

Deepening Ethical Awareness

1. Epistemology and Forgery: Tom Kummer's Apologia

Remixing and Resampling

The story is only too well known, at least most of it. On the fifteenth of May 2000 the magazine *Focus* substantiates and reveals what has long been bandied about as a rumour in the trade: Tom Kummer has — apparently for years — forged interviews for the respected *SZ-Magazin*, has elicited the most idiosyncratic statements from Pamela Anderson, Courtney Love, Brad Pitt and Sharon Stone, but has in all probability never actually met these stars.[1] Thus became public what one could have suspected or even known for a long time, had one really been interested in knowing it in precise detail and willing to find out. The conversations of the supposed master interviewer were essentially generated from his desk at his home. Some portions were copied from books, others were concocted from his own articles and archive material, and everything was assembled to yield new dialogues with a high-speed cut. Remixing and resampling — these are the terms for the preferred methods of this author who had already been uncovered as a forger several times before. In 1990 Tom Kummer had used a passage from a book by Richard Ford for the story 'Satanische Wildnis' published in *Tempo*, a fascinating reportage about a group of young devil worshippers. A reader informed the editor, and also supplied copies of the corresponding excerpts from the book. Tom Kummer finally lost his job with the magazine when he could not credibly disperse the suspicion of having fabricated yet another text, and particularly after he had complained about the anachronistic conception of journalism underlying the questions of the then editor in chief, Michael Jürgs, concerning the reliability of his research. Another time, the magazine of the Zürich *Tagesanzeiger* stopped collaboration with Kummer because the factual content of some of his texts seemed dubious. The magazine *Stern*, where the brilliant writer

---

[1] On the reconstruction of the affair, see Ott/Ramelsberger (2000) and Reus (2004).

but not equally competent researcher had been under contract for some time, had earlier terminated business relations because doubts had arisen and an interview had been challenged. The so-called facts, it became apparent repeatedly, are not of tremendous importance to Tom Kummer. What matters to him is the original quality of presentation, the emotional intensity of language, the styling of the writer. If the facts, sadly, are not original enough then this can only mean: hard luck for the facts that — owing to lacking media fitness — will not and cannot make it into the texts.

Patterns of Vindication

Less well known than this affair itself is the fact that there is now a proper literature of vindication with regard to the forgeries of this author. The apologia refers more or less directly to epistemological questions, partly even uses explicitly various set pieces of the constructivist discourse, but unfortunately in a misleading and terminologically imprecise way. There are, for one, the comments by Tom Kummer himself.[2] After having been exposed with effective publicity as a swindler by a magazine, he said in a first interview:

> It has always been my prime interest to question the definitions of reality and of fiction. […] I wanted to expand the theory of the media and to supply something scintillating to the magazine.[3]

And furthermore: 'Readers of my generation want to be entertained: Entertain me.'[4] A few days later a media theorist offered his support, this time with an explicit reference to constructivism: the borderline journalism of Tom Kummer, his thesis was, 'is neither a malignant outgrowth nor an accident of a society under a constant barrage of information.'[5] It is much rather 'the logical consequence of an escalation within the media industry, of a rat race for the ultimate scoop'.[6] Another statement runs:

> To see forgery no longer as an antagonist of truth simply implements the doctrine that [Ernst von] Glasersfeld, [Heinz von] Foerster and other radical constructivists elevated to the rank of an epistemological programme many years ago: reality is not discovered but invented. Translated into the journalism of the trendsetter Kummer this must read: true is what gives the audience the greatest kick; false is, by contrast, what reduces stimulation intensities to zero and induces the audience to zapping channels.[7]

In an article on the journalistic guiding difference of fact and fiction, one could read that the case demonstrated 'how essential it was to overcome

---

2 Kummer (2007).
3 Wellershof (2000) p. 110.
4 Ibid.
5 Maresch (2000), p. 3.
6 Ibid.
7 Ibid.

the alleged opposition between facts and fictions'.[8] They roughly identified the concept of fiction — with reference to the etymology of the word — with shaping, moulding and forming, i.e. processes that were simply inevitable. The conclusion is, accordingly, that fictionalisation in the sense of formative manipulation is the constitutive normality of the daily business of journalism. The upshot: 'Weaving facts into narratives, and enriching facts with fictions, is part and parcel of the business of journalism and does not *per se* constitute forgery.'[9]

Norbert Bolz has given such ideas even greater incisiveness by formulating the thesis that the moulding of available material always assumes the character of manipulation:

> There is always a presentational façade that is laid over an extremely bumpy reality and reshapes it, manipulates it by imposing some media-adequate form. The question of truth still applies, however, but it is answered differently today in comparison with earlier times. Previously, people would have said that questions of truth can be decided by capturing the characteristics of the relation between a representation and that which is to be represented — and that a more or less adequate form of representation can be established, i.e. *adaequatio* can be diagnosed. Today the only guarantee against constant deception is the competition between different kinds of representation.[10]

And he adds:

> Tom Kummer's trick and the intelligence of his self-vindication consists in a skilful change of argumentative plane: he is attacked on moral grounds and reproached with trickery; but he responds on an epistemological plane when he speaks of the indistinguishability of fiction and reality, thus retreating onto another level and no longer reacting on the level from which he is being attacked.[11]

Tom Kummer himself has presented various further arguments — having obviously done a bit of reading of literature that seemed relevant and possibly useful to him. In a more recent publication he writes:

> We have been born into the world of post-modernism, which is dominated by appearances and whose determining element is the show. In the show there is no truth, in the show there are only effects.[12]

He goes on to proclaim that objectivity, truth, and reality 'are nothing but pure myths in the media', and he offers the diagnosis, clearly harking back to the metaphors used in the appropriate secondary literature: 'The system of journalism has long become frayed.'[13] He then admits that he did indeed at least partially 'stage manage his interviews with the stars', but

---

8   Klaus/Lünenborg (2002), p. 103.
9   Ibid., p. 104.
10 Bolz, in conversation with Poerksen (2002a), p. 445 (author's emphasis).
11 Ibid., p. 448f.
12 Kummer (2005), p. 10.
13 Ibid.

he insists that his intentions had 'always been serious and matter of fact'. 'I never wanted to take the piss out of the readers.'[14] He raises the question himself if he 'is always writing the truth? No, the pure truth is of only marginal interest to me. Naturally, the facts must be right, and this has nearly always been the case with me.[15]

In a longer letter to the author of this book, Tom Kummer suggests organising a joint seminar for fledgling journalists and as alternative, a *School of Borderline-Journalism*. The topic to be treated is:

> How do journalistic realities arise? What was wrong in my system, or what about it could be groundbreaking for the future? [...] The handling of the routines of journalism, for instance, and the corresponding ideology of the purely factual, will require extended challenger strategies also in the future. The belief that someone really talks like the persons in an interview of the *Spiegel,* which has been scrutinised by seven fact checkers, deserves to be thoroughly shaken up whenever possible. Now, the deconstruction of authenticisms is one thing, the inventing and forging of figures and data is another, but this is totally clear to me.[16]

A year later, Tom Kummer comes under fire again: he had re-vamped a reportage for the *Berliner Zeitung*, which was six years old and had already been variously reprinted, according to the established pattern—remixing, resampling—without even bothering to adapt dates and ages.

Much less weight must, therefore, be accorded to the fact that even the above-mentioned letter to the author of this book will one day be re-exploited, too. Some of the sentences it contains have already re-surfaced in a portrait of Tom Kummer written by a certain Hannah de Meuron for the Swiss journal *Faces*. The text is full of admiration of the cool Kummer and his work and tries to correct the negative headlines. Only: Who is Hannah de Meuron? The editor in chief of the magazine is not quite sure; he says the author lives in the United States of America; his only contact is an e-mail address. On further questioning, he explains, however, that he shares the suspicion that it is Tom Kummer himself because the contact had after all been arranged by him.[17] The forger is now, in this most probably faked portrait about the fake, at least lord and master over the interpretations that are spread about him and that he is spreading himself.[18] The tenor: 'Tom Kummer still polarises and provokes even today—like no other print journalist ever before.'[19]

---

14 Ibid., p. 11.
15 Ibid., p. 12.
16 Kummer (2004), p. 2.
17 Personal communication by Patrick Pierazzoli, editor in chief and publisher of *Faces*, on 19 April 2005.
18 See Meuron (2004), pp. 34f.
19 Ibid., p. 35.

The Question of Form

The most worrying thing for authors who favour constructivist argumentation is, therefore, not the fact that Tom Kummer is a notorious forger and an unsavoury fraudster or that he apparently philosophises about his arts and his own significance under the cover of a pseudonym. One can remain wary of such deception, one must reckon with it, anyway, and one can always expose it by means of research without wasting too much thought and time. It is irritating, however, that his attempts at justification obviously impress people, and that they even appear consistent and substantial.

Are techniques of writing and rules of presentation, one may well ask, neutral as to the content involved? Is not every act of creating and moulding ultimately an act of fictionalisation, as various authors argue, because it pre-structures reality and thus undermines the apparently unambiguous distinction between fact and fiction?[20] Is there still—from the point of view of the audience—a recognisable difference and contrast between fact and fiction? Another thing to clarify is: How can the connection between epistemological insight and ethical or un-ethical action be best understood? Can the epistemological diagnosis that ultimate knowledge of truth must forever remain unverifiable, serve as a justification of arbitrariness? In what form can constructivists use concepts like *shaping, staging, lie, objectivity* etc., which are used by Tom Kummer and some of his advocates? Can these concepts—at the terminological heart of an ethics of journalism—be restructured and re-adjusted in an observer-relative way? Or are those communication theorists right who think that a journalistic ethics on a constructivist basis is bound to be impossible? Has Tom Kummer, justifying his methods in a book of his own and propagating rules for the promotion of journalistic effectiveness,[21] simultaneously written a 'manifesto of constructivism'?[22] Has he implemented practically what the epistemology of constructivism (supposedly) implies?

In the following, I shall attempt to tackle these questions in an extensive manner: first the work of Heinz von Foerster will be adduced to clarify how the connection between epistemology and (ethical-moral) behaviour can be envisioned; epistemological relativism does not, the argument will demonstrate, lead to ethical-moral arbitrariness as long as one follows the strict logic of his argumentation. Next, the problem of truth will be dealt with from the perspective of a constructivistically inspired ethics; this intends to show that the criticism of truth by constructivism may essen-

---

20   Quite in keeping with these reflections, Reus (2002, p. 78) has formulated the thesis that journalism has always 'crossed the boundaries of fiction' and that 'fictionalising' is present 'in all the forms of journalistic presentation'.
21   See Kummer (1997), p. 24.
22   Hömberg (2002), p. 296.

tially be understood as a new kind of truth theory. The subsequent sections will connect epistemological insights with the claims that have to be advanced for a constructivist ethics of journalism; concepts like *shaping, staging, objectivity* will be redefined, ethical-moral possibilities of orientation will be offered, not in the sense of prescriptions but with the goal of a comprehensive effort of reflection, of deepening ethical awareness, something indispensable for quality journalists. It will come as no surprise that the author of this book is convinced that Tom Kummer is completely mistaken if he thinks he can support his views by some hastily screwed-together set pieces he has torn from the discourses of constructivism or different theories, e. g. postmodernism. He does no more than practise what Heinz von Foerster, in a memorable moment of irritation, called *episto-babble,* characterising specific outgrowths of purely fashionable chatter and intellectual dilettantism.[23] One can only support von Foerster's appeal: theory work in the explosive field of ethics and morality will never be sensibly possible without conceptual acuity and great clarity of purpose.

2. Ethics of the Second Order: Excursus I

Ethics of Enabling Ethics

The connection between epistemology and ethics is the subject of the work of various constructivist authors;[24] it is central to the work of Heinz von Foerster. The very titles of some of his books — 'Wissen und Gewissen' [Science and Con-Science] and 'CybernEthics'[25] — express this connection. But a mere first glance at his work makes it appear doubtful whether the cybernetician has actually elaborated a constructivist ethics that operates with concrete rules of behaviour and defines in substantial terms what should be considered desirable.[26] Closer examination reveals that this is obviously not the case. It is his particular merit though to have embedded ethical reflection in a framework of interlinked lines of argumentation, which provides the foundations for ethical behaviour — of whatever concrete form. The constructivist ethics of Heinz von Foerster is essentially an *ethics of enabling ethics,*[27] or in other words, an ethics of the second order, i.e. the observation of modes of argumentation in the domain of ethics,

---

23 Foerster (1993), p. 364.
24 A survey of the concepts of ethics of Maturana, Foerster, Glasersfeld, Krüll and Krippendorff and other ethics-oriented representatives of constructivism is provided by Hungerige/Sabbouh (1995). The fact that the work by Foerster is dealt with in such great detail seems to me to result from the consistency and the elegance of his proposals — and the contradictions immanent to other proposals that will be discussed in the course of the following considerations.
25 See Foerster (1993a und 1993b).
26 See Kramaschki (1995), p. 266.
27 On this concept cf. Kramaschki (1995), pp. 262f.

which is itself in turn carried out with ethical intentions. Such an observation indicates the central preconditions of ethical and moral action. It is worked out according to the principle of the perspicacious avoidance of error, which is also of importance to the ethics of journalism. The relevant preconditions and premises of ethical-moral action, consequently, appear to be: the assumption of the freedom of choice for individuals; and the emphasis on, and the recognition of, individual responsibility, which must be granted to every individual. The specific connection of epistemology and ethics is not a relationship of derivation. Possible faults in design that might set this proposal against constructivist premises are the following: the recourse to unconditionally valid justifications; a kind of moral know-all attitude; attempts to impose ethical conceptions on others; the concretisation of moral and ethical orientations and stimulations for reflection in the direction of material prescriptions, laws and imperatives.

The work of Heinz von Foerster may thus be read from a double perspective: first as the attempt to create a transcendental ethics, secondly as the attempt to warn of the abysses of the merely well intentioned that does not see its self-constraining structure, does not want to see it or cannot see it.[28] The core question of the entire proposal is: How can an ethics (of the second order) be constructed that makes for transparency and contains the proclamation of its own goals—emphasis on freedom of choice, recognition of responsibility, avoidance of force—in all its differentiations of argument, and yet refers back to the central figure of constructivist thought, the observer?

From such a perspective, every beginning is fundamentally contingent. One may, however, initiate the process of argumentation convincingly with a pronouncement by Heinz von Foerster, which has already been quoted several times here but not yet in its entirety: 'Objectivity is a subject's delusion that observing can be done without him.' And furthermore: 'Invoking objectivity is abrogating responsibility, hence its popularity.'[29] Such a formulation involves a particular connection between epistemology and ethics that must be formulated more precisely: the ideal of objectivity is negated for epistemological reasons and criticised on ethical-moral grounds. The structuring principle of these reflections is again the contrast between an observer-independent and an observer-dependent conception of knowledge, which is here rotated in the

---

28 This warning is also directed at the constructivist community of fans that is overly eager to be furnished with prescriptions and recipes. In this connection an anecdote may be illuminating, which nicely illustrates the subversive constructivism of Foerster. He reports: 'My doctrine is not to have a doctrine. Of course that is a paradox, but it is a very dynamic one. During one of my lectures I once said, "Ladies and gentlemen, please, don't believe a word of what I am about to tell you!" Everyone laughed and apparently believed that they shouldn't believe what I had said. But I meant what I had said.' (Foerster/Poerksen 1998, p. 157).

29 Quoted in Foerster/Poerksen (2002), p. 148.

direction of an ethics of responsibility. *Objectivity, ontology* and (absolute) *reality* are characterised by Heinz von Foerster in the following way:

> These are all static notions that can be used by people to separate themselves from the world. They can be used as a justification for personal indifference by claiming that there is nothing you can do about it, since it is always a matter of an immutable existence that is rigid and timeless. [...] This means that you can contrast two fundamentally different positions. The attitude of uninvolved observers contrasts with the attitude of people who empathize and are involved and who see themselves as part of the world. Their basic assumption is, "Whatever I do will change the world." They are connected to the world and its fate and are responsible for their action.[30]

A different, a new, contrastive opposition has thus been brought into play: the point is no longer objectivity or subjectivity but the fundamental question as to whether the epistemological commitment can be invoked to separate oneself from the world, to assume the role of the distanced (non-participant) observer who de-personalises his observations by hiding behind the claims of an objective perception of what is given.

Reasons versus Decisions

The question is now if and how such emphasis on personal responsibility — strictly according to the logic of constructivist thought — can be justified. Certain authors have, at least rhetorically, suggested the possibility of an ultimate justification. Peter M. Hejl orients his pronouncements — even as a constructivist — explicitly by the mode of inference from existence to prescription; in this, and particularly in his, case: the inference from a reality that is declared to be a constructed reality to a conception of ethics that is admittedly equally constructed. He asserts a relation of derivation between epistemological assumptions and ethical postulates and thus purposefully moves, in thought and mode of argumentation, into the proximity of the pattern of justification that has been debated as the so-called *naturalist fallacy* in philosophy. The point of criticism of the opponents of such modes of justification is the rejection of the derivation of normative statements from descriptive statements, frequently by recurring to scientific knowledge that is accorded special dignity.[31] It follows: the substantial points dealt with by Peter M. Hejl in his proposal are constructivist points; the mode of argumentation that asserts a strictly verifiable derivation of ethics from epistemology seems to fit better into a realist tradition and is probably oriented by the model of positive law, i.e. guided by the

---

30   Ibid., pp. 157f.
31   On the formative principles of this argumentation see for instance Hejl (1995), p. 46 und pp. 52f.; on the debate about the suggested objection of the naturalist fallacy see Hejl (1995), pp. 49ff.

idea of an identification of law and morality, which is problematical in other respects.[32]

Humberto R. Maturana and Francisco J. Varela sometimes also use a jargon of irrevocability and a rhetoric of unconditional obligation, which in my view contradicts the essential line and style of constructivist argumentation; form and message come apart at the seams. At the end of the book *The tree of knowledge* one can read, for example:

> *The cognition of cognition obliges.* Knowledge obliges us to take an attitude of constant vigilance towards the temptation of certainty. It obliges us to see that our certainties are not proofs of truth, that the world as seen by everyone is not *the* world but *a* world that we bring forth together with the others. It obliges us to see that the world will only change when we change our ways of living.'[33]

In brief: the point is an ethics 'that is inescapable.'[34] Francisco J. Varela has apparently radicalised his view, probably due to the influence of Buddhism, in the direction of metaphysical speculation and has come to see ethical and moral behaviour ultimately as ontologically founded. In his book *Ethical Know-How,* he positively mentions the assumption that 'the authentic care is immanent in the foundation of all Being and can be unfolded to full flowering by sustained ethical education.'[35] Here an ultimate foundation is proclaimed in utmost clarity; ethical behaviour is moved into the proximity of the fulfilment of duties already given and immanent in Being.[36]

By contrast, Heinz von Foerster insists that his plea for responsibility and his decision for the attitude of the participant observer cannot be deduced from his epistemological insights and most certainly not from the original foundation of all Being.[37] His reflections on ethics have been inspired by epistemology, but they are not derived from epistemology, they are *not* a consequence that would immediately follow in a linear-causal way from the premises of epistemology. 'For if it were a consequence it would be a necessity. I assert however: it is not a necessity. It is an attitude that we can select from amongst all possible other attitudes.'[38]

---

32 See Schmidt (2000), p. 66.
33 Maturana/Varela (1992), pp. 263f. (authors' emphasis).
34 Ibid., p. 264.
35 Varela (1994), p. 77.
36 On a dispute about this question, see Varela in conversation with Poerksen (2002i), p. 105.
37 Comparing the approaches described so far will show that quite different conclusions may be drawn from constructivist concepts in epistemology; the heterogeneity of the different positions advanced, which appear similar only in some of their general aspects (emphasis on responsibility, acceptance of the plurality of reality conceptions etc.) is a strong indication of the fact that epistemology and ethics of constructivism cannot be brought or forced into a relationship of derivation and logical inference.
38 Foerster/Bröcker (2002), p. 64.

This means: Heinz von Foerster professes an *agnosticism by relational logic*[39] with respect to the relationship between epistemology and ethics, which will accept nothing but the exclusive choice by the individual; such an attitude is undeniably epistemologically inspired but contains no assertion or affirmation of an inevitable and inescapable connection between epistemological understanding and ethical-moral prescriptions of action, which could be spelled out in detail.

Decidable and Undecidable Questions

To make the possibility of choice and the inevitability of free decision quite clear, he introduces the distinction between *decidable* and *undecidable questions* and draws up an argumentative structure which impresses by its logical rigour and the revelation of individual ranges of play. The question of personal ethical-moral preference is considered to be undecidable, in principle, and is connected with the appeal to individual, i.e. self-responsible judgment. Heinz von Foerster:

> A decidable question is always decided within a framework that determines the possible and right answer from the outset. Its decidability is guaranteed by certain rules and formalisms, although they have to be accepted. Syllogisms, syntax and arithmetic are all examples of these types of formalisms. Within the framework of a logical-mathematical network, you get from one junction (the question or the problem) to the next junction (the answer or the solution). This is what makes the question of whether or not the number 2546 can be divided by 2 so easy to answer within seconds, since we all know that numbers that have a final digit that is even can be divided by 2.[40]

Undecidable questions touch the core area of metaphysics; they deal with the origin of the universe, the existence of a God etc. and must be considered to be irresolvable in principle; the question whether one considers knowledge as observer-dependent or observer-independent is a question undecidable in principle because its truth status can neither be proved nor disproved. Heinz von Foerster:

> You are being called on to make the choice. In a certain sense, decidable questions have already been decided by the framework in which they come to exist. The only thing you can do is to follow the rules in order to find the answer. [41]

Deciding an undecidable question (the very question of whether one is faced by an undecidable question is basically undecidable),[42] one adopts a

---

39 This concept is taken from Ott (1995), p. 296.
40 Foerster/Poerksen (2002), p. 153.
41 Ibid., p. 154.
42 Foerster: 'I would even go so far as to say that the question is undecidable as to whether an experiment can be found that unequivocally determines if a question is undecidable or not. The problem of undecidability cannot even be decided on the level of the second order.' (Foerster/Poerksen 2002, p. 155)

view of things that can never be conclusively clarified due to the topics dealt with and the impossibility of a verification of the assumptions. The decision of an undecidable question reveals individual responsibility and excludes the possibility of delegating such responsibility: 'You decide to view the objects, the world and your fellow human beings in a certain way and to act accordingly. You become responsible for the decision that you made and that no one else can take away from you.'[43]

Ethical-moral decisions, according to this line of argument, can only be justified by one single instance: individual preference, self-responsible choice in relation to the postulate of the freedom of choice.

The whole proposal thus acquires the character of a free-floating construction that combines relativistic epistemology and ethical-moral certainty in the case of having to make a particular decision. For this reason, an ethics that is designed in the clear understanding of its unavoidable relativity, does not permanently thwart itself: it is the decision by which one ties oneself down, excludes possible alternatives and defines the unambiguity required for action, but in clear awareness of its irrevocable contingency. The problem of justification is solved by the fact that the foundation of ethics is itself based on an ethical-moral decision. Any reliance on external instances (nature, God, laws and regularities, a *telos* of history etc.) is rejected; the constructivist postulates too (plurality of realities, autonomy of the individual, impossibility of ultimate justification, rejection of truth terrorism) and the possible 'correlates of such assumptions'[44] (tolerance, recognition of responsibility and autonomy etc.) can no longer be forced into a relationship of logical derivation. They are at best, if they are chosen with an ethical-moral intention, '*orders of investigation, postulates of reflection,* or *obligations of observation of the second order* […], which may in the given situation in question serve as a framework of finding a decision by the morally acting agents.'[45]

Ethics and Morality

A central point is that this framework of decision-making is not packed with commandments and interdictions of a material-substantial kind.[46] Consequently, a consistently designed ethics of the second order must needs appear vague and diffuse in the sphere of concrete action simply because its detailed formation is left to the individual. The *problem of mediation* must also be defined in a careful and intelligent way. What has been

---

43 Foerster/Poerksen (2002), p. 155.
44 Schmidt (2000), p. 65.
45 Ibid., (author's emphasis).
46 This kind of unfilled position or gap is also a feature of liberal democracies and of open societies in general. They constitute, metaphorically speaking, the frame but not the concrete picture, whose design and actual form of which must not be prescribed.

realised as right and correct cannot be propagated in the mode of certainty and with missionary zeal and furore because this would immediately provoke a rhetorical self-contradiction.

Heinz von Foerster and Humberto R. Maturana have suggested, in this connection, to distinguish ethics from morality, not least in order to characterise different styles of mediation. They consider morality as a matter of authoritarian demand, of preaching and prescribing; it is announced in the imperative mode. Humberto R. Maturana:

> The moralists stand for the adherence to rules, which they consider as the external reference lending authority to their statements and strange ideas. They lack awareness of their own responsibility. People acting as moralists do not see their fellow human beings because they are completely occupied by the upholding of rules and imperatives. They know with certainty what has to be done and how everybody else has to behave. People acting ethically, on the contrary, perceive others, consider them important, and see them. It is, of course, possible that persons argue like moralists but act in an ethical way. It is imaginable that persons are moralists without being ethical, or that they are generally held to be immoral while, in fact, acting ethically. In each of these cases, the possibility of ethics and of being touched arises only when the other human being is seen as a legitimate other, and when the possible consequences of one's actions for that other's well-being are reflected.[47]

One can only decide about one's own actions. Ethics must — and this is a key concept with Heinz von Foerster[48] — remain *implicit*, it should therefore be woven into the actions of the individual in order to avoid assuming the rank of an explicit prescription.[49] It appears to be somewhat paradoxical against this backdrop that Heinz von Foerster has himself formulated an ethical imperative like the following:[50] '*Act always so as to increase the number of choices.*'[51] On the one hand, such a formulation naturally fits the concept of an ethics of the second order; on the other hand, however, it does not. It seems fitting that the increase of possibilities inevitably raises the number of alternatives of thinking and acting, i.e. that it is a formal cri-

---

47 Maturana/Poerksen (2004), pp. 207f.
48 Maturana, in this connection, introduces the concept of *aesthetic seduction*. What he intends to express is a non-directive, respectful, form of persuasion that does not operate with compulsion and is based on the correspondence and harmony of speaking and acting; the self-expression of persons is decisive in this context. See Maturana/Poerksen (2004), pp. 50ff.
49 Foerster/Poerksen (2002), p. 157.
50 One can show, I think, that Foerster — who was first a cybernetician and bio-epistemologist, and later a cybernetically inspired thinker about ethics — has elaborated his ethical ideas and conclusions with ever-increasing consistency in the course of time; his ethical imperative appeared in one of his earlier articles, the relativisation of its claim to unconditional validity came later. His last books (Foerster/Poerksen 2002 and Foerster/Bröcker 2002) describe the history of his thought and illustrate the progressive radicalisation of his sceptical position; the recourse to the biological-epistemological foundation of autonomy and ethics is finally eliminated in favour of an emphatic idea of freedom of choice.
51 Foerster/Poerksen (2002), p. 37 (author's emphasis).

terion to raise the degree of freedom and thus to maximise the chances of self-responsible decision. Quite inappropriate, however, seems the presentation in the form of an imperative because the concept of the imperative (although not the content of the assumption) possesses at least misleading connotations that seem to be incongruent with self-responsible reflection. Heinz von Foerster has realised this himself and admitted that he had formulated this imperative 'in a slovenly manner', because it would create the impression that he, too, would like to 'order people around'. In his own words:

> That is my ethical imperative, although once again one might have the impression that I am trying to order people around, and this is just not right. I did not choose my words very carefully when I said that. It would have been better if I had written, "Heinz, act always so as to increase the number of choices."[52]

Decisions can only be taken about the sphere of individual actions if ethics is to remain implicit, if it is not transformed into explicit morality, and if it is not perverted into a strategy of suppression.[53]

Individual reflection, the decision about what is undecidable in principle, i.e. what cannot be separated from an observer and delegated to other instances of authorization, will thus remain inescapable. If one understands this proposal for an ethics of the second order as a theoretical framework of any kind of ethics, then it will also be of importance for reflection-intensive quality journalism: it will offer a logic of argumentation and well-founded unjustifiability combining means and purposes, ethical reflection and practice, in inseparable ways. It is everybody's choice and, therefore, everybody's individual responsibility, and according to this logic, everybody will have to face and manage their own freedom.

3. Consequence Theory of Truth: Excursus II

Conditions of Dominance

The variability of the possible views of the connection between epistemology and ethics becomes apparent when one compares the comments on the concept of truth offered by some of the protagonists of constructivism. 'I think', writes Humberto R. Maturana, amongst others,

> there is a fundamental alienation to which we are prone: the search for truth, the search for the absolute, the desire for ultimate stability through the denial of change; the desire that the world should be in the manner that satisfies our desires, and as such and with respect to that, stable. [...] But how do we act? We invent systems of consensual stability that we claim are absolute truths that must be protected against

---

52 Ibid.
53 Ibid., p. 157.

change because we deem their value to be universal. In their name, we deny the individuality of others that live in a different consensus and, without allowing them to disagree, we submerge them in a systematic social abuse that we expect they should accept as legitimate. This is our most frequent alienation: our blindness about the world of relative truths that we create with others, and in which man is the absolute reference, and our immersion in an ideology that justifies this blindness.[54]

Some speak of truth terrorism, some of 'reality terror'[55]. Paul Watzlawick writes that there is, 'hardly a more murderous, more despotic idea [...] than the delusion of a "real" reality'.[56] The claim to absolute truth, Siegfried J. Schmidt states succinctly, 'inevitably leads to oppression'.[57] Thus, all these and similar pronouncements, we may conclude, practise a form of criticism of an emphatic notion of truth that connects epistemology and ethical-moral concern. This kind of criticism may be taken to be a proper constructivist theory of truth and will from now on be called *consequence theory of truth*.[58]

To elucidate this thesis, some general remarks on the philosophical treatment of the question of truth will be helpful; only this necessary detour and unavoidable excursion into the domain of philosophy can yield the relevant criteria of description that will then enable us to explicate the peculiarities of a consequence theory of truth. What can be stated right away, in any case, is that the theories of truth discussed by philosophers are primarily the subject of epistemological, not ethical, reflection. With reference to a famous distinction introduced by Immanuel Kant, they deal with the key question of what human beings can know, and not the question of what they should do, how they should act (which would accordingly belong to the domain of ethics).

This localisation of the question of truth in the domain of epistemology is made additionally clear by the fact that all the different conceptions of truth, and ultimately also all the different types of truth theory, may be sorted according to the guiding difference *subject/object*, and that the kind of chosen relation between subject and object, i.e. between observer and observed, makes it possible to observe the differentiation of all the particular theories of truth. Depending on the specific relation established between subject and object, one may distinguish, in a first step, between three fundamentally different possibilities of characterising this relation. The first basic type results from

---

54 Maturana (1985), p. 29; author's original English text, unpublished.
55 Weischenberg, quoted in Neuberger (1996), p. 228.
56 Watzlawick, quoted in Neuberger, ibid.
57 Schmidt, quoted in Neuberger, ibid.
58 The concept of theory used in this context—in contradistinction to the more rigorously developed philosophical theories of truth—is obviously a diffuse one and means something like conception, understanding, view. It is not a *terminus technicus*. See also Gloy (2004), p. 5.

> preferring the objective side and neglecting the subjective. The domain of the objects is given absolute or at least relative dominance. It is assumed that the objects in their being and suchness, in their determinants and their relationships with other objects, exist *in themselves*, quite independently of whether there is a cognising being apprehending them or not. The things possess their own peculiar being in themselves as well as their own specific properties to which the human subjects must subordinate themselves in an act of apprehension. [...] In a process of acquiring knowledge, human subjects must subordinate themselves to what is given, must appropriate what is available. [...] This is the position of *common sense*, of the natural, everyday, pre-scientific way of handling things. Elevated to a philosophical position, it represents realism from its most naïve to its most sublime forms.[59]

According to the systematisation introduced here, the other epistemological extreme is marked by idealism; here the hierarchisation of subject and object is inverted, as it were; the world of objects becomes dependent on the cognitive grasp of the knowing subject. The third type of knowledge emerges

> when the two relata within the cognitive relation, the knower and what is to be known, are treated as equivalent and as of equal status, so that a correspondence is achieved between the world of the subjects and the world of the objects.[60]

Philosophical Theories of Truth

It is this variable evaluation and hierarchisation of subject and object, which leads to three different concepts of truth and types of truth theory:

- The assumption of *ontic truth* (also: objective truth, factual truth etc.) which is advocated within the framework of a so-called *theory of ontic truth*, assigns unconditional primacy to the world of objects; the subject's task here is to open up, to become permeable, in order to receive 'what there is such as it is in itself',[61] uncluttered and undistorted. The experience of truth, possibly supported by existentially dramatic feeling, consists in a kind of revelation, a becoming-apparent of the world of objects in its archetypal gestalt, and thus clearly exhibits mystical-metaphysical colouring: within such a conception, the idea of Being possesses qualities otherwise only granted to the Divine, as Karen Gloy has shown with reference to Martin Heidegger.[62]
- The position maximally removed from this understanding of truth relocates the apprehension of truth to the rational sphere of the subject *(logical truth)* and transforms the experience of Being-as-it-is into a perception of coherence, freedom from contradiction, or perhaps con-

---

59   Gloy (2004), p. 68.
60   Ibid., p. 69.
61   Ibid., p. 78.
62   Ibid., p. 78f.

sensus. The results are *subject-immanent theories of truth*; they have been given different forms and thus exist in diverse variants. The *coherence theory of truth* in its pure form restricts itself to 'the subjective domain of knowledge' and relies on 'the ability of a statement to be integrated into a system of statements, to be compatible with the other statements.'[63] Here truth means: freedom from contradiction, consistent integration.[64] The *consensus theory*, or *discourse theory*, *of truth* as proposed by Jürgen Habermas, for instance, also rejects any kind of reference beyond discourse, insists on subject-immanent argumentation; truth is here conceived of as the discursive satisfaction of claims to validity and is founded upon consensus manufactured in an ideal speech situation.[65]

- The concept of truth mediating between the object side and the subject side has recourse to the famous formula coined by Thomas Aquinas (*adaequatio intellectus et rei*) and aims to comprehend truth as *correspondence* between subject and object, as a relation of correspondence between the knowing subject and the object-to-be-known. The actual exposition of the diverse *correspondence theories of truth* leans heavily on *how* the kind of correspondence is specified, *how* the accommodation of subject and object is worked out in detail.[66] Is there a mapping relation, a mirroring of what is apprehended in the knowing mind? If so, this correspondence theory could be interpreted as a kind of reflection theory. Is there a causal nexus, a relation of cause and effect? Then the knowledge reached by the subject would be the result and consequence of the impression emanating from the object world, which is received by the subject, and which in fact imposes itself on the subject in its archetypal formation. In any case, each one of the variants of a correspondence theory must face up to the problem of how correspondence is to be understood and how all those essentially heterogeneous entities (subject, mind, cognition) and domains (world of objects, things, phenomena) are—or can at all be—integrated with each other in such a way as to achieve the desired ultimate state of assimilation and total structural isomorphism.

Criticism of Truth as Theory of Truth

If the observer schema that underlies the discussion of traditional theories of truth is also used for the reconstruction of the constructivist theory of truth, then striking differences become apparent. The systematic locus of the *consequence theory of truth* is not only epistemology but also ethics, i.e. the concern for the other that may be oneself. This means that there is a

---

63 Ibid., p. 168.
64 On the variants of the coherence theory of truth cf. Gloy (2004), pp. 170ff.
65 On this particular variant and also other variants of the consensus theory of truth cf. Gloy (2004), pp.193ff. and pp. 203ff.
66 On the variants of correspondence theory, see Gloy (2004), pp. 93ff.

characteristic uncertainty regarding its disciplinary placement, which may be summarised in the following formula: consequence theory can be justified epistemologically, its ultimate motivation, however, is an ethical-moral one. In the context of an epistemological discourse, one deals—quite traditionally—with the relationship between subject and object, observer and observed. Ontic and correspondence-theoretical concepts of truth are rejected, subject-immanent ones favoured. Arguing, however, from an ethical-moral perspective, causes a different relational structure to emerge: it is the relation between subject and subject, between various observers, possibly including ourselves as observers reflecting the cognitive costs and the consequences of our very own ideas of truth. Furthermore—and again in contrast to traditional theories of truth—the central problem for consequence theorists is not primarily the definition of the concept of truth or the specification of criteria of truth (evidence, consensus, utility etc.), i.e. the explication of the realisation of truth. Nor is it a primary aspiration to pass judgment on the truth or falsity of statements and to set up the corresponding criteria of differentiation, but much rather to ponder and bring to awareness the possible *effects* of the distinction true/false—therefore the chosen label *consequence theory of truth*. It asserts nothing about the essence of truth like traditional theories of truth, says nothing about its realisation, but deals with the consequences that result from the conviction of being in possession of unquestionable truth. One can distinguish, at least as ideal types, *logical-semantical consequences, individual-cognitive consequences* and *consequences for the domain of relations*.

The Logical-Semantical Level

Heinz von Foerster has graphically highlighted the logical-semantical consequence of the use of the concept of truth with his aphorism that truth is the invention of a liar.[67] It formulates succinctly that truth and lie depend on each other, refer to each other, and form a logical-semantical system of reference that remains in force even when the possibility of any access to truth is rejected. The meaningfulness of the concept is affirmed, in any case, and a conceptual master currency is introduced that directs one's orientation—however clear its restrictions. Tied to such a logical-semantical perspective, it is impossible to liberate oneself from concepts considered problematical by means of their negation because their very negation still accentuates their relevance. One can only get rid of them by simply not mentioning them, thus banishing them to a sphere of non-existence, depriving them of their pedestal and fundament as the transcendental condition of their topicalisation. They will then fall back into an amorphous and shapeless field that one cannot appropriate

---

67 See Foerster/Poerksen (2002), especially pp. 30f.; in addition, with reference to the distinction sickness/health, pp.76ff.

cognitively because it is unmarked by distinctions and designations. In this case, the fundamental statement by George Spencer-Brown, the first commandment regarding the creation of a concept of observation based on a logic of distinctions, would have to be changed. The requirement would no longer be: '*Draw* a distinction!' but: '*Drop* a distinction!' One puts distinctions, perhaps even systems of distinctions, behind oneself by flatly refusing to discuss, negate, affirm, defend or criticise them. Distinctions are deleted from the discourse because they no longer occur, because they are no longer needed.[68]

The Individual-Cognitive Level

It is one of the basic tenets of constructivism that there is an almost limitless plurality of reality designs, of concept arrangements, of ways to punctuate an event, to construct causality and to create meaning. By contrast, the defenders of a single truth reduce the multitude of potential interpretations of reality to one single certainty, to one ultimate determination of what is or should be considered absolutely right. One possible individual-cognitive consequence of such certainty about truth is, therefore, that it makes alternatives of thinking, feeling, and acting invisible, as it were, and that it may develop into the compulsion to say the same thing on all occasions, or to have to offer more or less similar answers all the time, to say he least. Although one may thus be protected from the endless circling in the labyrinth of undecidable questions, such certainty about truth may make the sympathetic re-enactment of other, contrary, views difficult, perhaps even impossible.[69] It may, moreover, eliminate the need for radical scepticism and may, according to Humberto R. Maturana, as long as it is not a question of securities required by the situation in hand,

> make all further reflection seem a waste of time: We believe we already know in advance the only possible result of any renewed reflection effort. What, in fact, do we really mean when we say we are absolutely sure of something? We say: There is no point in entertaining doubts; our beliefs are so overwhelming that it must appear completely absurd to think about the conditions of their origins.[70]

The Level of Relations

The majority of the writings from constructivist circles, which deal with the problem of the presumption of truth, however, do not refer to the logical-semantical or the individual-cognitive level. They are devoted to the sphere of human relations, the sphere of interaction. The basic point of reference is the relationship between autonomous individuals, a relationship

---

68 This operator is discussed in the conversation with Foerster in: Poerksen (2004g), pp. 20ff.
69 See Morin (2001), p. 82.
70 Maturana/Poerksen 2004, p. 45

constituting, as it were, the prototypical pattern of a potentially ethical or unethical relation. Two possible variants of consequence may be distinguished on this level: on the one hand, there is *the negation of the other* as well as of other views, which is inherent in the belief in absolute truth. Numerous protagonists of constructivism—recall only Heinz von Foerster, Niklas Luhmann, Humberto R. Maturana, Josef Mitterer, Siegfried J. Schmidt, Paul Watzlawick and Siegfried Weischenberg—have argued in this way, and have never failed to insist on the need for careful gradation.[71] Quite conceivable are concepts of truth that—although contradicting most of the definitions of truth—do not, or are not intended to, claim validity for anyone else but their advocates. They are excluded from the criticism, which targets only the generalisation of individual assumptions by means of dogmatically justified claims to truth. Truth in the sense of a concern based on consequence theory entails a static-dogmatic view of the concept that negates other views and considers the respect for these views to be wrong, counterproductive, and therefore dispensable, in the service of a good cause. At issue is the argumentative or pseudo-argumentative appeal to the truth concept and related ideas, which are, for the purpose in hand, considered equivalent, like *true, real, definite, certain, with ultimate certainty, objective, reality, the absolute*. They are functionally equivalent; they all serve comparable purposes, e.g. making something plausible, convincing and persuading people, but also discrediting and defaming people in conflict discourses.[72]

In one of Humberto R. Maturana's exemplary formulations:

> If we do not accept our interlocutor totally, or we want to assert our position, or we are certain that we are right, or we want to force the other to perform certain actions, we explicitly or implicitly claim that what we say is valid because it is objective (that is, founded on an objective reality), that we know how things really are, that our argument is rational, and that the other is objectively wrong and cannot honestly ignore it.[73]

Some of the possible consequences of this first consequence-theoretical reflection in the domain of relations would be: intolerance and a dogmatically fought quarrel, a lack of respect for other views, attempts at conversion, the menace of homogenising reality designs, demands for subordination, discrimination and defamation. The second variant of possible consequences deals with the *legitimation of violence*; in such justifications of aggressivity the use of power and, in the extreme case, even of

---

[71] Reflections on the links between the belief in truth and the negation of the other may be found in: Foerster (Foerster/Poerksen 2002, pp. 30ff.), Luhmann (1994, p. 11), Maturana (1998, pp. 226ff.), Mitterer (2001, pp. 64ff.), Schmidt (1991, pp. 47f.), Watzlawick (1994, pp. 204ff.) and Weischenberg (1993, p. 129).
[72] On the concept of *conflict discourse*, see Mitterer (2001), p. 77.
[73] Maturana (1998), p. 250.

physical force is endorsed with the argument that only in this way — thus runs the figure of thought elaborated by consequence theorists, and which is subjected to criticism — truth could regain its rightful place, and detrimental untruth be eliminated.[74] Paul Watzlawick has described in precise words this gradual transition from the initial desire to convert the other to the wish to subjugate them, ending finally in an act of purposeful aggression:

> The idea to be in the possession of ultimate truth will at first lead to a messianic attitude clinging to the conviction that the truth will prevail *qua* truth in any case. At this point, the protagonist of an ideology may still believe in the possibility of enlightening and perhaps convincing the heretic. As the world, however, soon proves to be hard-hearted, unwilling or incapable to open itself to the truth, the inevitable next step is what Hermann Lübbe has called the ideological self-empowerment for the use of force. The world must have its eyes opened for its own best interests.[75]

The appeal to an ultimate, dogmatically conceived truth, therefore, is generally seen to be a destructive incentive in the field of human relations. Truth in this understanding is not only a means to deform these relations and to ruin the climate of communication but may also lend an air of apparent necessity to violent disputes.

Between Epistemology and Ethics

The essential features of a consequence theory of truth have now been described, of a theory that oscillates between epistemology and ethics in a characteristic way, that analyses conflicts and reconstructs strategies of legitimating the privileged establishment and enforcement of views decreed to be true. It may, at this point, be a mere matter of speculation but it does indeed seem more than accidental that the very founders of constructivism developed reflections of this sort; all of them had to suffer under dictators, were confronted with dogmatically founded realities. Heinz von Foerster, working in Berlin during the period of National Socialism without the obligatory 'Ariernachweis' (proof of 'Aryan' descent), had to evade the inevitable checks by a careful tactic of procrastination. Ernst von Glasersfeld left Vienna after the National Socialists had seized power; Paul Watzlawick has repeatedly deplored how deeply shocked he felt by the NS-regime. Francisco Varela — after the death of Salvador Allende and the military coup of the putschist Pinochet — fled to Costa Rica. Humberto R. Maturana stayed in Chile — despite repeated threats — in order to experience, 'what it means to live under a dictator' and in order to observe, 'how people gradually go blind', even though

---

74   See Mitterer (2001), p. 64.
75   Watzlawick (1994), pp. 204f. (author's emphasis).

they may be well aware 'of the dangers of a blindness produced by ideology'. He recollects:

> I also asked myself whether I might be able to observe in such a dictatorial system how people gradually go blind, and what the causes of such perceptual deprivation were. Can one, if one has been duly forewarned and is aware of the dangers of ideologically produced blindness, prevent it from developing and retain one's capabilities of vision and perception?[76]

An instructive picture such as this one, illuminating the background of individual lives as well as the history of the practice of science, can of course contribute nothing to the plausibility of the criticism of truth and the criticism of truth theories presented here; however, it may speak in favour of examining more closely the links between theory development and individual biography. It also shows that the justification of the arguments introduced here can only be achieved in a wider context. The polemical overstatement, too, has no proper justifying quality, although it may be an acceptable corrective. It certainly is, as has become clear, a reaction against mental rigidity, against dogmatically defended reality designs, and against the form of the authoritarian-dictatorial presumption of truth, which declares the use of force in conflicts — explicitly or implicitly — a legitimate means of its practical implementation.

4. Journalistic Ethics: Key Concepts and Core Questions

Law and Morality

Breaking a rule reveals the rule; the public ascertainment of the confirmed violation of a norm demonstrates and stabilises the norm in question.[77] Such a mechanism of rule revelation and rule stabilisation through rule violation may be recognised in cases of media-ethical misconduct about which critical reports are published (with the obligatory portion of outrage) — in the media, of course. Such instances of misconduct include forgeries (spectacular example: the Hitler diaries), forms of sensationalist reporting about accidents and deaths (the photographs of the dead Uwe Barschel in the bathtub), the activities of certain journalists in the case of crimes (interviews with criminals during the hostage drama of Gladbeck). Other occurrences that are repeatedly found in the focus of media-ethical debate are, for example: infringements of personal rights (e.g. by the pillory methods of the gutter press), forms of direct or indirect corruption (rewarding of favourable reporting by lucrative advertisements etc.) and

---

76 Maturana/Poerksen 2004, p.168
77 In addition to what follows, see also Poerksen (2005c).

the excesses of television entertainment ('Big Brother' and other forms of experiments with human beings under mass media observation).[78]

What the debates about so-called media affairs frequently lack is terminological precision. In the processes of public discussion (and occasionally also in the context of scholarly and scientific analysis), the categories of morality and ethics, ethics and law, communication and media ethics, and naturally also journalistic ethics, tend to remain diffuse and vague. It is high time, therefore, to offer a few clarifying remarks on the terminology current inside the profession, not least as part of the preparation for the conceptual proposals to be made in the following sections. Ethics deals with internal regulation and control according to individual conscience; it works from the inside, as it were, and rests on individual, intrinsic motivation, this being its strength and simultaneously its weakness: it feeds on the more or less intensive commitment of the individual.[79] Ethical action is founded on individual readiness, individual insight and reflected decision in the face of given options of choice. Legal regulation, by contrast, consists in control and regulation from outside according to generally valid rules whose violation may lead to severe sanctions given appropriate circumstances. It is the compulsory character of law, and not so much individual insight and self-obligation, which effect a regulation here. The general rule is: not everything that is permitted — from the point of view of law — must therefore quasi automatically be accepted as ethically appropriate; depending on the circumstances, not even every punishable act is considered as ethical and moral misconduct. This means that law and ethics are not congruent or need not necessarily be congruent as far as the evaluation of actions is concerned. It may, of course, happen that the particular kind of ethics required and the locally valid law coincide, i.e. that ethical demands verbally reproduce existing laws.[80]

The scholarly literature often draws a distinction — even from the classical, non-constructivist, perspective — between ethics and morality, which has not, however, found acceptance in public language usage (where the two expressions are usually treated as synonymous). Morality designates, if one observes that strict terminological distinction, the totality of moral judgements and norms on the basis of which people, consciously or unconsciously, perform their actions. Ethics, on the contrary, is understood as the 'reflection theory of morality.'[81] Its purpose is the reconstruction of premises and central rationales, which guide moral action. In this understanding, ethics designates the (scientific) observation of actions

---

78 A survey and a typology of media affairs is provided by Weischenberg (2001a), pp. 254ff.
79 Debatin (2002), p. 260.
80 On the difference between ethics and law see, Krainer (2001), p. 40; on the problem of the verbal reproduction of law by ethical-moral demands, see Saxer (1999a), pp. 193f.
81 Weischenberg (1998), p. 189.

that are to be assessed morally — it does not constitute, as some constructivist authors propose, a mode of utterance that refuses to use imperatives and gestures of prescription.[82]

Journalistic ethics must be further distinguished from the wide field of media ethics and the even more generally delineated concept of communication ethics that embraces interpersonal *and* mass media communication.[83] Traditional media-ethical reflection concentrates primarily on journalists; consequently, a large number of publications — also under the rubric media-ethics — in fact deals with journalistic ethics. The concept itself, however, does not imply this conceptual narrowing down although it may be encountered frequently, because media ethics embraces all the possibilities and conditions of responsible media activity in general. The circle of responsible agents, therefore, contains not only journalistic practitioners but also media entrepreneurs, publishers, editors and artistic directors; even the media audiences are by some authors considered to be a decisive factor of influence because they may, by stronger or weaker demand, influence what will be supplied; they could therefore be considered co-responsible.

Reflection and Control

The special character of media ethics is defined by the fact that it combines — in this respect comparable to bio-ethics, medical ethics or environmental ethics — the needs of a professional domain (here: of all the media, or of particular media) with ethical reflection and moral orientation. It serves, on the one hand, the contemplation of the general premises, the theoretical foundations and also the concrete constraints underlying morally evaluated decisions. Media ethics, therefore, performs both the critical observation of existing norms and rules as they actually apply in media organisations and media systems; it makes these transparent (function of reflection of media ethics). It aims, on the other hand, at concrete implementation: media ethics supplies aids and instruments for the improvement of a given form of practice. It helps to increase the precision of professional rules and standards and thus also serves the orientation of the agents active in the media (function of control of media ethics).[84]

The same twofold function, which equally unites reflection and orientation, can, of course, also be claimed for journalistic ethics. Its central characteristic is, therefore, not a different specification of function, but consists in the fact that it refers to an even more narrowly delineated sphere of work. The journalists are the central agents here by definition; their professional activities must be reflected and connected with ethical-moral guide-

---

82 Siehe Foerster/Poerksen (2002), p. 157.
83 Siehe Thomaß (1998), p. 41.
84 See Debatin (1997), pp. 282f.

lines. The basic task is to clarify who is, or who should be, responsible for what forms of journalistic news reporting and for what reasons. Depending on the interests and perspectives of observers, the attempts at clarification and the answers that result show extreme variation.

The cognitive interests, the perspective and the theoretical-professional background of the following deliberations can be stated with great precision: the goal is to tackle three key questions of the ethics debate in the study of communication from the point of view of discursive constructivism.

- At the beginning, the basic question will be tackled how autonomous or free the journalists are of whom ethical-moral behaviour action is required. The suggestion offered here, which may appear somewhat contradictory, seeks to combine two positions that are, as a rule, seen to stand in polar opposition. It seems possible to envision a dialectics that can be activated according to situative conditions, and on whose basis autonomy and independence, freedom and lack of freedom, can be envisaged in combination and need no longer be considered as strict opposites.
- The second key question deals with the distinction between fact and fake, or between truth and lies, from a constructivist perspective. Again, the considerations offered here will most probably find little consensus: it will be suggested to view the differentiation of fact and fiction as a kind of *pact with oneself,* and perhaps even as a pact with and amongst others — and to discard the imaginary reference to some Absolute once and for all. Only if this is done with the utmost consequence, the core concepts of an ethics of journalism (objectivity, stage management, manipulation etc.) can be attacked in a strictly observer-relative way. What is understood as a fact, the argument runs, is a fact only for the reason that it has been declared to be a fact in accordance with one's own ideas; what is understood to be a lie is not a lie because one is stating an untruth in some absolute sense but because something is asserted the untruth of which one knows and believes at the very moment of utterance.
- The third and last key question deals with the problem, to whom actions and consequences of actions may justifiably be ascribed in the highly work-sharing processes of mass communication. It must be clarified what kind of responsibility can be assigned at all to individual persons because nobody — according to the postulate of autonomy propounded by constructivism — can control the effects of their own actions directly in a linear-causal way. The thesis to be defended is, therefore, that responsibility cannot primarily mean causation within the context of a constructivist argumentation, but can only designate an awareness of the possible consequences from the point of view of an observer at a particular point in time, consequences that may be suspected, expected, potentially foreseen, but can never be entirely determined.

5. The Question of Autonomy: Discourse-Generating Contradictions

The Construction of Responsibility

Debates about the morality and ethics of the media culminate in the search for the correct addressee. Who is to be made accountable for specific consequences of actions, and for what reasons? Whom do we have to turn to? The individual journalists? The chief editors in charge? The media system? To put the question in more concrete terms: when Sebastian Knauer, for instance, opened the door to a hotel room in Geneva, entered the room and took the photographs of the dead Uwe Barschel in the bath tub—was he alone responsible for his actions? Must one not also find the editor-in-chief guilty, for whom the magazine's reporter was working at the time, and who had most probably ordered him in strict terms to take the pictures? However, are not the editors themselves prisoners of a system that pays them money to deliver to the newsagents an optimally marketable magazine with a stirring cover image? Would it then not be a simple logical consequence to confront the top executives of the big media concern with the issue of guilt? Would it not be necessary to broaden the perspective even further and to analyse the logic of economic systems and processes as the timekeepers of any kind of decision? What will then happen to those in positions of responsibility? Will they continue to exist? Can one hold entire systems to account at all, including all the individuals who have no choice but to function according to the logic of these systems and who by doing so shrink to the point of invisibility? [85]

The problem of such constructions of responsibility becomes even more sharply delineated when two possible extreme cases are selected for closer scrutiny. There are, on the one hand, the fully self-employed journalists, independent as decision makers and accountable only to themselves, totally responsible for their own activities to the last. They are, in each and every moment, both potential agents and unique individuals, who impose their particular action sequences upon the world. And there are, on the other hand, the systemic imperatives of journalism, among them the orientation by markets and target groups; the pressures of competition, time, and success or failure; and the structural constraints of editing rules, organisational and management routines. The individual journalist, so the fundamental claim, is helpless and defenceless in the face of these constraints. Journalists have no freedom of choice and, therefore, can accept no responsibility for their actions; the helpless, the defenceless, and the victims cannot be found guilty.

---

85 On this case, see also Poerksen (2000, pp. 145ff.) in conversation with Weischenberg.

Heroes and Captives

Overall, neither of these positions appears convincing. The conception of ethics that styles the freely deciding individual as a 'moral hero' in the tradition of a normative idealism, is blind to context variation and far removed from actual conditions; the structures of journalism, which may affect the actions of individuals, are nowhere near accessible to such a conception. The attempt to tie ethics into a rigorous system, whatever its make-up, remains equally unconvincing because it denies individuals the freedom of choice — and thus negates the condition of the possibility of responsible action, i.e. blocks the ascription of responsibility by transcendental argument. Whoever wishes to act ethically and to assume responsibility for their actions must possess the freedom of choice and self-determined decision. In a formula: ethics presupposes freedom; ethics has no alternative.[86]

These two positions and all their differently aligned resultant problems have also shaped the ethics debate in media and communication studies. In the 1980s — following the publication of essential articles on the topic — two camps emerged, which engaged in a controversy that eventually proved to be fruitful.[87] One side assembled the representatives of a so-called normative-ontological approach (e.g. Hermann Boventer), who tried hard to nail universally valid standards onto the individual journalist in the tradition of individualist ethics. The other side gathered communication scientists of a strict systems-theoretical persuasion (e.g. Manfred Rühl and Ulrich Saxer). They were labelled as representatives of an empirical-analytical approach and drew special attention to the systemic imperatives that may frustrate the moral actions of individuals, and may even render them impossible. This example of an as yet not at all concluded specialist debate made, and still makes, clear: a rigorous individualist ethics overtaxes every individual; still, it must be maintained that no ethics can function without the concept of personal freedom of choice and individual responsibility. The systems-theoretical approach may indeed have destroyed the legend of the morality-driven lone fighter and may have demythologised the conception of journalism as a whole. However, as far as an ethics of the media is concerned, it has little else to offer than the acquiescent reference to systemic constraints and market mechanisms, so that it can all too easily be abused in the sense of a sort of *systemic fatalism*.[88]

---

86 See also Poerksen (2000, pp. 135f.) in conversation with Weischenberg.
87 For a reconstruction, see Weischenberg (1998): pp. 198 ff.
88 Ibid., p. 209.

Autonomy and Dependency

The attempt of a synthesis is undertaken by constructivist systems theory, which combines both perspectives. 'No doubt the reality projections of journalists are guided in great measure by professional rules and schemas and influenced by the structures of the media enterprises in which these journalists do their work, i.e. by economic, political and technical conditions', writes Siegfried Weischenberg about the ethical-moral dilemma of this position.

> Ultimately, however, it is the individual journalists that decide what sort of world views the media offer. Nobody can relieve them of this responsibility — nor of the responsibility for their ethical standards — no publisher, no director or chairman, and not "the reality".[89]

Media ethics thus becomes the ethics of responsible individuals who acknowledge their contribution to constructions of realities — and who remain, at the same time, aware of all the inescapable constraints that surround them. Consequently, it is possible to reject the exaggerated determinist theses of the *systems theorists* but equally well to rebuff the inflated demands on the autonomous journalist personality that supposedly makes decisions in total freedom.

This is to mean: such an attempt at synthesis helps to achieve a potentially fairer because better context-related assessment of individuals; the price to be paid, however, will probably be a somewhat inconsistent combination of autonomy and dependency, of self-accountable reality construction and other-determined world view. And this would, in the end, yield a rather contradictory description of an individual: on the one hand, as a largely closed entity that can hardly be influenced by its environment, and on the other, as an entity that can be moulded, formed and determined, that is open to external influences, directed by system-immanent imperatives, which guide all action. Such a combination need not necessarily be a source of irritation from the point of view of a constructivist interested in discourse. Quite the opposite: the potential theoretical incompatibility of the premises and postulates appears to be extremely fruitful from a practical-pragmatic perspective. One may put stronger emphasis on dependencies whenever assertions of autonomy seem exaggerated, one may exploit different ways of approaching things in order to generate material for discussion and to trigger a debate about standards of quality and the possibilities of ethical-moral self-obligation. In each case, such a combination of perspectives will stimulate the training of *double vision* for analysing both individuals and systems, journalists and journalism, to integrate autonomy and dependence in thought. This complexity-enhancing mechanism of reflection will help to elucidate: the

---

89 *Ibid.*, p. 227.

individual journalist is neither autonomous nor dependent, not just agent and not just victim, not in complete possession of power nor totally helpless, but, as a rule, and with varying intensity, everything at the same time. The journalist will always be, on the one hand, an individual agent, and, on the other, subjected to constraints exercised by editors, the economy and society. This means that the paradoxes of the position, at least in an ideal sense, operate as a generative factor; they provoke questions of the autonomy of the individual and also of the inevitably given constraints involved in working with editors and media enterprises. We are dealing with contradictions and fundamental anthropological assumptions, which ultimately lead to undecidable questions — for how could one finally, once and for all, as it were, prove the freedom and the lack of freedom of a human individual? Moreover, they are indispensable for getting an adequately complex conversation going at all, a conversation not reduced to Sunday sermons and raised index fingers. The irresolvable tension between the ethical responsibility of an individual and the imperatives of the media system potentially works like a sort of *discourse generator*. And even the excessive observation of constraints may turn out to be productive if performed in the spirit of a constructivism, i.e. a spirit geared towards working with paradoxical postulates. There is no need to exploit the perception of constraints solely for the exculpation of oneself and others; one can examine them in order to raise degrees of freedom, to open up new spaces for operation, and to uncover opportunities of self-accountable decision-making. The consequence: whoever becomes aware of their lack of freedom may possibly gain in freedom — as long as they are not just seeking simple excuses but much rather opportunities of productive action. They may perhaps be even better equipped to contest the determinations of their own actions or at least to choose from amongst the inescapable dependences those, which they know, which they are aware of. 'However, the reflection of one's dependence is also — in my view — a way of making oneself better aware of the options that are always available and of one's own autonomy', Helm Stierlin writes about the ethical-moral aspect of this approach from the point of view of a constructivist systems theory, 'so as to take on responsibility for one's actions within the limits of a finite life.'[90]

6. The Question of Fact and Fiction: An Observer-Relative Reformulation

Orientation and Relativisation

Guiding differences and fundamental dichotomies of an ethics of the media are *truth* and *falsity*, fact and *fiction*, *objectivity* and *subjectivity*, origi-

---

[90] Stierlin in conversation with Poerksen (2004j), p. 161.

nal and *fake* etc. 'That these distinctions (usually understood as indicators of journalistic quality)', Stefan Weber writes, 'have become dubious in the theoretical framework of constructivism, is plainly obvious.'[91] Consequently, he advises journalists to give up using these guiding differences and to make do without the customary vocabulary (truth, objectivity, factualness etc.), to abandon the separation of news reporting from commentary, of neutral information from evaluation, because such a separation has become superfluous.[92] What is propagated here, as a kind of escape route, is the exclusion of whole sets of concepts and the discarding of entire systems of distinctions for epistemological reasons. A proposal of this kind, however, is destined to remain unconvincing for various reasons. For one, merely discarding traditional guiding differences, even though they may be burdened with epistemological presuppositions and realistic connotations, does not automatically provide new viable orientations. From a practical-pragmatic point of view, a journalist is then told no more than that he has to change his language usage and the verbal surface of the discourse about ethics and quality. Only: what is he to do after he has been forbidden to employ a particular kind of vocabulary? What kind of proposed self-orientation could possibly replace established orientations?

Furthermore, the advice simply to discard systems of distinction that have become culturally entrenched, and have actually suffused the whole history of humankind, is hardly realistic. One fundamental distinction for the assessment and evaluation of human (not just journalistic) communication—even though one may lament it or consider it open to criticism for epistemological reasons—exists between facts and fictions, between invention and reality,

> between *Dichtung und Wahrheit*. Many further distinctions are connected with it—the distinction between original and fake, often enough the distinction between Good and Evil. All these distinctions create significant differences with many important social consequences.[93]

It seems sensible, therefore, not simply to reject established distinctions, or to advise against the use of available cognitive drawers for the varieties of designing media offers, merely for reasons of a misconceived kind of purism, but to specify them anew—in strict observer relativity.[94] The following objectives of such a constructivistically inspired conceptual enter-

---

[91] Weber 1999), p. 203.
[92] Weber (1995), p. 245; Weber (1999), p. 203.
[93] Meckel (2001), pp. 171f.
[94] One reviewer of an earlier version of this chapter remarked that it is important to emphasise that questions of 'fact or fiction' can—of course—be decided within the conceptual framework of constructivism. The point of reference is not an absolute truth but the realm of (previous) experiences of the person who distinguishes fact and fiction.

prise in the field of journalistic ethics will have to be postulated: any reference to an imaginary Absolute and to *the other world beyond discourse* should be avoided; the distinctions and orientations which are proposed must transparently be situated within experiential and life realities; it will be necessary to arouse the conscious awareness of responsibility in every individual journalist and at the same time suggest possibilities of orientation — despite the accepted insight into the relativity of knowledge; finally, dichotomous polarisations of *truth* and *lies* must be replaced by a continuum of distinctions that will do greater justice to the complexity of the daily routines of journalistic work.[95]

Construction and Design

According to the drift of these considerations, *constructing* could be understood as a largely unconscious process that is subject to biological, cognitive, social, and cultural conditions not under voluntary control. It is not a procedure for the conscious production of reality. The simple fact is, therefore: one cannot *not* construct.[96] *Design*, consequently, would entail taking hold of reality and shaping results in media-adequate ways according to the proper logic of journalism and the given options of media technology.[97] One organises investigative jobs in a certain way, chooses a specific language, a mode of presentation, a pattern of reporting; one orders materials dramaturgically, assembles strains of action, personalises and visualises an event, repeats, condenses and focuses, supplies contextual and background information, employs technical means (recording equipment, cameras, computer animation etc.).[98] One can maintain a high degree of awareness of all these ways and means of handling and shaping one's material; one can classify them as more or less appropriate and successful. One can train these operations of design, one can study them in a course programme, but they remain — although accessible to consciousness — the unavoidable condition of the possibility of medial message production. Therefore, this procedure of reality production can be similarly characterised by the formula: One cannot *not* design.

Dramatisation and Manipulation

Dramatisation, in this conceptual continuum, is intended to characterise a form of reality presentation that can indeed be easily avoided. *Dramatis-*

---

95 See also Baum/Scholl (2000), p. 100.
96 See Schmidt in conversation with Poerksen (2002f), pp.179f., and Weber (2003b), p.186. (This formula, to the best of my knowledge, derives from Stefan Weber.)
97 My position is thus clearly set apart from the identification of fictionalisation and design, which is advocated, for example, by Reus (2002, p. 80).
98 Cf. furthermore Hickethier's (2002) similar concept of narrative and its illustration by the example of television newscasts.

ation here refers to the intentional arrangement of what is to be communicated so that the aspects assumed as real are enforced, whereas others are deliberately suppressed. It is a sort of arrangement that is considered somewhat problematical by its practitioners themselves. They know that with such dramatisation they immediately break the conventional rules of reality orientation. They are fully aware that they themselves thus constitute and deliberately create the very events for a medial representation. Nevertheless, they consider this legitimate under particular circumstances and even justifiable in the service of a higher truth or a good cause. In actual practice, this may imply that a journalist pays skinheads money to perform the *Hitler*-salute on camera together with some defence sports exercises, simply because that is what people believe the skinheads to do normally, and because the public must by all means be informed about such activities. It may imply that the photograph of an oil-covered cormorant, which was taken on a different occasion, is used as a symbolic image for the environmental damage caused by the Gulf War, i.e. in order to reinforce reality assumptions in the desired direction. Perhaps the intention is also to trigger a campaign so as to spread warnings by means of visualised dramatisation.[99] It has become obvious, though: with dramatisation, one enters the domain of the ethically-morally reprehensible; construction and design are both unavoidable and not reprehensible; the dramatisation of events in the sense outlined here certainly is. One may dramatise, and one may refrain from doing so. It is a matter of a decision on an ethical-moral foundation.

An act of deception, however, need not be performed in the service of an alleged good cause or a higher truth. If the intention underlying the deception is wholly egoistical, then we speak of *manipulation*. 'Manipulation means', Humberto R. Maturana argues,

> to exploit our relation with other people in such a way as to give them the impression that whatever happens is beneficial and advantageous to them. But the resulting actions of the manipulated person are, in fact, only useful for the manipulator. Manipulation, therefore, really means cheating people.[100]

With reference to the business of journalism, for instance, a medical journalist might conceivably recommend certain pharmaceutical products and in return accept money or a share of the profits from the producers of those products. Manipulating journalists, as the example shows, thus exploit their news reporting for their own purposes. They simulate, explicitly or tacitly, neutrality although they are interested parties. They practise advertising under the flag of independent news reporting. They purposively keep the media audience in the dark about their own role, or they

---

99 See Weischenberg (2004b), p. 14.
100 Maturana/Poerksen (2004), p. 51.

Inventions and Lies

The highest level of ethical-moral turpitude is reached when expressions like *falsification, forgery, plagiarism, fabrication* etc. come into play. The semantic core of these undertakings is the *lie*, which (in strict observer relativity) is a statement form associated with a specific frame of mind; it is not (this would be the naive-realistic notion) the maliciously distorted representation of the Absolute. The point must be emphasised because although a lie can certainly be described as an untruth this would neglect the intentional component of lying.[101] If intentionality is taken into account, a lie will have to be understood as the conscious utterance of an untruth. But this still leaves us in the fetters of a tradition with ultimately realistic colours: it is the deviation from the truth, which forms the basis of the classification; one must know the truth in order to be able to lie; such is the presupposition, such is the necessary premise. It is an imperative of a constructivist perspective to detach lying from an emphatic idea of truth — and to shift the conscious intention to deceive into central focus. Lying, therefore, means saying the opposite of what one believes or thinks is right. More precisely and by way of a small typology of lies: 'There are', Hans Jürgen Heringer writes,

> strong, smooth lies, where one believes the opposite of what one says. And there are feeble lies, where one neither believes what one says nor its opposite; perhaps one just does not know anything. Then there is, apart from the direct lie, the more sophisticated indirect lie: one says ambiguous things, one makes a slightly skewed statement or challenges an over-precise assertion that is not even part of the actual debate.[102]

Variants of Correspondence

All these forms of problematical procedures have one thing in common: the intention of the agents. One knows what one is doing while doing it; one can at least be expected to know. And it is this connection with conscious insight (and not with an absolute reality), which is decisive. It is consistent within the constructivist framework, and it forms the basis for the ethical-moral assessment of the decisions of individuals, the basis of their responsibility. One can only be held accountable for what one does in full awareness. The ethical-moral relation, from a constructivist perspective, is primarily a pact with oneself and the others with whom one intentionally interacts in a particular manner. One takes decisions, makes an

---

101 Heringer (1990), pp. 14 ff.
102 Heringer (1990), p. 16.

agreement with oneself to the effect that one will definitely arrange things but not dramatise, manipulate or forge anything because any such action would be inconsistent — according to one's own views.[103]

Once these key criteria of agreement — and not of correspondence with an observer-independently given reality — are chosen, a closer look reveals that there are different forms of consensus: the *internal* and the *external consensus* as well as the *combination* of both these consensus variants.[104] The internal consensus is the correspondence between what one offers as a (journalistic) statement and what one oneself (perhaps even privately) holds to be real. The external consensus refers to the concurrence of the others that they accept as correct what is said. External and internal consensus may contradict each other — explicitly or tacitly — and it is even possible that such a contradiction goes unnoticed or is, although noticed, ignored. The combination of internal and external consensus implies that others equally acknowledge one's own assertion, which one holds to be true, as true. Such a typology of consensus variants permits the evaluation of different *stages and steps of agreement*, for instance, whenever the often controversial question is raised whether journalists have only professionally arranged things, or whether they are guilty of misleading dramatisation, intentional manipulating or perhaps even calculated forging. Whenever internal and external consensus cannot be made to match, more or less respectful negotiation processes will, as a rule, set in, which may naturally escalate into open fights for power. A lack of consensus and massively opposed interests are, in any event, sources of disputes and quarrels and even legal battles for *truth* and *reality*.

The specification of fact and fiction may also be embedded into the logical framework of constructivist argumentation, as one can now operate without the reference basis of an absolute reality for the diagnosis of facts. Consequently: *facts* and *fictions* are entities that are meaningful only within the reference system of a given experiential reality that is saturated with cultural conventions.[105] Facts and fictions are, with reference to the typology introduced earlier, signals of consensus or dissent, which are linked to the different steps of the agreement. A declared fact may be part of purely personal conviction (internal consensus), it may be considered as a fact by others (but not by the person making the declaration); it is also conceivable that one's own individual assumption that something is a fact meets with the agreement of others (combination of internal and external

---

103 The presupposition here is, of course, that one is honest with oneself and that one has the firm intention not to deceive. Imre Lakatos called this attitude 'intellectual honesty'. See Schmidt (1998), p. 126.
104 I have formed this typology on Immanuel Kant's elucidation of *Meinen, Glauben* and *Wissen*, which in my view necessarily presupposes a distinction between different forms of consensus. On Kant's proposal of a conceptual differentiation, see Gloy 2004: p. 61.
105 Glasersfeld (1991), p. 171.

consensus). The same is true of fictions: a fiction may be declared to be such by a communicator (internal consensus), but it may also be considered as such only by others (external consensus). It is, finally, also possible in this case that one's own personal assumption corresponds with general agreement (combination of internal and external consensus).

Of course, one must never discount the possibility of error. Constructivists justify its inevitable incidence by pointing out

> that error cannot be diagnosed as long as we are committing it. We can recognise an error only after we have committed it, i.e. when we are no longer committing it. We can never give an example of an error as long as we are committing it.[106]

At the very moment of living through an experience it is not possible to distinguish between perception and illusion, between truth and error; we always need a new experience as a basis of reference in order to classify a past experience as erroneous, mistaken or untrue.[107] The fragile and in principle irrevocable provisionality that is inherent to every classification of experience potentially raises one's awareness for the necessity of interminable scepticism. The assertion, therefore, that a journalist has coarsely exaggerated and distorted something can, therefore — from a constructivist point of view — never be derived from a comparison of the distorted representation with an absolute reality, but only from the comparison of different realities, possibly not even postulated at the same time, which are recognised internally, externally or in combination.[108]

The Ideal of Objectivity

Even the target value of journalistic news reporting, objectivity, may be construed as an observer-relative construct; according to the neurobiologist Humberto R. Maturana one can speak of *objectivity in parentheses*.[109] Proponents of a more strongly practical-pragmatic view seek to replace the emphatically conceived concept of objectivity by audience-related substitute terms ('usefulness', 'utility', and 'credibility'),[110] to offer an observer-dependent and communicator-related continuum of ascending constructivity for the assessment of relative objectivity,[111] or to comprehend objectivity with Gaye Tuchman as a *strategic ritual* — as a formal procedure for the journalistic production of statements.[112] Objectivity would then be a professional routine and an accumulation of the stan-

---

106 Mitterer (2001), p. 88.
107 See Maturana/Poerksen (2004), pp. 132ff.
108 Cf. also the somewhat differently oriented argument by Weber (1999a), pp. 18f.
109 See Weischenberg (1998), p. 227.
110 Weischenberg, in conversation with Poerksen (2000), pp. 143f.
111 See Weber (1999a), pp. 7ff.
112 Weischenberg (1995), pp. 165ff.

dards of a craft. (Such standards comprise, for example: the separation of news messages and opinion, the quotation of differing views in a dispute, the reference to supporting facts and expert statements for the confirmation of assertions). Independently of whether one defines the concept of objectivity in constructivist terms, the statement that one deals with *objective knowledge* must also be assigned its proper place in the stage model of conventions: the classification of a piece of knowledge is not static and true without end, it is woven into the processes of internal and external adjustment and definition and is, by consequence, always more or less amenable to consensus.

7. The Question of Responsibility: Ethical Awareness

Spheres of Action and Responsibility

The question of who is responsible in a particular situation is *the* central question of any media ethics. As the processes of mass communication are characterised by an extreme division of labour, it is necessary to establish to whom actions and the consequences of actions can be attributed with good reason, and how responsibilities are allocated. In journalism and communication studies, it has become established opinion to distinguish four possible spheres of action and responsibility.[113]

- The concept of an *individual ethics* concentrates on the individual journalist and makes him or her responsible for the predictable consequences of their actions. Such an ascription of responsibility as directed at the individual will always have to combat the objection that it idealises the realities of the profession, i.e. that it simply neglects the manifold constraints of (journalistic) activity.[114]
- A *professional ethics* is concerned with the moral standards of a professional group like the journalists, which are in part codified by professional societies and associations. It is expected to provide a certain amount of calculability for the whole profession and to implement the standards and rules in the daily work in media enterprises.[115] Such standards of journalism are, for example: careful research, precise quotation of references, the separation of news messages and opinions, and the constant effort not to deceive. The chief objective is to increase the factual content of journalistic messages.[116]
- An *institutional ethics* is intended to cover the individual media enterprise: the core question is here how a commercial orientation can be

---

113 See Teichert (1996), pp. 763ff., and Weischenberg (1998), pp. 217ff.
114 As already explained, from the perspective of discursive constructivism, the antagonism of autonomy and dependency may well be productively exploited.
115 See Weischenberg (1998), pp. 219f.
116 'Professional ethics' provokes criticism from a constructivist perspective, because it commonly argues on the basis of absolute values ('the truth').

connected with the ideal of social responsibility[117] and how economic rationality and media-ethical orientation can be connected under the conditions of a free market.[118]

- A *public ethics*, decisively shaped by Clifford Christians, reminds the individual users of the media of their own responsibility with regard to the available and the future media supply.[119] The task of a mature public is, consequently, the control of programming by targeted refusal and reasoned reception. Media consumption, from this perspective, appears as a moral challenge (and not merely as an activity undertaken for purposes of entertainment and relaxation), which readers of newspapers, listeners to the radio, viewers of television and users of online services must meet. Motto: we have the media that we deserve.[120]

A further point of discussion is whether there should also be — complementary to these different perspectives and levels — a more or less specifically elaborated ethics for particular media and their journalistic agents. This question has attained particular topicality due to the spreading of the Internet and the emergence of online journalism. The specific features of net media (interactivity, multi-mediality, hyper-textuality), the blurring boundary between news reporting and advertising (E-Commerce, *sponsored content*), the difficulty to assess the credibility of sources, the problems of data security and data abuse, the uninhibited spread of discriminating content (*hate speech*) and pornographic images constitute new challenges for journalistic ethics.[121]

These different variants of ethics have in common that they do not make the current conditions of the possibility of responsible action their topic; the question of responsibility is transformed into a problem of positioning, of a more or less plausible attribution of executive authority to individuals, to the profession, to media enterprises, or to the public, and even to

---

117 On the ideal of social responsibility, see Weischenberg (2001a), pp. 253f.
118 The attempt of an answer involves the concept of stakeholder management. Stakeholders are (in contradistinction to the purely profit-oriented shareholders) more broadly constituted claimant groups, who have interests in the enterprises in question and are affected by their decisions; they demand or should demand that their interests be considered whenever entrepreneurial decisions are taken. Ultimately, however, the fundamental problem remains unsolved how decisions ought to be taken in cases of conflict between profit-orientation and morally correct behaviour. On this concept, see Karmasin/Winter (2002), pp. 24ff.
119 See Teichert (1996), p. 770.
120 The problem is that this variant of ethics — simply because this is probably impossible in the case of the mass media — cannot specify any calculable possibilities of influence and formative contribution by the public. All that remains is the general plea, the call for the purposeful rejection of the media or the hopeful trust in the representation of the public and their interests by ombudspersons, by a critical media journalism and by media-watch organisations.
121 The chances, however, to establish securely an ethics in and for the net appear precarious, to say the least. The sheer extent and the impenetrability of the Internet render it extremely difficult to reconstruct positions of accountability, to identify sources, to follow rumours to their originators, and to clarify the questions of responsibility.

particular media. Here constructivism can contribute fundamental insights and open up new perspectives that spring from the friction between general premises (observer orientation, the postulate of autonomy, emphasis on personal responsibility) and the practical-pragmatic requirement of an unambiguous and concrete ethical-moral orientation of journalism. Assuming a perspective of the second order reveals that the ascription of responsibility is highly charged with presuppositions.

Responsibility and the Perception of Differences

It has become obvious that constructivists who maintain a consistent line of argument must keep a rationally defined distance both to a linear-causal control paradigm, which has been abandoned as archaic, and to a catalogue of moralising prescriptions that do not fit into an ethics of making ethics possible, as explained by Heinz von Foerster. It thus becomes clear that any proclamation of responsibility is highly charged with presuppositions. The attribution of responsibility to actions requires that agents possess the ability of reflection, meta- and self-reflection, so that they can recognise at least two alternative courses of action between which they are free to choose. The prerequisite of the power of individuals to decide as well as their ability to spot the differences that bring about an awareness of different courses of action, are indispensable premises revealed by the constructivist perspective.[122]

The reflecting agents must choose from amongst the perceived alternatives and can then describe their choice with linguistic means as responsible or irresponsible. 'People are aware of the circumstances and reflect the consequences of their activities', Humberto R. Maturana argues.

> They ask themselves whether they want to be what they are as they are doing what they are doing. In the moment of self-observation, all the certainties and securities of the state without reflection disappear. When, through the linguistic operation, a form of contemplation and an awareness has been generated that allows observation, then people will, at the next step, act according to their own predilections and preferences, that means they will act responsibly.[123]

Insights of this kind make it possible to elucidate a central objective of a media ethics on a constructivist basis. The objective should be, one can conclude, to transform performed actions into objects of observation and, in this way, to make alternative courses of action visible, in the first place—e.g. by means of a casuistic approach, by role playing etc.—in

---

122 Maturana/Poerksen (2004), pp. 75 ff.
123 Ibid.

order to practise gaining and maintaining the necessary distance for one's own individual decision.[124]

Responsibility and Causation

From a constructivist perspective, *responsibility* must be clearly distinguished from *causation*. Various authors, by contrast, defend the assumption that responsible action can only be based on the 'calculability of potential acts ' and the capability of 'exercising predictable influence.'[125] Action sequences must be foreseeable at least in their rough outline in order to justify an ascription of responsibility at all. [126] The consequence would be that this concept of responsibility is inextricably tied to the notion of instructive interaction, the notion of the computable determination of other beings or a given environment. Thus, if we do not believe that the effects of our activities can be securely planned, we will find ourselves landed with a *paradox of responsibility*. We would be held responsible for something the consequences of which cannot be assessed at all: doing good deeds might conceivably lead to horrific results (and vice versa).

Now, authors with constructivist training assert that action sequences can never be pre-determined with absolute certainty because predictions are inevitably observer-relative, and because systems inevitably react to any impingement attempt according to their own proper laws. In the extreme case, therefore, good intentions may indeed produce horrifying effects of various kinds and degrees of intensity, even though one had thought to be in a position to predict something very different.[127] To act responsibly, therefore, does not mean to achieve the desired results in every single case. Nevertheless, it means that the *possible* consequences of an action must be pondered and that actions must be directed according to the consequences that may be presumed on the grounds of the best knowledge available and the best judgment by the conscience of each agent. In this view, responsibility becomes primarily a matter of awareness. 'Persons act or fail to act in the awareness of all the possible and desirable consequences of their actions', Humberto R. Maturana argues. 'It is not necessary for the consequences of an action to be fully calculable and foreseeable; there may indeed be undesirable consequences in the end.'[128] And

---

124 Ethical-moral decisions, following Humberto R. Maturana (1985, pp. 310 f.), may be defined as the expression of preferences against the background of alternative courses of action; they are determined by the will to realise the potential consequences of the preferred action.
125 Neuberger (1996), p. 226.
126 Pohla (2003), p. 72.
127 Predictions—from a constructivist perspective—are an expression of the expectations of observers; they think they know the relevant factors of influence and believe that a certain state will result from another state, which will then again be accessible to their observation. See Maturana/Poerksen (2004), p. 79.
128 Maturana/Poerksen (2004), pp. 78 f.

this also means that one is fully responsible for what one intends and does in the light of one's own understanding, but one is not responsible for how others receive and interpret one's utterances and actions and how they appropriate them and apply them in performing their own actions.

Meta-Rules of a Constructivist Media Ethics

From a constructivist perspective, ethical-moral recommendations for actions should have the character of meta-rules. They should not take the form of a directly pre-set requirement that would negate individual responsibility and transform ethics into morality. The postulate of autonomy, the preference of difference, and the understanding of the plurality of realities are the figures of thought that provide orientation here. They may not only be interpreted descriptively but also normatively — and may be reformulated as ethical-moral meta-rules of an ethics (of journalism). These rules can be expressed in the following way: *Sustain or expand the space for autonomy; spare or maximise differences; preserve or increase the plurality of projected realities.*[129] Such formulations yet again demonstrate the double claim of a constructivist ethics of responsibility. On the one hand, it wants to provide orientation, on the other hand, however, it seeks to encourage individual reflection and safeguard the possibility of initiatives with due regard to personal responsibility, even though we may be dealing with ethics and thus ultimately with the distinction between *good* and *evil*. For this reason, the quoted meta-rules will unavoidably appear diffuse, but they do point in a particular direction that must be spelled out by agents in their individual ways. The demand to create and expand space for autonomous action in media enterprises and in editorial offices does not entail a concrete direction for action. However, it foregrounds what must definitely be rejected: the intimidation of editorial team members because of divergent views; the more or less subtle enforcement of conformity, and the corruption of independence by means of rewards in the form of either direct allowances or favours, gifts, promises of promotion; finally, the socialisation of new colleagues in the sense of a standardisation of ideology-based perception.[130]

The challenge to guard and increase the difference and plurality of world views, likewise, does not possess the character of a concrete recommendation for action but proves its relevance equally well when we consider illustrative examples of the breaking or jeopardising of these

---

129 As for these meta-rules, cf. also Heinz von Foerster's *ethical imperative* that has already been quoted several times (Foerster/Poerksen 2002), and the *categorical imperative of the world society*, which Bolz (2001: 55) formulates in the following way: 'Spare the differences!'

130 On the socialisation in an editorial office and the quasi-osmotic processes of acquiring norms and behavioural standards, cf. the pioneering study by Breed (1973) that has lost nothing in topical relevance; on the problems of autonomy and adjustment in editorial offices, see Groß (1981), especially pp. 81ff.

meta-rules within the sphere of the media. It is thus categorically necessary to criticise the increasing number of press mergers and the continuing concentration of media enterprises because this may lead to a potential loss of possibilities of observation, to the marginalisation and discrediting of reality projections, and to the homogenisation of perspectives. There is the menace of the loss of the diversity of mass communication organs for the market of opinions. Censorship must be rejected for comparable reasons because it aims at excluding specific observations (of the first or of the second order) and at restricting the public forum for the communicative treatment of heterogeneous realities. In the extreme case, individual decision-making will largely be predetermined by the pre-structured selection of media offers. 'As soon as the access channels to information become barred categorically', Ralf Gödde states,

> sources will be rigidly aligned, controlled according to vested interests, and manipulated. As a result, the self-determination and autonomy of the system of journalism will be so drastically restrained that the free formation of opinions as the indispensable prerequisite of responsible individual and societal action will basically become impossible.[131]

Finally, these meta-rules of a constructivist media ethics imply the general plea and support for democratic conditions. Democracy, it is well known, thrives on alternative and competitive reality projections, which must never be decreed to be absolute, though. [132] It is, to quote the clear-cut formulation by Adolf Arndt, 'the political life form of the alternative'[133] — a space of freedom that presupposes its responsible fashioning within the given limits of well tested rules. As errors can never be excluded, the reversibility of decisions should always remain feasible, and a maximal range of selections with regard to ever new and diverse assessments and decisions should thus be maintained.[134] Autonomy, difference and plurality are, consequently, ideal core notions of liberal-democratic conditions that existentially require functioning media for the independent self-observation of society, but that must also stand up for them and must, if necessary, fight for their survival and continuity.

8. The Indispensability of Trust: Idealistic Closing Note

The critical examination of a media ethics on constructivist principles, as has become evident, has to tackle dangerously loaded issues. For one, critics claim that constructivist assumptions encourage arbitrariness and wil-

---

131 Gödde (1992), p. 283.
132 That democracy presupposes relinquishing all claims to absolute truth is explained by Weischenberg (1998, p. 85) on the basis of a comment by the constitutional lawyer Hans Kelsen.
133 Arndt (1966), p. 2.
134 Luhmann (1987), p. 39.

fulness, that they may be exploited for the justification of deceit and lies. By contrast, constructivists argue that their position is particularly suitable as a foundation for ethics because it inspires a maximum sense of responsibility. The question as to whether someone can be right in an absolute sense must be taken to be an undecidable question in the understanding of Heinz von Foerster. Nevertheless, the quarrel itself, the irritation of ethical-moral certainties on both sides, is a decisive quality in its own right. From the point of view of discursive constructivism, the provocation of a debate is the decisive thing, quite independently of whether one considers the proposed points of approach, theories and concepts to be plausible or perhaps only productive; the essential point is that one's awareness of the limits and blind spots of one's own perception is deepened and one is encouraged, as a theorist or practitioner of journalism, to reflect one's own standards and truths—again independently of the position one has adopted.

In addition, this means, as a matter of course, that the creation of ethical sensibility cannot ever terminate in a direct programme of action, concrete prescriptions of behaviour or a gospel-like plea for a constructivist media ethics, but must aim at the refinement of the individual capabilities of reflection and the individual sophistication of distinctions and their rationales. This kind of plea for *the great discourse* about standards and their rational justification may give the impression of being a rather feeble proposal inspired by a spirit of resignation. It may even appear disappointing, at least at a first glance. The peculiar strength and perhaps even appeal of this position and attitude, however, rest in the trust that is accorded to others and their pacts with themselves. It could be that this ideal of the mature, responsible and trustworthy fellow-human knows no alternative whenever and as long as there is a discourse about ethics. One must presuppose and transform into practical application whatever one intends to accomplish; the means and methods of persuasion are then the immediate expression of the objectives to be obtained.

WAYS OF LEARNING

Chapter VI

Deepening Awareness of Autonomy

1. The Formal Anthropology of Constructivism

Trivial and Non-Trivial Machines

Immanuel Kant articulated the core issues of philosophy succinctly in four questions. The first question touches upon the sphere of epistemology: What can I know? The second question summarises the concern of ethics: What should I do? The third question relates to the domain of metaphysics: What can I hope for? All three questions, according to Immanuel Kant, could finally be condensed into a single question that would formulate the core interest of philosophical anthropology. This question is: What is human?[1] According to these reflections, anthropological commentaries and more or less clearly spelled out images of humanity, comprise epistemological and ethical assumptions and perhaps even speculations that must be termed metaphysical, all mixed together in varying proportions. And they are of prime significance to any form of pedagogical-didactic activity because they provide models of action, incorporate their own particular internal logic of observation and action, and promote, at least implicitly, specific modes of interaction.

At the start of a discussion of ways of learning, which in the following sections will be made concrete step by step in the direction of a specialist didactics for journalism studies, a critical examination of what could be called 'constructivist anthropology' is indispensable. Its core question, barring the suggestive ontology of Kant's formulation, can be formulated in the following way: How can humanity be understood — without any claim to finality but inspired by the figures of thought of constructivist discourse? Such a question is not aimed at the apprehension of a determinable core essence, of an ultimate static set of properties of Being, which could be ascribed to *the Being Human*. Heinz von Foerster[2] has worked out

---

1   See Landmann (1982), p. 35.
2   On the following, see Foerster/Poerksen (2002), pp. 54ff.

a particular demonstration of how he would try to answer the question of constructivist anthropology, which has provoked an intensive debate in pedagogy and didactics. He distinguishes—with reference to the very broadly conceived concept of the machine by Alan Turing—trivial and non-trivial machines. *Machine*, in this understanding, is a formal concept. It is not necessarily 'an assembly of cogwheels, buttons and levers, or chips, discs, and connectors',[3] but an abstract entity with well-defined functional properties, which may naturally very well assume the figure of a classical machine.[4]

To characterise a trivial machine in detail, one must first distinguish a cause or an input and a rule of transformation, which changes the cause into an effect or the input into an output (see figure 3). Heinz von Foerster:

> You need to imagine a group of events that we can denote with A, B, C, and D and with the numbers 1, 2, 3, 4. In the case of a trivial machine we will see that there is a regular relationship between these events. This means that following a predetermined rule, the machine receives a stimulus, a cause or an input and produces a corresponding response, effect or output, reliably and flawlessly. For example, you give the machine an A and it outputs a 1. Give it a B, and it will output event 2. The trivial machine constantly delivers us a certain output. It remains this way without ever changing.[5]

In the case of the trivial machine there is a given, unchangeable and ever dependable relation between input and output, cause and effect, stimulus and response; internal states that one may suppose to exist in this perpetually opaque entity, remain forever unaffected. The trivial machine is synthetically determined, history-independent, analytically determinable, and predictable. Should the expected effect not arise after all, then it is possible—with the help of the logic of defect research immanent to the machine—to diagnose the cause of the fault in the output production and to put the machine to rights again so as to make it return to calculable behaviour and perform accordingly again. The operation of repair with the goal to restore calculability and to secure predictability will, in the language of description chosen here, be called *trivialisation*.[6]

---

[3] Foerster (1993a), p. 357.
[4] The concept of machine used by Foerster (in this specific sense) has provoked criticism. The objection is that talking about machines always creates the suggestive image of calculability and transparency. The metaphor of the machine implies that all aspects of the entity under discussion can be deciphered. The essential point of Foerster's demonstration is, however, the opposition of triviality and non-triviality. (Foerster/Poerksen 2002, p. 58)
[5] Foerster/Poerksen (2002), p. 54.
[6] See also Rotthaus (2000), p. 109.

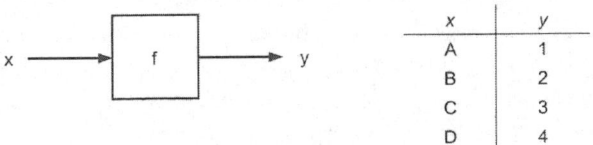

Figure 3.
The Trivial Machine Yields Predictable Results

Non-trivial machines, by contrast, transform the rules according to which they carry out transformations, and thus cut the nexus between cause and effect, which had previously — with the trivial machine — been recognised as secure. Once again one can mark a group of events or inputs formally by the letters A, B, C and D and distinguish them from a group of possible results (again, for example, 1, 2, 3 and 4). Heinz von Foerster:

> Again a simple experiment can be performed. For instance, you might input the letter A, and the machine will output the number 1. Then you repeat the procedure, and this time the number 4 is output. You input an A again, and a 1 is output, but when you input an A again this time it outputs another result. [7]

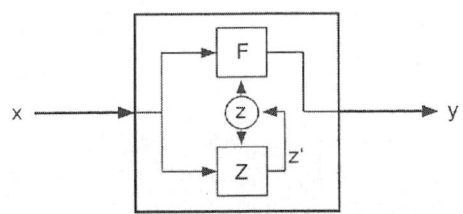

State I				State II		
x	y	z'		x	y	z'
A	1	I		A	4	I
B	2	II		B	3	I
C	3	I		C	2	II
D	4	II		D	1	II

Figure 4.
The Non-Trivial Machine Exhibits an Internal State Z,
Which Keeps Changing in Dependence on X and Earlier Internal States

The explanation of this incalculability of a non-trivial machine is that it is capable of changing its internal states; the regularities underlying these

---

[7] Foerster/Poerksen (2002), pp. 55f.

changes, however, remain inaccessible to an observer.[8] Non-trivial machines, furthermore, interact internally with their own states. They process inputs in recursive loops so as to create outputs that are generally variable, and they sometimes produce no output at all (see figure 4).[9] The resultant value y is not only dependent on the input value x but also on the internal state z in which the machine is at a particular moment. If z were constant and remained invariable forever, this would be no problem for the predictability of y. As this is not the case, however, and as the internal states of the machine change in dependence on x as well as on z, new internal states will constantly emerge and make the rules of transformation indecipherable for an external observer. The consequences: the output value can no longer be predicted; nor is it possible, as can be shown, to specify the operative properties of the machine in a finite series of experiments. Any kind of apparent lawful regularity that may be inferred from the (unforeseeable) relations between input and output, cause and effect, must remain speculation and will be refuted by ever-new variations in the results.[10] The internal dynamics of the changes of state remain necessarily hidden from the observer; the rules of transformation cannot be extracted from the perspective available to him. In brief: the non-trivial machine operates contrary to the elementary wish for certainty, calculability, transparency, and controllability; it is synthetically determined, history-dependent, analytically indeterminable, and unpredictable.

The Premise of Non-Triviality

Quite in keeping with these considerations, Heinz von Foerster has pleaded for the conception of human beings as non-trivial machines, not least with the intention of protecting humans with the aid of this definition and the corresponding strict logic of argumentation against the more or less degrading attempts of trivialisation, which he has criticised in the most ardent terms with regard to systems of schooling.[11] From this perspective, human beings are transformed into *beings of potentialities*; they are no longer stimulus-reaction machines that can be induced with the right kind of knowledge to produce regularly an expected output in reaction to a given input. Their defining property is their indeterminacy; the fundamental unforeseeability of their modes of behaviour is to be counted

---

8   See Simon (1999), pp. 45ff.
9   See Müller (1996a), p. 47.
10 For a relevant mathematical illustration by Foerster, see Simon (1999), pp. 47.
11 'Many people are of the opinion that the awful thing about children is that they do not behave in a predictable manner. They don't act like trivial machines that always generate the same output when a particular input is entered. Since our education system is set up to produce predictable citizens, its purpose is to eliminate those annoying inner states that allow unpredictability and creativity.' (Foerster/Poerksen 2002, p. 65).

amongst the central features of their normality.[12] Their 'nature' is not some fixed stock of substantive items but a law of constitution that precedes and simultaneously shapes every sort of concrete item of content; its central feature is the production of the unexpected, the generation of the surprising, and the unfolding of the possible. What happens within them, how their internal states transform and continually re-constellate themselves in dependence on external influences and past experiences, momentary insights and moods, must forever remain impenetrable.

trivialising view	non-trivialising view
analysability	unanalysability
predictability	unpredictability
controllability	uncontrollability
other-determination	self-determination
cause/effect	self-organisation
input/stimulus	perturbation ('disturbance'; 'stimulation')
output/response	behaviour/action
function	process
static	dynamic
linearity	non-linearity
faults and disorders	motives and interactions

Figure 5.
Features of the Trivialising and Non-Trivialising View of Human Beings
(With minor modifications from Lindemann (2006), p. 133)

An anthropology that argues in strictly formal terms[13] is not understood here as an ontological fact but as an inspiring and potentially fruitful way of thinking. As will be shown later in detail, such a way of thinking is especially viable for university didactics, chiefly for the following reasons:

- It provides a justification for the necessity of practising respect for the autonomy of other human beings by acknowledging their essential impenetrability as something given. It corresponds, furthermore, with an increased readiness for tolerating surprises and unforeseen effects

---

12 On the interaction of non-trivial machines (human beings) and the emergence of stable modes of behaviour (eigenvalues), see Foerster/Poerksen (2002), pp. 59ff.
13 On the concept of a formal anthropology, see Landmann (1982), p. 195.

of incidents that may previously have appeared totally insignificant ('butterfly effect').[14]

- One must part company with a didactics of instruction that is fundamentally oriented by the principles of trivial procedures of control: teaching is no longer understood to be an activity that can be organised according to the pattern of linear-causal instruction. Interventions will therefore be transformed into stimulating suggestions; planning and apparently situation-independently viable prescriptions, which are expected to secure specific learning results, will lose in importance. This is no plea for rejecting planning altogether or for indifference, but a plea for discarding a model of knowledge transmission that negates the autonomy of the addressees.[15]

- It is the individuals who are expected to learn, who move into the foreground, who will become the centre of attention because they will inevitably play the major role in the projected processes of teaching and learning, which may change into expeditions and quests leading to unexpected results. [16] It will be necessary to orient teaching by the rules of reality construction applied by the learning individuals, and to replace the model of external control according to external premises by the concept of a directed kind of self-organised control according to their very own personal kinds of logic. This means: it is no longer possible or necessary to define the 'right' kind of input independently of internal states in order to produce the 'correct' output; the question that has to be posed is what kind of input could, according to the properties of the addressees, function in a productive way.[17]

The goal is certainly not, as Niklas Luhmann suggests in his discussion of the distinction between triviality and non-triviality, to propagate the 'antagonistic model of an education towards unreliability, towards a creativity of surprises, or towards the production of nonsense'[18]; such a model would not only 'stand little chance of being realised but would also contradict the legitimate societal interest in predictability.'[19] Of central importance, however, is the possibility of formulating the core problem of all pedagogical-didactic effort more precisely and more clearly, and to work towards a 'de-trivialisation of the concept of transformation',[20] which lies at the conceptual centre of processes of learning and education.

This core problem may be expressed as follows: How can one — while simultaneously acknowledging the autonomy or non-triviality of all participants — communicate and interact in a manner that will stimulate

---

14 See also, in another connection, Bardmann (1991b), p. 29.
15 See Siebert (2003b), p. 133.
16 See Arnold/Siebert (2003), p. 43.
17 See Lindemann (2006), p. 131.
18 Luhmann (2002a), p. 78.
19 Ibid., p. 79.
20 Baecker, quoted in Wimmer (1999), p. 169.

non-accidental effects? How can one, in a fundamentally uncontrollable field of processes of learning and interaction between non-trivial machines, produce comparatively calculable effects?[21] What kinds of contexts and learning cultures should be promoted because they are able to offer stimulation for self-directed learning? How can one, when understanding self-organisation as the central mode of cognition, penetrate to *an organisation of self-organisation*,[22] which would facilitate an adequate balance between inspiring pre-settings and opportunities for individual self-governed implementation?

On the bases of considerations like the ones developed in this context it is obviously impossible to answer such questions by means of pre-defined didactic prescriptions and universally applicable methods, which would further suggest the possibility of a sort of ultimate and quasi mechanistic planning programme for learning processes. The following discussion will devote less space to checks and examinations and hopeless attempts at external control. It much rather aims to create a *didactic field of reflection* by means of distinctions and conceptual development, to organise and build up a productive relationship of mutual stimulation between constructivism and didactics that would illustrate the profitability of this epistemology for the understanding and the execution of learning processes.[23] For this purpose, I shall begin with a summary of paradigmatic considerations and consequences,[24] and I shall quote role models for university teachers, which are intended to transform their self-image according to the premises introduced. I shall then devote myself in the following chapters to specialised didactics, I shall reconstruct the structure-forming relationship between theory and practice for journalism studies on a constructivist basis, I shall describe working with so-called *informing irritations,* and will characterise postulates of observation that are useful for quality journalists.

2. Paradigmatic Considerations and Consequences

The Paradox of Education

To begin with, another profound insight by Immanuel Kant will be helpful. In his essay *On pedagogy*, which was published for the first time in 1803, we can read:

> One of the greatest problems of education is how one can unite the subjection under legal compulsion with the capability to make use of

---

21 See Willke (1987), p. 351.
22 See Simon (1997), pp. 123ff.
23 No exhaustive research report can be given here with regard to the numerous conceptions of pedagogy and didactics that have been inspired by constructivism. The state of discussion is adequately rendered in the book edited by Voß (2005).
24 See also Poerksen (2005b).

one's freedom. For compulsion is necessary! How can I cultivate freedom under concurrent compulsion? I am expected to make my pupil suffer the suppression of his freedom and I am, at the same time, expected to direct him to make the best use of his freedom. Without this, everything is pure mechanism, and the human being who is released from education does not know how to make use of his freedom.[25]

Education (and one may add for our purposes: erudition, too) may be understood as the unfolding of a central paradox.[26] On the one hand, one wants to release free, self-determined human beings from the institutions dedicated to education and training (schools, universities); on the other hand, one imposes a syllabus on the future individuals, forces them to attend, punishes their failures by bad marks and persecutes their negative responses — in the extreme case by expulsion. One would like to open up new vistas and to stimulate intellectual creativity, but one goes on practising schoolmasterly instruction by insisting on traditions, on established and canonised stocks of knowledge, and by proclaiming rock-hard results. One would like to do justice to the individuals in their peculiarities, but one keeps orienting oneself at the same time by the average tempo that is needed by a more or less imaginary learner for tackling the set tasks. One would like to appreciate individual characteristics and personal knowledge levels, but one is continually forced to give the experts their due on the grounds of their superior knowledge. One wants to respect differences but makes sure at the same time that these differences will not become too great.[27] There is a necessary relationship of tension between the ends and the means of pedagogic-didactic efforts, as the assessment offered by Immanuel Kant suggests. Ends and means contradict each other because, according to the quoted sentences, both compulsion and the cultivation of free thinking appear to be necessities. However, from the perspective of a constructivist university didactics that presupposes the non-triviality of (adult) learners, the *paradox of education* shifts in several directions.

- On the one hand, it becomes the core task and the key criterion of a self-critical evaluation to discover means and methods with which the paradox just presented could at least be defused. This is to say that the means must be chosen in such a way as to express and support the pervasive objective of encouraging and improving autonomous individual reflection, whatever the changing combination and mixture of such means owing to differing circumstances might be. The unfolding of the paradox, one may conclude, has achieved particular quality whenever the tension is no longer, or hardly at all, recognisable or perceptible for the learners: they do what they do in their own particular ways, and their self-determined actions will still remain coupled to

---

25 Kant (1983), p. 711 (original spelling).
26 I owe this insight to the Kant-reception by Baecker (2000), pp. 51ff.
27 See Ackermann (1995), p. 341 and Reich (2002a), pp. 115f.

superordinate learning objectives. The self-determination that is demanded will then actually be learnt by the concretely practised self-determination that is granted to others; reflexive competences will then be acquired by the stimulation of reflection independently of pre-set results; the contradiction between means and ends seems to have been partially suspended.[28]

- The paradox clearly identified by Immanuel Kant also shifts, in a constructivist view, due to the reason that the formal anthropology of non-triviality elevates the uselessness of linear-causal concepts of compulsion to the rank of an irreducible premise. The paradox of education consequently changes into a *paradox of intervention*,[29] a relationship of tension and contradiction between the two poles of external intervention and internally given autonomy: one knows about the non-controllability of learners and must therefore find ways and means to make it possible that 'self-controlled processes of learning move into the desired direction out of the free will of the learners';[30] didactics then appears — as seen from this angle — as the 'art of seduction into paradox'.[31]

- The strategies of intervention in cognitively autonomous systems have been labelled as *context control* by Helmut Willke. The essential assumptions involved in this concept, which is central to a constructivist didactics because it defuses the paradox of intervention, are formulated in the following way: 'Interventions in autonomous, self-referential systems must take the indirect way of non-hierarchical context control; they would inevitably fail otherwise, due to the barrier of the operative closure of these systems. Self-referential systems are not amenable to linear external control by way of secure access, because external influences can only exert effects if they can be transformed into information, i.e. if they appear on the monitors of the system as relevant distinctions according to the appropriate guiding differences of the system itself. [...] Autonomous systems, which are tied to their own mode of operation, can receive external influences only as information that punctuates, supports and inhibits their own internal processes, and connects them with external conditioning processes at internally defined points of transference. Therefore, interventions may appear possible only in the form of a sort of *politics of options*. This is to say that only such options of intervention can successfully be offered to a system as are adequate to its specific mode of operation and its own degrees of freedom and do not violate its systemic autonomy (and are additionally supported by corresponding contextual conditions), although they may still produce, for instance,

---

28 See Maturana/Poerksen (2004), p. 127.
29 This concept derives from Schmidt (2005b), pp. 111ff.
30 Schmidt (2005b), p. 112.
31 Ibid.

other and less weighty negative externalities.'[32] Put in a formula: results cannot be implemented by force; they can only be influenced by boundary conditions (occasions of learning, learning environments, impulses of an *enabling didactics/didactics of empowerment*[33]). The decision about the relevance of contents and envisioned competences is ultimately taken by the learners themselves. They alone refine and revise or stabilise their use of distinctions.

- Finally, the ways and manners of unfolding the paradox are also influenced by the institutions of education and training in question. One can argue that schools — quite independently of whether one likes this or not — tend to realise and implement the tension between freedom and compulsion, goals and means, in favour of compulsion. Apart from the so-called free schools, the predominant mood is one of unquestionable obligation. In a university — put quite generally again — the paradox is more easily resolved or unfolded if the compulsions are reduced and if the pedantic checking of attendance and performance is given up; freedom has a greater weight here by tradition. Naturally, the main reason for such an approach is the fact that one deals with adults who have knowingly chosen a discipline and a curriculum in order to gain an academic qualification.

- The core problem of university learning is the problem of a beginning that is not a beginning any more. Learning here is inevitably follow-up learning and not primarily learning from scratch.[34] To stimulate learning processes thus necessarily means: to work with what is available, to take into account pre-experiences in larger measure, to link up with what is already there. One begins the personal unravelling of the paradox within the field of tension created by what has already been unravelled. One has to ask oneself what kind of starting point for creative interaction one may be able to discover if those who are to be taught are young adults, formed by their family homes, by their schools and by the peculiarities of their cultural environment. How does one deal with human beings that one does not really know at all, as a rule, and that must be understood as nontrivial and therefore fundamentally impenetrable? One may of course ignore the problem, to quote Heinz von Foerster (the strategy of ignorance). One can trivialise it, i.e. cut it down to an apparently manageable size and — for whatever reasons — proclaim again the calculability of the incalculable (the strategy of trivialisation). One can finally try to make the constructivist epistemology of non-triviality the point of departure for one's own reflections about learning and teaching, which starts out

---

32 Willke (1987), p. 355 (author's emphasis).
33 See Arnold/Siebert (2003), pp. 6f.
34 See also Siebert (2003a, p. 17), with reference to the special situation of teaching adults.

from the autonomy of the knowing individual and strives to enhance its general acceptance and appreciation.[35]

Linear-Deterministic View	Systemic-Constructivist View
Epistemological Change of Perspective	
linear models	non-linear models
knowledge as representation	knowledge as construction
mandatory truth	plurality of reality constructions
objectivity	relativity
right/wrong	viable/relevant, non-viable/irrelevant
normative/instructive	interpretative/reflexive
trivial image of humanity	non-trivial image of humanity
ethical (pre-)supposition	responsibility
Pedagogical Change of Perspective	
pedagogical direction	basic pedagogical attitude
pedagogue is agent of development	everyone is agent of own development
immature pupil	autonomous subject
directed instruction	subjective construction of knowledge
provision of answers	stimulation of questions
learning of facts	learning of learning
schoolmasterly instruction	accompanied learning and development
a single correct path of solution	variable paths of solution
faith in methods	multiplicity of methods
learning programmes	learning opportunities
depreciate and avoid mistakes	appreciate and exploit mistakes
uniformity	differences
objective evaluation	subjective assessment
external evaluation	meta-reflexion
external determination	self-determination
command	dialogue
responsibility and maturity as objective	responsibility and maturity as path

Figure 6.
Paradigmatic Differences in Contrast (From: Lindemann (2006), pp. 181f)

---

[35] See Foerster (1993a), p. 360.

If one chooses this third strategy — in full awareness of all the possibilities of failure — then one will clearly see: the linear-deterministic outlook must be replaced step-by-step by a systemic-constructivist approach and this epistemological change of perspective must be made operational with respect to pedagogic-didactic situations (see figure 6).

Against the backdrop of these postulates and decisions, a didactic field of reflection emerges — ideally — whose purpose is essentially to provide stimulation, to lend contours to concrete actions, while making sure at the same time that its autonomous implementation by teachers and learners remains indispensable. The following considerations, theses and concepts are of importance for the change of perspective as it has been sketched out:

- The principle and the ideal of knowledge transfer, which together with trivialising ideas of communication form the basic epistemology of hierarchic teaching and learning processes, call for of revision.
- *Learning* and *knowledge* — key concepts in all didactic efforts — must be reformulated from a constructivist point of view.
- The constructivistically inspired interpretation of the distinction between *knowledge* and *ignorance* — a sort of guiding difference for educational processes — allows for the more precise structuring of one's own position and reveals in what ways epistemologies influence the choice of learning methods.
- The postulate of autonomy and the orientation according to the horizon of knowledge of the addressees, inspire one's attempts to redefine systematically one's own capabilities of communication, to practice a self reflexive form of listening, and to pay a different kind of attention to so-called *mistakes, errors,* and apparently *illogical* assertions; after all, such evaluations on the part of the teaching person might possibly be the most revealing manifestations of the autonomy of the learner.
- The ideas sketched out finally terminate in a plea for a dialogically oriented creation of knowledge that fits particularly well with the epistemological assumptions of constructivism, as will be shown in the following chapters.

The Ideal of Knowledge Transfer

The point of general importance is: the foremost and perhaps most important re-orientation consists in parting company with the ideal of a linear transfer of knowledge.[36] This ideal matches up, as a rule, with a strictly hierarchical distinction between the knowing and the ignorant, and thus establishes a communicative matrix that eventually tends to poison the cli-

---

[36] In these and the subsequent explanations of the self-role-image of a constructivist university teacher, I shall be working with the technique of ideal-type reduction. Ideal types, in the understanding of Max Weber, are the result of exaggerations, instruments of order, to throw into sharp relief modes of action and properties of social frameworks, which — although empirically of substance — cannot be identified as such in reality.

mate of learning. The teachers who embrace the idea of the transfer of knowledge in the understanding implied here always know precisely and long before an actual interaction what kind of subject matter they want to transfer, they always know the optimal ways of presentation, they know how to divide the stock of knowledge into digestible portions, how to raise the level of understanding and knowledge step-by-step; and in this way they slowly spiral upwards from the simplest thoughts to the most complicated processes of reflection. The learners are assigned the role of the passive recipients; they are expected to listen and to take notes, to try hard to understand what the teachers are saying and thinking. In a final phase, what has been learned is revised, then subjected to inevitable examinations and marked; the concluding act is the certification of the state of knowledge achieved. A comprehensive knowledge of facts, the guiding assumption is, will in any event improve competence.[37] The transfer of knowledge is the central mechanism of control performed by the teacher in order to manoeuvre the learners in the direction of the desired learning objectives.

The epistemology hidden in this kind of approach is that its practitioners believe that there are general, situation-independently valid, principles governing the optimal transfer of subject matter; they think that knowledge can be instilled into the heads of the ignorant — comparable to some substance — in order to redeem them from their raw and still uncultivated state of being (according to the pattern of the traditional metaphor that sees learning as the alchemist's transformation of base matter into precious material). Knowledge appears to be a transferable resource, an entity that may be turned into an object; it can therefore be stored in a memory from where it can be retrieved whenever necessary.[38] Thinking is accordingly a form of data and information processing and human beings, as the computer metaphor that has been so immensely influential in this context suggests, could be modelled as information processing systems that take in, transform, store, and re-activate information.[39] Items of content, and apparently observer-independently existing kinds of information and elements of knowledge, enjoy unquestioned primacy; the particular configuration of relations, which makes these items of content at all communicable so as to make them develop powers of fascination, does not appear to be of central importance.[40] 'The pedagogues' chief interest is', Kersten Reich writes,

---

37 See Siebert (2003c, pp. 25f.) on these and other myths populating the educational system.
38 On the concepts of memory and recall connected with the ideal of knowledge transfer, see Schmidt (2005b), pp. 114f.
39 On the computer metaphor of the mind and its trivialising implications, see Foerster/Poerksen (2002), pp. 106ff.
40 See Reich (2002b), pp. 260ff.

> whether the transport has been successful and whether their goods have reached the memory and the behaviour of their addressees. [...] The decisive thing about the content-related connection between pedagogues and learners is that it seems to be of a complementary nature: the pedagogues possess something that the learners need. A symmetrical relationship in which both parties would interact on the basis of equal rights seems to be excluded by the superior knowledge and better information on the part of the pedagogues.[41]

Constructivism and the formal anthropology of non-triviality fundamentally oppose such a conception of a simple linear-causal transfer of knowledge. The individuals destined to learn are positioned in the foreground; according to the premises of this approach, the important thing is to learn learning and to observe the learners in order to be able to teach them something, which is held to be of potential importance to them. The erroneous view of communication, the principle of knowledge transfer, is replaced by the postulate of the irreducible subjectivity of meanings. From a constructivist point of view it seems impossible to expect that the utterance of a speaker releases precisely those ideas in another individual which the speaker had intended to refer to with his/her utterance, and that consequently some content could be formulated in such a way as to make the receiver reconstitute it in precise correspondence with the sender's intention. Constructivism raises the awareness of the normality of misunderstanding, of the improbability of successful communication and the multitude of presuppositions that are involved in every act of communication. It is necessary for the partners in a communication process to master (a) language, to know the rules of the situation, to be familiar with the adequate genres of speech and, finally, to be motivated to engage in utterances and corresponding follow-up reactions. What may be observed and reconstructed whenever communication occurs is the more or less single-minded attribution of meaning by cognitively autonomous individuals. The so-called receivers of messages turn into active constructors: it is ultimately the receivers that determine the meaning of an utterance.

Learning and Knowledge

The definition of learning and the understanding of the acquisition of knowledge are equally subject to change. Learning refers to a specific type of observable and correspondingly commented change of state: the state of a non-trivial system *before* learning is compared with its state *after* learning, and this comparison by an observer then yields an explanation of the change of state centred on the concept of learning.[42] The change of state is thereby, as a rule, related to an external influence, and considered to be the

---

41 Ibid., p. 260.
42 See Schmidt (2005a), p. 100.

processing of a *perturbation* or irritation that has released self-controlled processes of learning.[43] The concept of perturbation or irritation replaces more or less consistently the concepts *stimulus* and *input*, which generally suggest a direct linear-causal impact and stem from the language of causality. Perturbation is a strictly formal concept — and in the terminology developed by Humberto R. Maturanas denotes the observation of an external influence that hits a system but does not destroy it and allows it to maintain its organisation and to change its structure.[44] Learning by consequence no longer appears to be the result of a successful process of transference that may be determined by the teacher with the help of immediately effective stimuli but turns into the construct of an observer who registers the processing of perturbations and resulting changes of behaviour, interprets these behavioural changes as processes of learning, and possibly attributes knowledge to the observed individuals. Humberto R. Maturana:

> In general terms then, the observer grants knowledge to another observer or organism in a particular domain when he or she accepts as adequate or effective the behaviour or action of that person or organism in that domain. Or, in other words, knowledge is behaviour accepted as adequate by an observer in a particular domain that he or she specifies.[45]

The distinction between the knowing and the ignorant, which clearly derives its forms from a realist interpretation of the process of knowing and may create inhibiting and frightening reactions and perhaps even intellectually unproductive attitudes, loses in importance, relevance and weight from this constructivist perspective. In the sphere of conventionally valid knowledge and the observation of recognised behaviour there exist differences, intersubjectively valid agreements, conventionally accepted standards and more or less clearly specified experiences, but in contradistinction to the claimed reference to absolute knowledge — that could only be topicalised in discourse anyway — there is a fundamental equality of students and teachers. They change into co-learners, formed, inspired and fascinated in a strange way by the certainty of uncertainty.

---

[43] See Arnold/Siebert (2003), p. 115.
[44] *Organisation* means here: relations between elements that define the system as a member of a particular class of systems. The organisation will exist as long as the system exists. The structure of a system can be modified, however, without the system losing its identity, without its organisation being destroyed, although structural changes may naturally also be driven in the direction of the dissolution of the system. What is thus shown is: the concept of perturbation stands for a vast spectrum of possible external influences or corresponding diagnoses of external influences by an observer, which may transform the system but leave it undamaged so that its identity is not lost. On the concepts of perturbation, the distinction between organisation and structure, and the possibilities of the changing of systems while simultaneously maintaining their identity or organisation, see Maturana/Poerksen (2004), pp. 71ff.
[45] Maturana (1998), p. 284.

Knowledge and Ignorance

Heinz von Foerster, quite in keeping with these reflections, has spoken of a 'theory of knowledge that remembers the unfathomable character of our knowledge.'[46] He writes of the 'tip-of-the-iceberg epistemology that is aware of its floating state'.[47] But what does that mean? Heinz von Foerster: 'The knowledge we have of our world is to me like the tip of an iceberg; it is like the tiny bit of ice sticking out of the water, whereas our ignorance reaches far down into the deepest depths of the ocean.'[48] A new kind of modesty results from this 'tip-of-the-iceberg epistemology' that is recognisably connected closely with constructivism, a modesty that may be made productive in teaching. The insight into the ineluctable temporariness of all knowledge makes intellectually fruitless hierarchies crumble — ideally — travelling with such an epistemology, one is more easily inclined to keep reconditioning oneself and to get off the couch of fixed truths. Whoever knows that he knows or believes that he knows turns into someone who knows that he knows nothing or that he does not yet know, and who is therefore — strangely enough — eager to know.

Some might like to perceive here a distant echo of Wilhelm von Humboldt's understanding of science and scholarship, which is astonishingly like the view of knowledge and the more general idea of understanding entertained by constructivism. In Wilhelm von Humboldt's work, one can read that science and scholarship, in contradistinction to schools, have nothing to do with 'ready-made and conventionalised knowledge'.[49] Of central importance is to him

> that in the internal organisation of the higher institutions of scientific learning everything must be founded on the endeavour to maintain the principle that science is something not yet found and something that will never be found in its totality and that must therefore be searched for tirelessly without end.[50]

It is worthwhile to introduce at this point a pair of concepts set up by Ernst von Glasersfeld.[51] He suggested distinguishing *training* from *teaching*, i.e. the mere learning by rote, the simple repetition, the basic routine, on the one hand, from the active, creative development of concepts and ideas, which is associated with the communal discovery of different ways of solving a problem, on the other. This is to say: a kind of thinking that does not engage in the confrontation of the unknown and not yet certain, is by consequence not scientific or scholarly reflection. The inculcating of the

---

46 Foerster (1993b), p. 133.
47 Ibid.
48 Foerster in conversation with Poerksen (2004g), p. 23.
49 Humboldt (1964), p. 256.
50 Ibid., p. 257 (original spelling).
51 See Glasersfeld (1997), p. 167.

secure and the established, mere *teaching*, cannot be the acceptable objective of the learning and teaching processes at university.

All the same, the total condemnation of simple repetition and basic routines and the wholesale rejection of all methods of instruction would not be considered compatible with the position taken here. On the one hand, the arsenal of possible methods must not be restricted independently of practical situations, because that would mean faith in methods in the form of fundamental preferences.[52] On the other hand, a kind of instruction that is practised offensively by a teacher may naturally not eliminate the mode of cognitive self-organisation on the part of the learners or even render it invalid. 'Even externally organised learning', Siegfried J. Schmidt writes,

> happens within the framework of the basic mode of cognitive self-organisation of the learning system, even though imposed learning, places of learning, steps of learning, and evaluations of the success of learning are applied to the learning system from outside; living beings do learn, but they cannot be instructed.[53]

The orientation by the learner and the comprehensive strengthening of the awareness of their autonomy also imply that there is and cannot be *the* one and only method;[54] the constructivistically induced change of view supplies a number of supporting insights and possible strategies that will now be presented by way of a survey.

Refining Communicative Capabilities

The orientation by the learners must induce teachers to refine their style of communicating. This will have to include the reflection of individual preoccupations, the re-examination of guiding decisions, and concerted efforts to come to terms with the consequences of internally initiated perceptions of reality. One orients oneself — for fundamental reasons — according to the horizon of the partners, observes the forms of reality construction practised by them and varies one's own communicative offers accordingly in order to attract attention and to communicate in as acceptable and fruitful a way as possible. A further step may be to transform the relationship aspect of current communicative processes into an object of observation, i.e. to practise meta-communication on the relation-

---

52 One could, after all, argue that even methods of instruction (lectures, written papers etc.) may be advantageous in specific situations; the labour invested may produce a more transparent structuring of the subject matter, a more illustrative presentation, and a more responsible reduction of complexity. See Siebert (2003c), p. 88.
53 Schmidt (2005b), p. 103.
54 A survey of the spectrum of constructivist-didactic methods, which cannot be described here in detail is supplied by Reich (2002b), pp. 235ff.

ship level in order to identify possible disorders and disturbances or at least to defuse them.[55]

The concrete teaching behaviour of a constructivistically oriented didacticist will, therefore, always exhibit the features of a more or less successfully achieved adjustment, which is, of course, additionally regulated by the temperament and the talent of the teaching individual as well as by the specific logic inherent to the subject matter in question. One practises, to introduce a distinction by David E Hunt, *reading* and *flexing*.[56] *Reading* denotes the capability to decipher the mood of a group, to perceive difficulties of learning, misunderstandings and disturbances, blockades or possibly sudden insights, always in the awareness that the perceptions of others will definitely represent more or less viable constructs. *Flexing* represents the adequate reaction to a given situation, which results from the training of such participant-oriented perception.[57] Such an insight into the necessities of adjustment may result in certain forms of institutionalised rules of operation (repetitions and summaries, accompanying sessions of reading, support and revision with the help of tutorials). But it may also happen implicitly and in the process of direct interaction: one begins to speak more slowly, for example, visualises thoughts that may appear to be too abstract, initiates a discussion, practises meta-communication, or changes the form of language or the level of style in dependence on what seems required (variety switching).[58]

Variants of Listening

This kind of direct interaction, during which opportunities for self-transformation are to be created, fundamentally requires a very special way of listening. From a constructivist point of view, the distinction between different forms of listening is elementary in several respects. On the one hand, the criticism of a static culture of schoolmasterly instruction and the 'traditional primacy of pedagogical speech'[59] basically suggest greater attention to listening. On the other hand, one's own listening is frequently tinted by personal assumptions about reality as well as by declarations of truth.[60] One often listens in ways that are directed by questions as to whether one agrees with the others, whether one likes what the others say,

---

[55] Reich (2002b, p. 60), in his conception of an interactionist-constructivist pedagogy, pleads for the primacy of relationship communication; he writes: 'The fundamental idea of meta-communication as communication about relationships is of the greatest importance to pedagogues. We will call it the pedagogical primacy of the relationship level.'

[56] See extensively Siebert (2003a), p. 102.

[57] See again Siebert (2003a), p. 102.

[58] Cf. in this context the distinction between different seminar languages (heuristic language, empathic language, tactical language, official language, role-specific language etc.) in the book by Siebert (2003a), pp. 120f.

[59] Garrison/Neubert (2005), p. 109.

[60] See Maturana/Poerksen (2004), pp. 129ff.

whether one finds it sympathetic, true or plausible etc. Such a form of listening, which tests every utterance for its subjectively sensed correctness, is not intended here, of course, because in such a situation one does not really listen to the others but primarily to oneself. The personal system and its mental model of predilections, interests and dislikes, function as filters: the stronger the agreement with the personal model of reality construction the more useful and truthful will appear what is being heard and so much greater will be the degree of harmony in the conversation.[61]

A constructivistically shaped manner of listening no longer proceeds from the question of whether what the others are saying concurs with one's own thoughts. Agreement is no longer central. One would much rather find out in an act of non-egocentric attention in what area that which is being said by the others is valid. Under what conditions is it right? In what world is it relevant? What are the internal criteria to be applied for finding a decision about the validity of what is being said? Is what is being said right if one applies these criteria of validation? Whoever listens in this way and asks questions in this way, will at least get to know the others better and may learn how they listen themselves or why they perhaps refuse to co-operate. In such situations one may carry the observation further, enter the concept of listening into a reflexive figure of thought, and train oneself in a further step, *listening to listening,* to find out the conditions that must obtain for the others to be prepared to take note of what one is saying at all. Are they sensing a devaluation of their position? Do they feel respected? Do they feel invited to cooperate? One may get to know individuals whom one has to teach something, by listening to them, and by listening to their listening — on a constructivist basis — in order to extract the conditions of potential blockades in communication.

Such unconditional concentration on the learners changes the view of so-called *mistakes, errors,* apparently *illogical* assertions and learning results that are classified as *insufficient*. So-called mistakes must be met with a mixture of tolerance and sharpened attention because: 'forbidden mistakes are forbidden developments'.[62] This kind of insight does not entail the complete abandonment of assessments, or even adopting the permanent and wholesale praise of failure,[63] but it makes the diagnoses in

---

61 Students have a masterly understanding and command of the subversive aplication of this principle: they study model examination papers in order to pass examnations successfully; they do not orient themselves by a subject, by the topical matter itself, but by the cognitive horizon of the examiner. Should they be successful in understanding their examiners they will achieve excellent marks. What is examined is obviously not the knowledge but the ability of the students to bring about an experience of intellectual harmony and to feel themselves united with others in their view of the world.

62 Kahl (2004), p. 130.

63 Reich (2002a, p. IX) has suggested, however, that the practice of marking be at least supplemented by a discourse about the agreement on goals and proper support. He argues that such attempts at a crossing of perspectives would be implied by a constructivst attitude.

question lose the character of universally valid assessments and changes them into tokens of a difference in perception that may be of the highest relevance to the process of communication and the adaptive behaviour of the teachers. So-called mistakes thus quite clearly reveal themselves to be symptoms of the autonomy of the others, of internally consistent modes of approach. However, they are not considered effective in reaching the pre-set goal from the perspective of the external observer.[64] The teachers are confronted with a strategy of problem solving that does not correspond with the strategy of problem solving that seems acceptable to them, either for reasons of pure accident or for systematic reasons that consequently merit particular interest. The observation of such mistakes, which consists essentially in an exemplary reconstruction of differing principles of construction, supplies decisive indications of possible ways of improving communication. Humberto R. Maturana:

> The opinion, for instance, that the ideas of a pupil are illogical and false means, as a rule, nothing but that what was said belongs to a domain of logic that is different from the logical domain, which is the basis of the observer's listening and judging. In other words, a mistake is a statement made in a particular domain of reality, which is heard and evaluated in the context of another.[65]

Universalising the Dialogical Principle

The considerations presented serve the particular design of communication of discursive constructivism, which will be called the *universalising of the dialogical principle*. A dialogue is accordingly characterised by the following key features:[66]

- Dialogues require a common topic and take for granted that the different partners in dialogue enter into a communal, a shared world, and that they interact — more or less directly but not necessarily — in the *face to face* mode. The orientation by a common topic further implies that the partners refer to each other when voicing comments, that the partners react to mutual objections, anticipate them and deal with them. The contributions of the partners are of fundamental interest to each other.
- Dialogues are furthermore characterised by the fact that they cannot be planned down to the last detail and that they necessarily exhibit a certain measure of spontaneity and improvisation. Ideally, something attains expression in language that has never been thought before,

---

64 On this understanding of mistakes and the differentiation of different types of mistakes (old, correction-resistant mistakes and new never-before-made mistakes) see also Müller (1996a), pp. 48ff.
65 Maturana/Poerksen (2004), p. 132.
66 My understanding of dialogue is particularly indebted to the work by Cissna and Anderson (2002), which refers to Martin Buber and Carl Rogers, amongst others; see e.g. Cissna/Anderson (2002), pp. 9ff.

that has never been said before. Openness towards results and the readiness for the revision of preconceived opinions are essential features of dialogical competence; conducting dialogues in a merely strategic and non-truthful way, which is additionally bent on deceiving partners and dogmatically insists on personal positions can never be genuine dialogue. 'Dialogue partners base their relationship on the presumption of authentic or genuine experience', Kenneth N. Cissna and Rob Anderson write. 'This means not that people always tell the truth, but that no sense of genuine dialogue can be based on a participant's self-consciously untruthful, hidden, deceptive, or blatantly strategic set of interpersonal calculations. Rather, in dialogue, commmunicators are assumed to speak and act in ways that match their worlds of experience. Where such trust breaks down, dialogic potential dissolves.'[67]

- All dialogue thrives on the mutual recognition of the different qualities of the partners involved. This does not mean that such differences will necessarily be welcomed or approved of in their concrete appearance; but the main point is that these different qualities are perceived and respected as actual facts. The recognition of such differences does not mean, however, as the dialogue theory by David Bohm and his followers suggests, that all quarrelling must be avoided and that any hard and fast debate about some topical matter must be sacrificed in favour of a harmonious climate of communication with high values of self-experience.[68] Dissension is an existential component of dialogue. Wolfgang Welsch convincingly argues: 'Whenever the necessity or even the sensible opportunity of dispute and debate are eliminated, conversations lose their value, lose their intensity, and the culture of conversation degenerates into mere chatter. Mere 'contributions to conversation' will in the end be nothing but contributions to entropy. From the very beginning, they are produced in a vacuum devoid of challenges and in an atmosphere of arbitrariness, and they do not lead to insights and clarifications but only to palaver [...]. It is not enough to say something, it is important to say something better, something revealing, something important. No discourse can be really alive that is not also anti-discourse. [...] One cannot get round sensible debate.'[69]

- A successful dialogue is always an expression of the fundamental constructivist thesis that *the* reality does not exist; the only thing that exists is a multi-verse of different interpretations. One may contradict each other and one may quarrel; one may attack an insight, which might otherwise remain unchallenged in its generality if uttered by a single contributor, from various angles without aiming at total final

---

67   Cissna/Anderson (2002), p. 10.
68   Bohm (1998) and his followers understand dialogue as the cooperative investigation of processes of thinking, prejudices, blockades in encounters. Struggles about matters of content or disputes relating to personal beliefs that are aggressively presented, are practically demonised.
69   Welsch (1996), p. 221.

harmony or a synthesis to conceal all the contradictions. The process of the genesis and the manufacturing of thoughts is turned into the genuine stable focus of what is to be achieved. The attitude of claiming a comprehensive and unbroken representation, which is generally required by ultimate truths and monolithic structures of thought, is thus disrupted. The form is the message and the message is the form; the result of a dialogue that merits the name is not victory or defeat of one side or the other, but mutual understanding, perhaps even a separation based on mutual respect.

The phrase *universalising the dialogical principle* is intended to mean that even inevitably monological forms of presentation—e.g. lectures, the writing of articles and books etc.—can be understood as dialogues on the part of the speaker, as elements of a superordinate conversation positioned within a university. For whoever directs their very first utterances in the spirit of a dialogue, will speak and write differently; they will provoke in a strategic way, take up the objections of their audiences, orient themselves according to the horizons of their audiences, and will recognisably strive to reach their actual or imagined addressees. The ways of speaking and writing will thus always be geared towards communicative connection and follow-up. Totally different realities are legitimately involved in such presentations.

3. Role Models and Self-Images

Guiding Images for Teachers

The described rules of the game of university teaching match up, as has already become noticeable, with a change in attitude, a different self-role-image.[70] It will no doubt be easy to imagine that constructivistically inspired teachers—independently of their original disciplines—can no longer present themselves as omniscient hierarchs; they can no longer be the untouchable experts but must see themselves as catalysts of a highly important culture of dialogue, which they have the responsibility to facilitate and keep alive. In such a situation of practically never-ending turbulence and permanent conversation, the teachers themselves become learners in a very serious sense, and they orient themselves and their own communication according to the principles of the construction of communication formulated by Klaus Krippendorff.[71] Of particular importance amongst these principles is the *imperative of self reference* ('Make yourself the component of your constructions!'), the *ethical imperative* ('Grant to the others who appear in your constructions the same kind of autonomy that you claim for yourself when constructing them!'), and the *social imperative*

---

[70] The self-role-image is the sum of personally entertained expectations that are connected with regular modes of behaviour and specific attitudes. On a definition, see Donsbach (2005), p. 415.
[71] See Krippendorff (1990), pp. 65f.

('Communicate with others in such a way as not to restrict the domain of possible decisions!').[72] Basically, teachers enter the dialogical space of a university — carrying these three imperatives in their bags[73] — in at least five different roles. These roles will now be described in the following pages in a rather fragmentary and cursory manner:

- The teachers act as practitioners of *Socratic maieutic techniques*, employing preferably the communicative pattern of questioning, which is particularly close to constructivism because it helps to understand how realities are created in a co-operatively organised and consensually oriented way.[74]
- The teachers understand themselves as *moderators*, constantly aware of the immanent dramaturgy of successful dialogues, and struggling intensively with the paradox of a non-directive control of conversation. The moderators are supported in their occasional stretches of meta-communication by some of the participants from the group of learners, who are here called *seminar observers*.
- The teachers act according to the self-role-images of *researcher* or *leader of an expedition*. From this perspective, teaching and learning change into cooperative research. The concept of education that is so difficult to capture is transformed into a processual concept involving the deliberate alternation between knowledge, not-yet-available knowledge, and fundamental ignorance. The group making up a seminar turns into a sort of community of explorers.
- Teachers of this kind maintain a distance to their own convictions, keep reflecting their personal prejudices in a more or less humorous way and manner, and thus practise a form of self-reflection that Richard Rorty has made the guiding image of his contingency theory: ironically-unironically, he calls such a person *ironist*.[75]
- Finally, the teachers act a role that Siegfried J. Schmidt has called *irritation agent*; their concern is to pluralise opportunities of perception and to shake up certainties, involving even instruments of provocation, as will be shown in detail later.[76]

All these role models differ in the techniques they use but they share a common goal: it is the creation of a climate in which fascination and enthusiasm for thinking will (again) find sufficient room; it is the universalising

---

72 Krippendorf (1990, p. 67) considers his social imperative to be an expansion of the ethical imperative of Heinz von Foerster; the expansion consists in the embedding of the plea for new opportunities into interpersonal practices of communication.
73 I have already pointed out elsewhere — in a constructivist view — the problematical connotations of the concept imperative, which indicates compulsion and external determination.
74 See Müssen (1995), p. 180.
75 See Rorty (1992), p. 14.
76 See Schmidt in conversation with Poerksen (2004f), p. 152.

Socratic Maieutic Techniques

As a practitioner of *Socratic maieutic techniques,* a constructivistically trained teacher pursues the goal of bringing the children of knowledge into the world. Socrates himself has described his activity in this way and compared himself to a midwife that takes care of the 'birth-giving souls'[77] of the knowers. His practice consists, as is well known, in posing searching questions, in an examination of what the interlocutor who claims to know actually knows.[78] He discusses with the military leader what courage is, and asks the orator for his knowledge of rhetoric. He never sets his knowledge against the knowledge of the others but always starts out from ignorance himself when examining the knowledge of the others by means of questions, exaggerations and counterexamples, orienting himself by their horizons but still remaining the questioner that controls the conversation. He thus reverses the traditional asymmetry between the questioner and the responder: it is the fundamental doubt, which is of recognisably higher value than the answer that is temporarily considered to be definitive.

The attempts at justification and the clarifications striven for by the dialogue partners of Socrates often end in aporias, in highly stimulating moments of doubt and uncertainty, which turn out to be occasions for new beginnings and drive the process of self-understanding forward. Whoever has become entangled in the webs of a Socratic dialogue, begins to think afresh once more because this kind of reaction to the underlying 'principle of guided self destruction'[79] now appears to be self-evident. All of a sudden they see themselves as deprived and needy. Socrates is the teacher who does not teach anything but creates conditions in which the hunger for knowledge is excited and increased, in which the happiness about achieved knowledge and independently fabricated insight can be experienced directly: what has been considered common knowledge has been made strange, personal truths have been made the object of doubt, perception is de-automated in this comprehensive procedure of the philosophically motivated demolishing of what was previously certain and secure.[80]

The Socratically inspired practitioners of maieutic techniques proceed in quite similar ways, train themselves in the art of conversation of their historical model, but without the intention of setting up rules independently of situations, as has been tried by some several times, without wanting to lay down directions for the choice of initiating dialogues and the

---

77 Quoted in Böhme (1998), p. 134.
78 See especially ibid., pp. 117–41.
79 Schwanitz (2002), p. 67.
80 Ibid., pp. 66f.

first examples to be introduced.[81] The Socratic practitioners search for questions — without however subjecting this search to a canon of rules — which will create turmoil in the mind of the partners, disconcert them, unsettle them and shake them up. They do not solve problems; they create problems. They create environments in which learning will take place because it is recognised and experienced as necessary by the partners, the students.

The counter-image of the figure of the Socratic practitioner is the expert who knows and proclaims his knowledge. He supplies answers without knowing the questions that would make these answers important in the first place. He starts his way to knowledge at the goal, and spreads results and finished thoughts around the circle of the ignorant. Thinking experiences and intellectual events, which would bring about an embodiment of personal thoughts in the first place, are no longer possible. The Socratic practitioners, by contrast, pose questions that make horizons visible and available to awareness, against which sensible and revealing dialogues about questions become possible. Their goal is not *the* truth or even (as the somewhat softened variant) the claim to truth, but the more or less stable consensus of the participants, the plausible insight.[82] The central principle of their procedure is that they create the problems, which then generate answers and solutions that may finally be treated and debated. The Socratic practitioners create the foundation for learning, and they illuminate the minds and feelings of their listeners and Socratic co-practitioners with the kind of inner brightness of which Socrates speaks when he refers to the awareness of his own and everybody else's self.

The Moderator

However, should the general helplessness — perhaps due to a surplus of Socratic games of confusion — become too overwhelming and the situation teeter on the brink of the abyss of unproductivity, then another kind of constructivistically trained teacher may seize the initiative. It is the *moderator*, who will try to keep the dialogue that has been started and the desire for answers alive. Moderators will pay attention to the contours of the dialogue, demand definitions and terminological precision, if necessary. They will prevent the participants from drifting off into presumably unproductive marginal spheres, will intervene in paralysing power games, establish relevant differences that may advance the learning process as topics of the agenda, point out the already existing canon of knowledge when necessary, not however presenting it as a context-

---

81 For a more rule-governed and therefore inevitably somewhat schematic understanding of the Socratic dialogue, see Horster (1994), especially pp. 55ff.

82 On the question of truth in the Socratic dialogue and answers given by authors that do not argue from constructivist premises, see Horster (1994), pp. 26ff., pp. 33ff. and p. 47f.

independently valid accumulation of ultimate truths but—like a good constructivist—as a tradition of interpretations whose knowledge may be necessary.[83]

Moderators know that dialogues that are to be successful and fascinating need a particular dramaturgy, a constant interplay of vision and abstraction, exaggeration and refinement, tension and relaxation, experience and knowledge. This kind of interplay oscillates between different aggregate states of thoughts, between the rigidification and the renewed liquefaction of what has been created as knowledge. The understanding of the moderator role involves a certain modesty, by definition; it must furthermore be based on a mixture of result-orientation and didactic-pedagogical tact. Moderators condense, summarise, set topics, and make people talk to each other, whom they consider, on the basis of moment-bound observations of the first and the second order, to be independent and whose views have to be of interest to them for professional reasons. The counter image is the figure of the hierarch who controls communication linearly. He does not cooperate, he decides, he sets tasks, regulates the flow of information in connection with robust power interests. Moderators, by contrast, trust the surprising powers of self-organisation, they know about the effects that particular stimulations—initiated at the right moment and in the right kind of dosage—may produce. The standard of quality is no longer the quantity of the imposed subject matter but the intensity of participation, the measure of contradiction, correction and necessary supplementation, the common maximising of internal coherence and consistency. The implementation of the dialogical principle is the proper standard for the evaluation of the success or failure of meetings.

The Seminar Observer

Moderators primarily guard and preserve the culture of communication that has been created; they are supported from meeting to meeting by a changing circle of individuals that may be called *seminar observers*.[84] A seminar observer is a specialist in evaluation for one meeting. They are recruited from amongst the students and their tasks consist in the observation of observers. They execute the situation-bound evaluation of teaching, which is thus no longer carried out at the end of term in the form of an anonymous debate, but at a point in time where there is still opportunity for change, i.e. in the course of business as usual. The seminar observers summarise criticisms, suggestions for improvement and encouragements directed at all participants in a few minutes at the end of a meeting; they confront the real with the possible; they draw conclusions suggesting advisable changes in the approaches of the participants on the basis of the

---

83 See also Siebert (2003b), p. 86.
84 I owe this consideration to a conversation with Otfried Jarren.

observable contrast between what has been achieved and what might be seen as yet distant goals; and they facilitate by such changes of view the relativising of petrified attributions.[85] It is the elementary concern of such observation to infiltrate meta-observations and alternative conceptions into the process of communication, and to make it possible furthermore to re-include continually — over a longer period of time — the dynamics that has been built up into what is going to happen next.[86] What will, ideally, result is a process of communication, 'in which the processes of transformation drive themselves forward in an iterative pendulum-swing between impulses of change and the processing of the reactions released by them.'[87] Furthermore, such institutionalised and term-wide practising of other — and self-observation may possibly shake up unproductive power relations.

Researcher and Expedition Leader

Another role model, another metaphor, which will be sketched here and will be interpreted by way of ideal-type reduction, is the model of the *researcher* or — perhaps better — the *expedition leader*.[88] Researchers or expedition leaders do not work with clearly defined horizons of expectation; on the contrary, they are the permanently controversial leaders of expeditions, active and participating, never passive and supposedly neutral. One travels together and on the understanding that one will be dependent upon each other, into as yet unknown territory, interprets teaching and learning as the common investigation of something one does *not yet* understand, i.e. one exploits the fundamental constructivist insight that there can be no absolutely valid stocks of knowledge, for the purposes of pedagogy and didactics in the university. In the course of the expedition, an exploratory and tentative style of moving forward will naturally dominate. What one knows may be wrong and outdated or insufficient, it will need supplementation, it will have to fit the ever-singular circumstances and environments. The leader of the expedition can define goals and objectives only in a relatively crude way at the beginning; he can distinguish quite precisely between the security of the process and the security of the results[89] that must be established with regard to details of content, simply because he must always try to keep the degree of strategically induced uncertainty manageable so as to avoid any sudden suppression of creativity by imposing details and all too schematically elaborated paths

---

85 See, in another context, Willke (1987), p. 349.
86 See the fundamental discussion by Wimmer (1999), pp. 167ff.
87 Wimmer (1999), p. 169. (Wimmer deals generally with the transformation of organisations; in my view, the results of his analysis can equally be applied in the context under discussion here.
88 See Mack (2001).
89 See also, in another context, Wimmer (1999), pp. 170f.

of solution. The expedition leader has the special task in these processes of the generation and the absorption of uncertainty, to redefine and to mark constantly the ever-changing boundary between what is known, what is unknown, and what is practically unfathomable, in order to feel his way — on the grounds of what is already known — into the unknown territory. He must, to put it differently, constantly and in interaction and consensus with the other participants in the expedition, distinguish between *legitimate* and *illegitimate* questions. Illegitimate questions, according to a definition by Heinz von Foerster, are questions the answer to which is already known; whoever asks illegitimate questions asks for something that he already knows. Legitimate questions, however, are genuine questions; the answers to them are not yet known, one does not know them *yet*.[90]

Whoever takes this activity of a researcher or expedition leader seriously, namely to distinguish between legitimate and illegitimate questions, and consequently interprets teaching systematically as cooperative research, will finally arrive at a special definition of education, which is highly dynamic but at the same time also involves working with established stocks of knowledge. Education does not mean any longer: to reproduce ready-made knowledge, to impress others with one's reading and with quotations from the classics or other established pieces of knowledge. Education is then no longer individual capability or potential or the individual process of development that produces a singular individual. Education will also no longer be defined as the higher development of humanity. And education will no longer refer, as it still often does today, to the training and qualification that is executed and certified by the relevant institutions. Education will then mean, as Heinz von Foerster formulates, *to learn to pose legitimate questions*.[91]

This is a definition that deals with the distinction between knowledge and ignorance, between the known and the unknown. It lacks pathos and pragmatism; it unites a static and a dynamic moment; it also unites the inevitable knowledge of facts and the equally necessary feeling for the limitations of available hitherto valid insights. One must know something in order to decide whether a question is legitimate or illegitimate; at the same time, however, one always acts on the basis of the knowledge of the legitimate questions in the awareness and against the background of one's own ignorance. This is to say: in the course of an expedition, one oscillates in a characteristic and hopefully productive way between knowledge and ignorance. And whoever changes a legitimate question into an illegitimate question, secures, and sorts stocks and results, will discover, as long as he thinks along constructivist lines and does not want to reach out for an imaginary absolute, new legitimate questions that will again point

---

90 See Foerster/Poerksen (2002), p. 73.
91 See Foerster (1993a), p. 209.

towards something unknown. They will restart the naturally never-ending game of educating oneself once more; they will give the concept of education a content through the very process of self-education itself, without pre-set objectives with regard to the substance of this process. Researchers and expedition leaders favour this concept of education and thus inevitably upset university seminars when promoting the corresponding idea.

The Ironist

A new self-role-image does not only require, however, that energy for change is directed at the external environment and at others, and that one tries hard to organise reasonably calculable modes of action in a non-trivial system of interaction. Of central relevance is also the conscious reflection of one's own approaches and procedures, one's own use of language, one's own role.[92] This means: the irritation of the others must always be accompanied by a measure of self-irritability, in order to set oneself apart from a meta-dogmatism and a missionary kind of instruction of a supposedly higher order. A figure that has made this self-irritation a permanent and constitutive element of a form and way of life may be found in a book by Richard Rorty, entitled *Contingency, irony and solidarity*.[93] Rorty calls this figure *ironist*, and thus characterises individuals who have realised that their central beliefs are contingent and who have therefore decided to change their use of language in such a way as to reflect this fundamental contingency. Ironists, therefore, avoid any so-called *final vocabularies*, any ways of talking in a mode of ultimate certainty and any possibly connected idea of linguistic reference as relating to apparently observer-independent entities.

Richard Rorty defines the ironist as someone who fulfils three conditions:

> (1) She has radical and continuing doubts about the final vocabulary she currently uses, because she has been impressed by other vocabularies, vocabularies taken as final by people or books she has encountered; (2) she realises that argument phrased in her present vocabulary can neither underwrite nor dissolve these doubts; (3) insofar as she philosophises about her situation, she does not think that her vocabulary is closer to reality than others, that it is in touch with a power not herself.[94]

Self-irritability can be shown to maintain itself through the confrontation with ever-new language games — an ever-new vocabulary. The re-description of what has already been described within the changing

---

92 See Lindemann (2006), p. 190.
93 Cf. Rorty (1992).
94 Ibid., p. 127. [Orig.: p.73.]

networks of different varieties of language usage is one of the central techniques used by ironists. They experiment with worldviews, but not in order to penetrate to some ultimate foundation but to maximise the number of perceptual opportunities—and to push back at least partially the influence of the one and only world view that is, due to its monopolistic position, particularly powerful. Further results of the applied philosophy of language and the awareness of contingency and the resulting practice of self-relativisation, as recommended by Richard Rorty, are the humorous distance of individuals to themselves as well as, obviously, the ironical attitude that has given the approach its name. Ironists are, one may read

> never quite able to take themselves seriously because always aware that the terms in which they describe themselves are subject to change, always aware of the contingency and fragility of their final voabularies, and thus of their selves. [...] The opposite of irony is common sense. For that is the watchword of those who unselfconsciously describe everything important in terms of the final vocabulary to which they and those around them are habituated.[95]

Whoever speaks humorously and ironically, such is presumably the premise of the unfolded argument necessarily integrates different perspectives, folds and crosses them, turns a state of mind into an commonplace practice that is multidimensional, connects diverse things for purposes of exhilaration, mixes spheres. Humour thrives on the

> insight into the deficiencies and the provisional nature of human thinking and acting, Humor includes self-irony, i.e. the awareness of one's own weaknesses. [...] Humour excludes absolute claims to truth; the epistemological principle of humour is relativisation.[96]

A humorous, ironical, and self-ironical attitude and style of presentation can accordingly be considered a practical illustration of contingency.

The Irritation Agent

The last role model that will be proposed as a didactically relevant guiding image, has to do with the figure of the *irritation agent*. Premature consensus, intellectually unproductive rigidification, boring or subjection-oriented disputes are all occasions for summoning irritation agents. They implement the theory of constructivism as a sort of subversive practice, they disturb and create unrest within the harmony of the well-meaning, and they de-ideologise the conversations of the seminar. Irritation agents are radical, perhaps even polemical, unfair and one-sided; dancers without fixed positions and without a prescribed choreography, players without an immediately recognisable morality or ethics. Not quite

---

[95] Ibid., p. 128. [Orig.: pp. 73f.]
[96] Siebert (2003a), p. 164.

accidentally, this kind of not at all obedient and humble attitude can best be illustrated by an example from the sphere of the arts.

It was Joseph Beuys who, in the summer of 1964, made a statement of far-reaching consequence, which well reveals the concrete approach of an irritation agent. Beuys — still a professor at the art academy in Düsseldorf — is, at the time, in the initial phases of a dispute both with the North-Rhine-Westfalian ministry of the Interior and his colleagues at the academy, which finally ends with various court proceedings, an occupation of the academy, police actions, instant dismissal, and an enormous boost of the reputation of the sacked professor. One of the statements by Beuys that was evidently considered a public nuisance by the state ministry of the Interior and caused it to launch a parliamentary inquiry, is printed in the programme brochure for the Aachen 'Festival of the New Arts' under 20 July 1964. In a sketch of his life and work Joseph Beuys writes the following sentence: '1964 — Beuys recommends raising Berlin Wall by 5 centimetres (better proportion!).'[97] Within the questionnaire sent to him by the evidence collectors of the state ministry of the Interior, he formulates the following response:

> A contemplation of the Berlin Wall from a point of view that focuses only on the proportions of this building must definitely be considered permissible. Defuse the Wall at once. By inner laughter. Destroy the Wall. One will no longer remain stuck to the physical Wall. The view is directed at the spiritual Wall, and overcoming it is certainly the main thing. So the Wall will first be overcome by me, for me. Motto: Under my government of the heart, the Wall would not have sprung up at all. Spontaneous question: What essential member in myself or other human beings has brought this thing into existence? How much has each one of us contributed — and is still contributing — to making this Wall possible? Is every human being sufficiently interested in the disappearance of this Wall? What anti-egoistical, anti-materialistic, what reality-adequate spiritual schooling is given to young people to overcome it? Quintessence: The Wall as such is totally irrelevant. Do not talk so much about the Wall! Provide the foundations for a better morality of the human kind through self-education, and all Walls will vanish. There are so many Walls between you and me. A wall as such may be very beautiful if the proportions are right.[98]

Enhancing the Sense of the Possible

What Joseph Beuys suggests here is a new orientation and a re-orientation of public perception, which is not amenable to ordinary patterns of dispute. He refuses to conform to the general style of discourse; he creates a new reality that is aimed at increasing the dynamics of a merely commonsense form of thinking and thus applies central principles of the irritation agent. He does not condemn the Wall explicitly — as the monument of vio-

---

97 Quoted in Stachelhaus (1989), p. 166.
98 Quoted in ibid., p. 167.

lence, as the symbol of permanent compulsory socialist happiness turned to stone—but he recommends seeing it in a different light and raising it a little for reasons of proportionality. He works strategically with the principle of affirmation and a (most certainly provocative) kind of de-focusing and re-focusing of attention. The classical procedure in those years of the Cold War would have been to demand for the Wall to go: 'Tear down that wall!' Ronald Reagan, full of outrage, once shouted from West to East Berlin. It would have been customary and discourse conforming to become outraged about the forceful billeting of one half of the nation. But Joseph Beuys does not negate the Wall; he affirms its existence but he envisions the necessity of a small-scale correction. Like a therapist trained in the techniques of paradoxical intervention, he recognises the reality of the symptom (i.e. the Wall), and he even reinforces it to a certain extent, but at the same time he shifts the attention quasi unnoticeably in the direction of the proposed treatment: the ideological consciousness must be dissolved. From the point of view of constructivism, such acts of subversion by irritation agents may be understood as the imposition of extremely uncommon modes of observation. The act of distinction, as is well known by now, may be understood as the fundamental operation of thinking that may entail cascades of follow-up observations: they create another universe, make another view of the world emerge.

What Joseph Beuys actually performs with his statements and the additional remarks in his curriculum vitae is to propagate another basic distinction. He does not look at the Wall along fundamental and ordinarily accepted differences like *good* and *evil*, *powerful* and *poweless*, but begins with the distinction between *beautiful* and *ugly*, in order to arrive at the observation that the Wall should be raised by five centimetres for reasons of proportionality. In brief: he de-focuses the discourse of the moral and political level—and focuses it on the aesthetic level, and then presents the aesthetic as a moral and a political category and dissolves the boundaries between established modes of distinction. The question of power appears to him to be a question of awareness.

It is the intellectual sophistication of this strategy, which contains the essential features of the subversive constructivism of an irritation agent: irritation agents reject the exacting patterns of dichotomous thinking and forms of thought petrified as conventions. They do not make the mistake to become entwined in a rejected reality—and thus have themselves transformed into dogmatic anti-dogmatist who exhibit just as much rigidity and hard-heartedness as their antagonists. They do not proclaim a new dogma but consider their impulses to thinking and their conundrums as a medicine against dogmatism itself. Their positions are only meaningful in a particular context, and they derive their legitimacy only from the mental rigidity of their opposite sides. They must not melt into the conversational situation, they must not allow themselves to be tied down, and they must never give up their positions. The irritation agent represents a philosophy in which even programmatic impertinence belongs to the arsenal of instruments of knowledge. Their authority is not derived from a superior state of knowledge, and definitely not from a claim to the sole possession of truth, but from the virtuosity with which they cut their capers of reflection, finish half-matured thoughts, and play with their internally developing consequences. It is their goal, to quote Robert Musil, to enhance the sense of the possible and to maintain the awareness of the multiplicity of available worlds.[99] They would like to demonstrate what might exist, what possibilities and opportunities are contained in a reality that appears to be unambiguous, what realities could be developed out of this reality or could be read off it with scepticism and humour. It is the task of the irritation agents to provide these creative moments, to make sure that experiences of contingency are permanent companions — in the sense of an antidote to certainties — and to show that combating contingency will only lead to new contingency that may then perhaps no longer be experienced as contingency. Whenever the liquefaction of a static reality has been achieved, the strategies and patterns of interaction of a university teacher operating in such a manner will have accomplished their tasks. In the moments of relative unambiguity, and thus in situations of a certain freedom, one may begin, even in the venerable halls of a university, to start one's quest afresh. It will be a creative and a beautiful moment. A beginning.

---

99 Cf. Musil (1996).

Chapter VII

The Reality of the Study of Journalism

1. The Distinction Between Theory and Practice

Between Scholarship and Application

The guiding formula of the study of journalism represents a sort of promise. And this promise reads: integration of theory and practice, closer linking of academic study and real life, combination of reflection and action, elimination of the distance between the university and its environment.[1] This promise, however, to forge a closer connection between the system of academic scholarship and the system of application[2], has been the subject of a long-standing debate within the field of journalism study. What Bernd Blöbaum noted in his book 'Zwischen Redaktion und Reflexion' [Between editorial office and reflection] a few years ago is still applicable today: What is precisely meant by practice? How can theory and practice be tied to each other by means of new forms of teaching and learning? How can they be anchored in the environment of a university or college? How can journalistic knowledge of routines and recipes be reconciled with the demands of reflection required by a university? With what other institutions for the training of journalists will competition primarily be sought? All this still remains the subject of controversial debate.[3]

This kind of discussion, whenever it is not conducted in the mode of mutual accusation with politicians responsible for science and research or practitioners, who operate with a black-box concept of practice that is supposedly accessible only to insiders and people with exceptional talent,[4] this kind of discussion revolves, as a rule, around the semantic vagueness of the key concepts *theory* and *practice*. It brings into focus fundamental problems of autonomous reality construction, which are of great interest

---

1   See Blöbaum (2000), p. 11f.
2   On the distinction between the systems of science and scholarship and the systems of application, see the fundamental work by Luhmann (2005).
3   See Blöbaum (2000), pp. 12ff.
4   See Rühl (2002), p. 4.

from the point of view of systems theory, because the demand for integration may be coupled with the idea that a scholarly discipline could be controlled by the requirements of practice in a quasi linear way, or that, in the reverse direction of influence, practice could be more or less directly instructed with the help of quality knowledge. Finally, such discussions of the difference between theory and practice are especially loaded today because in the course of the Euro-wide reforms of curricula (the Bologna Process) an increased orientation of universities by the labour market is demanded and enforced, so that the hierarchies of relevance are now changing, not least due to external pressures. Practice-relevance, something that has been demanded everywhere and all the time, has long acquired the character of a universally usable catchword.

In what follows the quoted points of debate will be commented from a dual perspective. On the one hand, aspects of the theory of science and of systems theory will be introduced into the considerations; on the other hand, field internal comments from the study of journalism and communication will be summarised. At the end of the chapter, I shall attempt to throw some light on this promise of integration from a constructivist perspective, and will propose the concept of *informing irritation*, in order to characterise the relationship between theory and practice and to inspire the specialised didactics of the field.

The Problem of Definition

As already noted, it is unclear what the terms *theory* and *practice* really mean in these contexts. In the study of journalism, the concept of practice is 'extremely well suited as a plane of projection'[5] and refers amongst other things to the job world of journalists, their craftsmanship and skills (research, writing of news reports etc.), or to the specifics of a form of teaching that may be characterised by a particularly high degree of exercises concerning communicative competence.[6] The frequently valuative dichotomous separation of theory and practice can only mean that the world of training colleges is contrasted with the world of universities, that reflections *about* journalism and *practising* journalism are compared with each other, or that different forms of teaching and learning are contrasted and set against each other.[7]

It is a general fact that the concepts are not, as a rule, used in a strict sense. Practice does not stand for a spectrum of activities specified in greater detail but much rather exhibits the character of a positively connoted cipher, which is intended to signal rootedness in concrete realities. Practice means: entering an action-based relationship with the world.

---

5 Blöbaum (2000), p. 13.
6 See ibid. and Weischenberg (1998), pp. 26f.
7 See Machill (2005, p. 209), with reference to Blöbaum.

Practical is what directly serves such activities.[8] Theories in this context are not systematically connected and consistent assertions for the purpose of the explanation of specific states of affairs. [9] The concept also has the character of a cipher. It stands for detachment from practical action, for abstractness, and it is even used occasionally to name a defect: what is labelled theoretical, the assumption is, has very little or no relevance for the sphere of everyday actions and jobs, it is simply useless, perhaps even a hindrance. Theoretical knowledge or the too intensive-extensive involvement with the action-relieved production of interpretations and meanings[10] is considered or feared to disqualify people for handling the practice-bound requirements of the lowly spheres of ordinary life. In brief: the distinction between theory and practice is simply of asymmetric build and operates with contrary connotations. Peter Fuchs states in stringent words:

> Practice appears real, close to reality, down-to-earth, it is saturated with experience. It possesses the aura of incontestability, self-evidence, and worldliness. [...] Theory is cold, operated by overpaid egg-heads, who vegetate in ivory towers, suffer from cold feet or at least, like Blaise Pascal, from toothache.[11]

The Problem of Integration

It is controversial whether the promise of integration by the study of journalism can be realised at all. This fundamental doubt is justified by the simple fact that the study of journalism and journalism belong to different systems, and that the 'discrepancies between the system of science and the system of application'[12] cannot be bridged in a simple way. Niklas Luhmann writes about the science system in terms of systems theory:

> The necessity to proceed in a method-adequate way internally, to reflect theoretical connectibilities and to pay attention to applicability, is a restriction when observed from inside, is freedom when observed from outside. Under these conditions, science can never totally enter into the service of specific interests of application, can never be fully instrumentalised. Its scaffolding of traditions is too cumbersome, its methodical apparatus not environment-specific enough. Science thus becomes autonomous [...] precisely because of its differentiation as a component system of society and the corresponding multiplication of system references. Autonomy is the mode of its societal existence and means something like: self-restriction is expressed by proceeding and acting according to proprietary rules.[13]

---

8   See Fuchs (2000), p. 62.
9   See Weßler (2002), p. 23.
10 See Beck/Bonß (1989), p. 27.
11 Fuchs (2000), p. 64.
12 Luhmann (2005), p. 375.
13 Ibid., p. 374.

Journalism may also be considered to be a social system, which operates strictly according to proprietary rules, which has restrictive effects internally and requires the unconditional socialisation of its agents, but which still indicates autonomy with regard to the possibilities of external control. This specific mode of operation manifests itself in the search for the exceptional, the special and the uncommon, in contradistinction to the common, ordinary, normal, and lawful. Long-term, quasi lingering processes, therefore, tend to fall through the grid of journalistic world perception. Science, by contrast, searches for regularities and general insights, orients itself by long-term problems and not by actualities. Its agents work according to a different temporal rhythm and with other economic resources, they communicate with different audiences (orientation by lay people versus orientation by experts) and favour a different concept of truth and objectivity, which implies different routines and methods.[14] With reference to the problem of integration discussed here, this means: science and practice come into contact with each other inevitably on the bases of their own proper rules and hierarchies of relevance; even the individual journalist who is engaged in professional work deals with scientific knowledge according to criteria of exploitation that are internal to journalism. Put in a formula:

> Journalism changes everything into—journalism. The system of journalism, therefore, also observes the system of science, in particular the study of journalism, strictly from the framework of its own *logic of operation* and will only be irritated and motivated within the framework of its own rules and objectives by external observations.[15]

Having such recourse to the systemic autonomy of science and of the system of application is of momentous consequence. On the one hand, efforts of integration with the objective of totally subordinating scientific knowledge acquisition to practical demands could only be realised at very high cost: the specific scientific mode of reality construction would have to be relinquished. In this case, *integration* would actually imply the *dissolution* of science in the medium of the university-bound education of journalists—a demand that cannot sensibly be articulated in the halls of a university and (happily) will not stand a chance of being enforced in the near future. If the plea for the dissolving of science (or also of professional practice in the medium of science) is given up, then this will mean that the hoped-for quasi-smooth amalgamation of science and application must inevitably be disappointed.[16]

---

14 See Weischenberg (1990), pp. 55f.
15 Weischenberg/Kriener (1998), p. 25 (authors' emphasis).
16 Bolz (2005, p. 163) defends the even more far-reaching thesis that the individual professor—despite all protestations to the contrary—will inevitably be overtaxed by the task to coordinate the contrasting jobs of research, teaching, and concrete practice-oriented activity in a harmonious way.

In the study of journalism, science and application are coupled spheres that cannot, however, be completely enmeshed. What Manfred Rühl formulated several years ago is still true:

> An immediate transfer will not be accomplished in the near future, for instance according to the wishful thought: input to the automaton of the study of journalism: current problems of journalism; output: application-ready solutions for journalism.[17]

Every attempt of an integration of theory and practice is therefore compelled to take into account the systemic single-mindedness of the participant agents if it is not just intended to overpower and destroy identities. Such a scaling down of the claims in the perpetual dispute of the participant factions need not necessarily be interpreted as an expression of systemic fatalism; it has a relieving quality and might even relax the relationship between theorists and practitioners. The mutual accusations of irrelevance and the broad spectrum of possible recriminations and misunderstandings[18] result obviously from '*a lack of understanding of the differences between the rules that determine the production and the use of knowledge.*'[19] This means: Whenever scientists (theorists) accuse journalists (practitioners) of distorting scientific reality in their representations, they must accept from a systems-theoretically informed perspective that, due to the operative closure of the systems, it can never be otherwise. What is classified as distortion may probably be a most professionally designed media product that proves unsatisfactory to scientific rationality for that very reason. In brief: the mutual *painful suffering from autonomy* belongs to the inevitable accompanying phenomena of all attempts to bring theory and practice into contact or even to integrate them and to position the study of journalism in the boundary area of science and application.

The Problem of Relevance and Hierarchy

The debate is exacerbated by the fact that *theory* and *practice* have advanced to the status of most powerful catchwords in the present contro-

---

17 Rühl, quoted in Weischenberg (1998), pp. 26f.
18 The criticism of the practice of science, for example, is as follows: research possesses only little usefulness for the solution of scientific problems, supplies too few well-secured insights, lags too much behind developments (accusation of lacking up-to-date-ness). Occasionally practitioners explicitly suggest that people should not study journalism if they wanted to be journalists. People who had not been successful as journalists had for that reason withdrawn themselves to a comfortable chair in the ivory tower of science. From that position far removed from everyday life these people would then offer norms and standards to journalism that simply would not fit the really existing job of journalism. On the other hand, there is the repeated complaint among the representatives of the study of communication: practitioners would systematically ignore results of research or would represent these results only in a crudely distorting and fault-ridden way; journalists are judged to be fundamentally hostile to science and theory. On the spectrum of such accusations, see Hohlfeld (2002), p. 168, Ruß-Mohl (1987), p. 13, Weber (1999a), p. 28.
19 Beck/Bonß (1989), p. 11 (authors' emphasis).

versies about the reform of universities. The simplistic plea for practice-orientation is naturally not at all uncontroversial. Norbert Bolz, for instance, declares the demand for greater practice-relevance to be a 'death sentence'[20] for the social and cultural sciences, which are particularly hassled by such pressures: their theoretical curiosity is turned into a vice. Stefan Weber deplores — also in a more recent publication — the 'new epidemic'[21] of increasing hostility towards theory work and lists the following indicators of the 'tyranny of practice'[22] that he claims to have observed:

> Just think, for instance, of the sneaking transformation of numerous German-language university institutes for the study of media and communication into better multimedia laboratories of the sort that one has known in connection with the degree courses of technical colleges or even in institutions of further education.[23]

Several professors in the field of the study of journalism have pleaded for a clear primacy of journalistic practice for many years; they support the approach that the university-bound education of journalists should 'not be organised according to the criteria of university science and scholarship, but with respect to sensible and meaningful media practice'.[24] The study of journalism constitutes, according to their argument, 'a *semantic* system of statements of *pragmatic* relevance', and this implies that the decision about the relevance of theory 'cannot ultimately be taken by theory but must be taken by practice, by the world of experience.'[25] Ulrich Pätzold has tightened these arguments even more by stating further conditions that a theory must meet in the study of journalism if it is to be considered adequate to the subject matter: it must admit only assertions about journalism

> that can be followed and fulfilled by journalistic practice. The standards applicable to the theory of journalism study cannot be taken over from other fields or philosophies. They cannot be set as ideas against reality. They will remain accepted only and only as long as they correspond to the observed and researched reality of journalism. In other words: the theory of the study of journalism must meet the requirement to be capable of integration into the practice of journalism.'[26]

It remains unclear, however, how all these criteria can be made operational, if this requirement is really upheld. Who will have the right to decide whether a theory cannot be integrated or does not possess sufficient practice-relevance? What happens then? Could one not imagine that

---

20 Bolz (2005), p. 163.
21 Weber (2003a), p. 12.
22 Ibid., p. 175.
23 Ibid.
24 Haller (1987), p. 306.
25 Haller (2000), p. 122 (author's emphasis).
26 Pätzold (2000), p. 425.

theories may appear to be irrelevant at first, but begin to unfold their significance for the professional reality of experience only at a later stage of elaboration?[27] Would it therefore not be better to introduce a kind of *time lag* into the evaluation of theories? On closer scrutiny, however, such a decision would only postpone the problem of a sufficiently consensual evaluation for some time. And finally: perhaps the total lack of practice-relevance is, in fact, a particular form of practice-relevance; it can be very useful and, in the long run, extremely productive to absolve a stretch of training the faculties of the mind, which does not at all match personal ideas and attitudes with regard to what is relevant evidence.[28]

Modes of Observation of a Hybrid System

If one chooses a decidedly constructivist perspective at this point, a perspective that deals with the observation of observers, then one will realise: on the one hand, the distinction between theory and practice obviously serves, in a pragmatic respect, as a means of articulating mutual disclaimers and complaints about irrelevance, or even, to use a stringent expression by Peter Fuchs, as a kind of *scepticism-generator*, as a mechanism for churning out persistent messages of distrust, puzzlement, and suspicion.[29] On the other hand, however, when disregarding the debate with its concrete comments, and approaching the situation with a more formal interest, then one will discover that scientific theory formation and journalistic practice belong to different levels of observation. In the moment of practical operation (or also: of the successful simulation[30] of practice in the form of project work etc.), the observer is completely involved, immersed in his activities, cannot cope with the plethora of possibilities but must systematically exclude alternatives for a period of time in order to move forward and to avoid obstructing himself. 'One could also say: actions are moments of the self-oblivious observer, moments during which he operates without observing himself in his operations of distinction.'[31] To practise science in the real sense (i.e. to practice research) always means, however, to observe other observers or to reconstruct their modes of distinction, and this also naturally always means: to act. Teachers, who try hard to instigate learning processes, coordinate these different levels of observation. They act too — and they reflect their own and the actions of other observers; they try to animate the students to perform this

---

27 One can — for instance — show that the brand of systems theory elaborated by Niklas Luhmann has been rebuilt and further developed by current management science and has thus been turned into a highly practice-relevant theory after a critical stretch of time.
28 See, for a positive reaction, Bolz (2005), p. 168.
29 Fuchs (2000), p. 58, 62.
30 Simulation may be defined as 'the controlled representation of real phenomena in environments and processes of teaching'. Weischenberg, quoted in Blöbaum (2000), p. 98.
31 Hansen (1996), p. 71.

alternation between levels of observation, and they try to acquaint them with new perspectives of observation.

From a constructivist perspective, the handling of uncertainty distinguishes the core activities of an academic researcher in the study of journalism from each other (research and teaching in the areas of theory, empirical investigation and experiment, and media application practice). In projects of research, uncertainty is accepted, as it is the motive behind the investigator's questions, it is the starting condition of the possibility of scientific research in general. What appears certain at some point in time, need not be investigated. In university teaching, established knowledge is to be passed on against the backdrop of its fundamental dependence on supplementation. Teaching at a university means: to pass on certainties that possess a strange kind of instability; they will one day be disproved, declared to be outdated or inadequate. 'To be overtaken in science', Max Weber already diagnosed in his work *Science as profession*, 'is [...] not only our decreed fate but our purpose. We cannot do our work without the hope that others will go further than us. Fundamentally, this kind of progress moves towards the infinite.'[32] However, to do practical professional work means, by contrast, to eliminate as much uncertainty as possible and to trim down one's own activity to routine action without alternative, i.e. to suppress the essential contingency of all operational processes in the moment of ongoing action. 'To act means to reduce the multitude of imaginable possibilities to one and only one possibility. To act is to select, is to decide. Action is always unambiguous.'[33] The permanent reflection of possible uncertainties and simultaneous journalistic or media-practical activity are barely compatible. Whoever cannot curb the uncertainty and contingency of their routines will inevitably become incapable of acting, they will turn into the notorious centipedes that due to their amazement by the marvellous coordination of their instruments of walking, and overcome by the multitude of possible paths and right and wrong tracks, could only continue moving themselves forward laboriously if at all.

Journalism study, according to the introduced distinction of levels of observation, has the task of *reconstructing* current and ordinary modes of observation[34] practised by journalism, and to display and spread available knowledge. It has the task of *deconstructing* in teaching and learning processes all too dominant perspectives in order to tutor the use of alternatives and to increase the degrees of freedom. And one of its tasks is to *simulate* media practice in tutorial meetings so as to make students forget

---

32 Weber, M. (1995), p. 17.
33 Hansen (1996), p. 70.
34 Journalism appears, in the light of constructivist analyses, interpretations and evaluations, as the fundamentally changeable, multiply conditioned, autonomously operating, and fact- and actuality-related construction of realities in and through media.

about the scientific approach in the course of such observation activity of the first order, at least until the moment of subsequent reflection.[35] This means: whoever wants to integrate theory and practice, wants to couple different levels of observation; in the course of this coupling activity, he moves from the level of observation of the first order (the simulation of practice) to the empirical-theoretical reconstruction of journalistic observations (which are observed, as is usual in media journalism, by journalistic observers whenever feasible), and then further to the next higher levels of observation. These 'higher steps' do not carry and award particular privileges of knowledge or even lead to a greater proximity to an imaginary pole of truth. They only mark other modes of observation, which are constitutive for a system of science and thus also naturally possess their own blind spots.[36]

Integration as Reciprocal Irritation

Bearing in mind that theory and practice belong to systems that are operatively separated, there can by definition be no theory-practice integration in the sense of the reciprocally induced dissolution of guiding differences in favour of the creation of a new unit. The levelling of systemic differences, furthermore, can be no acceptable goal because it would not help the training of the handling of differing perspectives but would inevitably only lead to trivialisation and levelling reductions of complexity. Fledgling quality journalists would suffer from being insufficiently stimulated, inspired and encouraged by such attempts to dissolve difficulties in favour of trivial popular science and a sort of practice that is hyped up by means of pseudo-scientific slogans. Consequently, the question arises how — on the presupposition of systemic autonomy — the relationship between theory and practice should be modelled so as to fulfil the promise of integration. Different authors, arguing from the point of view of systems theory and constructivism, have specified the relationship between theory and practice as an, ideally, possibly most productive relationship of irritation,[37] and have called the study of journalism a study in irritation.[38] Alexander Görke, for instance, puts it quite acutely:

> Journalism study *must want to irritate!* What journalists will do with these irritations, whether they will discard them as theoretical fantasies or whether they will see the scholarly insistence on selectivity, perspectivity and viability, as propounded by the academic study of

---

36 Cf. the complete presentation by Weischenberg (1998).
36 See Poerksen (2004a, p. 343) with reference to the work by Stefan Weber and Siegfried Weischenberg.
37 See Görke (1998), p. 4 and Weber (1999a), p. 28
38 See Weischenberg (2004a), p. 10.

journalism, as an opportunity to create new degrees and spaces of freedom for journalistic observation, will have to be left to them.[39]

As the quotation shows, the concept of irritation is obviously problematical because it may be understood in too broad a way. Irritation or perturbation[40] is, from the perspective of systems theory, everything that, from the point of view of an observer, influences a system from outside, does not destroy the organisation of the system, i.e. bring about a destructive change. Whoever irritates people, may annoy them, disturb, amuse, or excite them, may provoke a shrugging of shoulders as a sign of indifference, or satirically intended commentaries, may hurt, frighten, deeply upset them, may inflict bodily pain, arouse resistance, release emphatic appreciation etc—the whole spectrum of such forms of reaction may be summarised as irritation whose central feature is that it remains beneath a threshold of destructive impact.

Such a concept of irritation results from the distinction between organisation and structure, as proposed as significant or constitutive by systems theory. But the concept of irritation itself is not specific enough to characterise sufficiently and precisely the productive relationship of exchange between theory and practice as well as learning processes. If the orientation by the learners is taken seriously, then an irritation must be relevant for both teachers and learners, in the long run; it must not, for example, be permanently deflated and rejected as a theoretical craze, because that would only lead to annoyance and rejection. If the relationship between theory and practice is, however, considered as a relationship of reciprocal irritation, and if learning is considered to be the result of successful irritations, as suggested here, then the concept of irritation needs to be specified more precisely in detail. It will come as no surprise that this will now be done in the next section of the chapter.

2. The Management of Contradictions: Informing Irritations

External Stimulation and Internal Relevance

A mere feeling of irritation is definitely insufficient and inadequate with regard to successful processes of teaching and learning. From a constructivist perspective, a sort of *bridging concept* is needed, which would connect the external processes of stimulation with the system-internal affirmations of relevance. According to the fundamental presupposition of the essential non-triviality of all the participants, traditional emphatic categories of control and regulation, suggesting calculable stimulus-response schemas and causal interference in the cognitive system of

---

[39] Görke (1998), p. 4 (author's emphasis).
[40] On the equalisation of the concepts of irritation and perturbation in systems theory, see e.g. Luhmann (2002b), pp. 124ff.

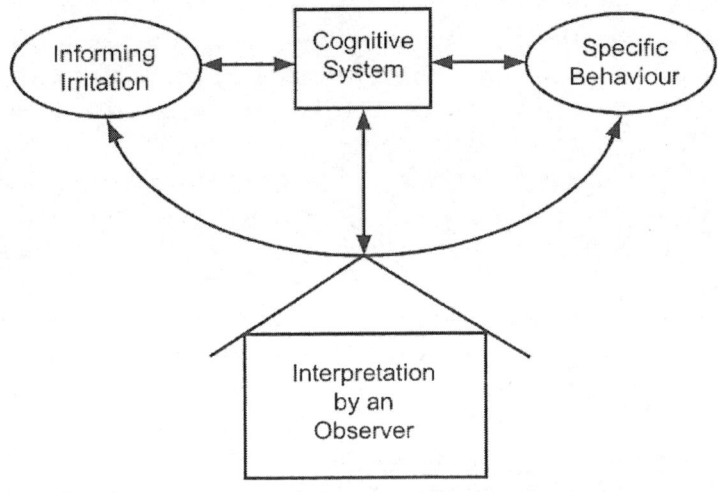

Figure 7.
Visualisation of an Informing Irritation,
Diagnosed by an Observer in Coordination with a Learner

the learner, are definitely out of play. The concept of *informing irritation* proposed here is intended to represent the didactically indispensable linkage between system-external observability and system-internal specificity of resonance (see figure 7). The event that is counted as irritation is attributed primarily from outside; it is considered as an external influence by an observer (e.g. the teacher), and nothing is said about its further processing within the system.[41] Consequently, all diagnoses of irritation are actually observer-relative suppositions. Whoever asserts an irritation isolates single factors or bundles of factors in the accessible field of perception, and attributes specific effects to these factors. Whoever then infers an informing irritation, i.e. successful learning, believes to be able to observe and communicatively verify an affirmation of relevance by the system in question (the learner): specific distinctions become objects of communication; they are taken up and dealt with. The external irritation — in the view of the observer — has turned into system-internal information because changes of behaviour or changes of state of the system have been observed. A comparatively non-specific irritation has now become, to use Gregory Bateson's definition of information,[42] a difference that makes a difference, i.e. which is internally perceived and accordingly processed further as a difference.[43] Informing irritations are thus external stimulations that are

---

41 On the system-external and the system-internal attribution of irritations, see Luhmann (1995), pp. 61ff.
42 On this definition, see Luhmann (2002b), pp. 128f.
43 On the concept of information and the distinction of different variants of *intellectual capital* (data, items of information, knowledge) see Willke (2004), pp. 28ff.

classified by an observer as system-internally informative or relevant. The learner now works recognisably with the distinctions constructed into their environments, combines them with individual guiding differences, re-arranges systems of distinctions, possibly exchanges them, and keeps them in memory for shorter or longer periods of time.[44]

The fact that external observers judge the internal processes of other individuals, and evidently can do so only on the basis of their external perceptions of those individuals, entails the consequence that no universally valid criteria of differentiation can be made available to distinguish a permanently unproductive perturbation, which generates only annoyance and refusal, from an informing irritation. What may at first produce only annoyance and refusal, will perhaps at a later stage be assessed as productive and inspiring and will possibly release an irreversible re-orientation of the learners. What is necessary is the constant effort of checking and folding and crossing perspectives; what is required is the dialogue with those whom one wants to subject to informing irritation; what must be clarified is whether what one believes to be stimulating fits the internal criteria of relevance of the learners. Nevertheless, the fact remains that the construction of a direct connection between irritation and information or the consequential internal change of state will forever retain the character of a supposition. All one can do as a teacher is to generate suppositions about system-internal criteria of relevance, and then test them in ever-new run-throughs and ever-new attempts at refinement and revision.[45]

The Construction of Informing Irritations

These tests of relevance are not completely dependent, however, on experimenting in a potentially infinitely large space of possibilities. The production of informing irritations can be carried out with the help of a genuine constructivist strategy that will here be called *problem design*. Design is hereby understood as that process of decision, judgement and creation, which lends shape to a set of ideas within an interesting domain.[46] Problem design means that one makes transparent aporias that promote learning, difficulties, contradictions etc., that one works them out in a concise way, dramatises them by means of case examples, reports on experiences, and role-playing etc. in order to transform apparently valid answers into questions, supposedly ready-made recipes into open situations of decision, which require self-responsible action. The central concern of so-called problem designers is that they bring the contradictions, the paradoxes and the aporias of quality journalism to awareness in order to gener-

---

44   See also Luhmann (2004), p. 40.
45   See also Willke (1987), p. 334.
46   On this understanding of the design concept, see Ackermann (1995), p. 348 and Floyd (1997), p. 116.

ate informing irritations and to stimulate resulting reflected decisions. They will be successful if they manage to sketch the problems in such a way as to make them appear to the students as the students' own problems, which they will have to solve for themselves. Some of these contradictions, aporias and paradoxes of journalism will now be quoted – albeit only in an exemplary way and without any claim to completeness.[47] They can be exploited for the problem design of teachers within the context of the study of journalism.

- In daily routine work contradictions may arise between the complexity sensed by individual journalists and the ever necessary reduction of complexity; between comprehensive research work and the deadline-determined production of some article; between the adequate discussion of an issue and the inevitable strain due to lack of time.
- The pressure exerted by lack of time and imposed deadlines enforce action and thus the continual balancing of basically contradictory goals: journalists may not have done sufficient research due to lack of time but they want to see their story printed so that it can still achieve the expected impact. Quick publication may attract attention and beat the competitors, but a premature publication that is proved faulty will undermine credibility and damage the image of the medium in question. This kind of dilemma entails the consideration of the consequences of journalistic action in as accurate a way as possible.
- Conflicting goals may fundamentally arise between comprehensive information and the simultaneous necessity of selection and reduction, between an emphatic ideal of objectivity and the insight that it is impossible to meet this ideal in an acceptable manner in the practice of news reporting.
- It may also happen that the will of journalists to pursue political aims does not appear compatible with the simultaneously propagated claim of independence and neutrality. In this way, discrepancies arise in the self-role-image of journalists, which may require well-reflected re-orientation.
- Among the essential features of the daily routine work of journalists are the more or less relaxed tension between individual points of view and external influences (exerted by skilful PR-people, colleagues with vested interests, ideologically committed chief editors, nervous marketing departments etc.). This kind of tension may also manifest itself in the form of aporias (personal ideal versus instruction by chief editor etc.).
- The insistence on personal independence may conflict with the necessity of maintaining the job position, i.e. to secure economic survival: there are the situations in which a specific tendency in the reporting of

---

47 The presentation of these contradictions follows Krainer (2001), pp. 269ff.

news is enforced in connection with more or less direct threats of dismissal.
- In daily routine work, potential contradictions may arise between personal professional ideals and the general goal of enlightenment, on the one hand, and the commercial interests of the employing media enterprise, on the other. This is a fundamental dilemma and a 'built-in schizophrenia'[48] of open media systems: the conflict between the commercial orientation of the media enterprise and the personal claim and publicly voiced demand to engage in ethical-moral objectives of the community. On the one hand, media entrepreneurs pursue particular interests. They want to, and they have to earn money, make profits, and fight competitors for shares in the market. On the other hand, journalists want to serve the goals of enlightenment and the political maturity of individuals, and to orient themselves according to the ideal of comprehensive information.[49]
- The ideal of responsibility (understood as the awareness of the potential consequences of the reporting of news and of the orientation of individual actions by these presumed or expected consequences) may, in the extreme case, fundamentally contradict the actually occurring consequences, particularly and especially in the highly work-sharing processes of mass communication. Thus, responsibility may have to be shouldered for something in whose process of production journalists have neither part nor influence.
- The fundamental rights to the protection of the privacy of individuals may collide with the *grundgesetz*-guaranteed freedom of the press (in Germany), the legitimate interests of the public in relevant information, and the desire of journalists to organise and create publicity; in such cases of legal or ethical-moral conflicts, well-reflected management of contradictions is necessary. Barbara Thomaß comments: 'In this field of conflicts, journalists have to cope with divergent claims, i.e. they have to maintain the fundamentally guaranteed rights and avoid any damage by infringing the privacy of the objects of their reporting, but they also have to supply the information demanded by their customers, the market, their professional ambition etc.'[50]
- While planning their careers, journalists may possibly experience the contradictions between their own personal moral claims and the quest for the scoop, the revelation that creates a stir. A scoop will secure the attention of colleagues and the public, open up opportunities of professional advancement, may however be researched only at the price of the temporary suspension of personal moral norms. In such situations, a clear distinction must be made between professional standards and the craving for sensations, between individual morality

---

48 Weischenberg (1998), p. 171.
49 See Altschull (1990), p. 43.
50 Thomaß (2003), p. 164.

and the methods of cheap, basely career-motivated, snooping journalism.
- The treatment of informants always entails a 'balancing act'[51] between closeness and distance. Keeping too great a distance will endanger being supplied with sufficient background information; delving too deeply into the environment or milieu that is to be described, may threaten the neutrality of the journalists, and they may become agents in the events and happenings about which they are supposed to report. To maintain individual independence and still to acquire relevant information will, therefore, always require the careful exploration and assessment of the relationship between closeness and distance, participation and neutral observation.
- Quality journalists are inevitably forced to serve different audiences and publics, to subject interests in information and requirements of entertainment to carefully balanced assessment, to reflect constantly personal self-images and to re-arrange anew and continually the (potentially contrary) objectives of individual activities (criticism, control, orientation, entertainment etc.).
- In the education and training of quality journalists, contradictions will unavoidably arise between the necessary market-orientation and journalistic responsibilities. It is certainly appropriate to educate and train by market-adequate criteria — yet at the same time insist on ethical-moral standards that may prove to be something of a hindrance in the elastic adjustments of journalists to encountered professional realities.

The implication is that such problem design will always include the requirement of a sort of best-reflected management of contradictions — but no concrete criteria or standards pre-set by the teacher, no precise exposition of concrete ways and means to be employed in the treatment of actually identified contradictions. Whenever such problem design is successful, there is an oscillation between contrary possibilities of thinking and diverging alternatives of action; there emerges a feeling for conflicts between objectives and conscience, for the sensitive treatment of informants, for attempts at influence and manipulation, and for the potential threats to the duties of care and the protection of personality rights. In all such cases, reflection is indispensable and decisions are necessary. Fledgeling quality journalists will be capable of balancing these aporias of the media business, which are deeply entrenched in the political organisation and control of Western media, naturally in changing personal-individual combinations and mixtures. If they manage to comprehend these aporias and can accordingly interpret and explain their own experiences, they will have been informingly irritated, but they will not have been told

---

[51] Krainer (2001), p 162.

what they ought to do in detail.[52] It cannot be emphasised often enough, however, that such abstinence with regard to concrete advice need not necessarily be a disadvantage.

It is definitely not the task of the study of journalism in universities to supply recipes for all conceivable eventualities, thus negating the autonomy of the individual students, i.e. certifying their immaturity by order. The consequences of a mode of action can be demonstrated by means of casuistic approaches. Such consequences can be identified, and decisions can be prepared and stimulated by selected examples, also in order to explain the relativity of supposedly universally valid rules of decision. Finally, it can always be shown that there is the choice of what is to be recognised as a potential choice, i.e. that there is always the choice of potential choices.[53] The first and foremost objective of the study of journalism must therefore be to prepare the creation of a *school of seeing*, through which the aporias of the daily working routine of journalism become perceptible as part of a framework of conditions. These contradictions are ambiguous, they cannot be dissolved according to the pattern of *right* and *wrong*, because there are always arguments for every kind of position. Recognising, processing and reflecting such contradictions must be the general subject matter and the central topic of the study of journalism.[54] The pedagogical-didactic imperative of the entire discipline should therefore be to present these aporias to the learners in a problem-oriented way, to confront them with the multiplicity of realities and opportunities of decision[55] in order to make them capable of choosing in a self-responsible way what they have perceived as the potential choices available.[56]

An existential presupposition of this position is the constructivist postulate of autonomy: the refusal to provide concrete models of action with particular content in a world of contradictions presupposes that there is a fundamental trust in the students and their personal ability to take self-responsible reflected decisions.

---

52 On the essence of contradictions and the features of aporias, see Krainer (2001), p. 299.
53 See Floyd (1997), p. 108.
54 I am indebted to Krainer (2002, pp. 157f.) for these considerations, which she formulates with a view to media ethics (and not the study of journalism).
55 Concrete didactic strategies for securing such a variety of perspectives are, for example: the historical contextualisation of statements, the comparison of different programmes of construction, the reduction of assumptions about reality to a specific system of the interpretation of the world.
56 See Müller (1996b), p. 76.

3. The Parable of the Blind Spot

The proposals of a constructivistically inspired study of journalism, as presented here in detail, may be recapitulated in the form of a little experiment that has been publicised by Heinz von Foerster.[57] The execution of this experiment requires a piece of paper showing a black star and a black spot. The spot is fixated, the left eye is closed, and the piece of paper is moved back and forth along the axis of seeing until the black spot disappears. If the star is fixated intensively enough, the black spot remains invisible even though the piece of paper is moved in parallel to the spectator from left to right or up and down. The physiological explanation of this phenomenon of sudden non-seeing is that the black spot at this specific distance is projected onto an area of the retina where there are no rods and cones because there the optic nerve leaves the eyeball.[58] As there are no visual cells at that particular spot inside the eyeball, human beings could very well be expected to walk about the earth and through the world with a visual hole of a certain size. This is undoubtedly not the case. The visual field appears to us fully closed, unless we perform experiments with our visual capabilities and happen to discover the existence of the blind spot.

Figure 8.
The Experiment with the Blind Spot (From Foerster/Poerksen (2002), p. 112.)

'We do not see that we do not see', is the paradoxical formulation by Heinz von Foerster relating to this phenomenon. 'We are blind to our blindness.'[59] There are no gaps because it is our cognitive system that supplies the missing information and constructs the experience of an unbroken continuous space.[60] The interpretation of the world and human perception and knowledge seem appropriate, comprehensive and without alternative. We are not aware of our contribution to the generation of this interpretation of the world, but we can bring it to awareness if we want to.

This seeing of not seeing and the discussion of this phenomenon of the not-seeing of not-seeing turns into a provocation that can be rejected and eliminated only with great difficulty because the impact of its ordinary evidence is so overwhelming. One gradually begins to discover this individual blindness outside the experimental setup as well – in dealing with paradigms and dogmas and statements of belief, in the confrontation with

---

57 See Foerster (1993c).
58 See Foerster/Poerksen (2002), p. 112.
59 Foerster (1993c), p. 19.
60 On the interpretation of this experiments, see also Maturana/Varela (1992), pp. 21ff.

prejudices and ideologies, in the analysis of the pressures of conformity, of group behaviours and the mechanisms of manipulation, in the reflection of personal mistakes and errors committed in the conviction to have been doing the right thing. One begins to understand what it means to research without prejudices, what it means to pre-condition answers by particular ways of questioning, by methods and approaches, and to force the so-called facts into a corset that presses them into pre-determined tracks and forms. The seeing of not seeing and the realisation of individual bias and limitation imply that one does not perceive and understand the world exactly point by point in its essential modes of Being, but that one may understand that there is no perception without a blind spot, and that every act and kind of perception ignores the conditions of its own constitution in the act of perception, and that it is compelled to do so.[61]

In the context of an ideal construction of the study of journalism, this experiment acquires the character of a key story, the status of an instructive parable that tells of the general human inclination towards self-affirmation, and stimulates and inspires, at the same time, to confront this kind of self-affirmation with the analysis and critical examination of processes of perception.[62] This parable of instruction indicates the predispositions and the blind spots of every observer claiming to approach a supposedly independent object of description. It deals with the fact that every perception is constructed, and also with the necessity to relativise personal certainties, to reduce their claim to validity by their reduction to the conditions of observation. And it stimulates and encourages the readiness to study systematically this personal blindness and the blindness of others, and to take seriously the fundamental phenomenon of personal blindness to personal blindness and to the blindness of others, with the specific goal of creating a new kind of openness.

---

61 See Bolz (2001), p. 17.
62 Cf. in another context also Pöttker (1998), p. 240.

Chapter VIII

Summary in the Form of Theses

Arthur Schopenhauer once said that the point of a dispute is not to defend *the Truth*, but to stand up for a personal argument, a personal thesis.[1] Theses are — one might add — a form of communication that is used to highlight the fundamental relativity and the deficiencies of one's message. Theses represent exploratory movements in the realms of thought, employing the instruments of overstatement for purposes of intellectual stimulation and inspiring debates. At the end of a book whose core assertions consist in the plea to take seriously the essential contingency of all knowledge and the definitive farewell to the Absolute, a summary of the essential considerations in the form of theses seems appropriate.

Chapter I: Premises and Postulates

- Constructivism, as it has been elucidated here, is an epoch-specifically grounded kind of scepticism, an invitation to critical reflection and 'the radical and creative re-examination of personal habits of thinking and acting — particularly for journalists who all too quickly adopt a group mentality in their processes of professional socialisation, which they then fail to question ever again. Constructivism teaches journalists to probe and query their certainties.'[2]

- The constructivist discourse can be characterised more precisely by pointing out the common core problem of all constructivists, i.e. the investigation of processes of knowledge acquisition. It may be portrayed in detail by referring the particular theories and models to specific disciplines, and by correspondingly distinguishing philosophical, psychological, cybernetic, biological and knowledge-sociological currents of constructivist thought. Ultimately, constructivism may also be understood as a set of recurring figures of thought (observer orientation, autonomy postulate, interest in circularity and differences etc.).

---

1 See Steinfeld (1991), p. 11.
2 Weischenberg (1992), p. 175.

- The reception of constructivism by journalism and communication studies has been accompanied by robust disputes. It, has in point of fact re-opened and recast a fundamental and apparently long virulent conflict between realists and relativists within the profession. Quite obviously, there is still in force a largely standardised catalogue of accusations (the accusation of trendiness, the accusation of arbitrariness, the accusation of perspectival reduction, the accusation of solipsism etc.). Some of the accusations must be accepted as justified even by constructivists, particularly those advanced in the ancient and early history of constructivist thought, when it still operated excessively with metaphors of irritation and excitation and a suggestive rhetoric implying the possibility of total individual re-invention at any moment, of the arbitrary creation and re-creation of realities.[3] Such views and attitudes must be cast aside because the act of observation clearly either reproduces old orders or systems of distinction, or produces new ones against existing backgrounds. The degrees of freedom and the arbitrariness of constructions are thus massively constrained; the world — understood as the sum of the constraints affecting an individual — simply does not permit the permanent re-invention of individual selves.
- The numerous accusations and objections advanced towards constructivistically arguing researchers in communication — partially warranted, partially unwarranted — may be condensed into three fundamental problems of constructivist theory formation. 1. The *problem of self-contradiction* involves the contradiction between the posited premises and the claims to validity raised either implicitly or explicitly; self-contradictions not only result from the apparent violation of logical rules, they also result from a thoughtless use of language (rhetorical self-contradiction) and from terminological imprecision (cf. the analyses of the problem of referential confusion). 2. The *problem of self-dogmatisation* arises whenever constructivist insights are elevated to new creeds and exclusive theory offers — for whatever reasons. The position of discursive *constructivism* promoted in this book is intended to make constructivism an instrument of de-conditioning and a communicative strategy for the reconstruction and deconstruction of dogmas and certainties about reality, all following the general aim of stimulating debate and to inspire dialogue. Discursive constructivism is seen as a fundamental kind of scepticism turned into a form of communication that is aimed at the intensive self-reflection of personal prejudices. 3. The *problem of practice-relevance* results from the largely unclarified relationship between epistemological understanding and daily professional practice, between epistemological principles and their practical implementation. This book advances the plea to consider this relationship between epistemology and daily professional practice as a sort of *relationship of stimulation*. The general postulates

---

3   See Schmidt in conversation with Poerksen (2004f), p. 144.

are undoubtedly not completely without consequence or completely irrelevant ('*non-relationship*'). The assumption is much rather that they inspire practical action but do not determine any action according to the scheme of linear causality (*relationship of derivation*). Constructivism therefore obviously lacks an immediate quasi recipe-like relevance for the practice of journalism. Its more indirect usefulness is that, as a school of thought, it provides productive irritations, opens up opportunities for reflection, and supplies new possibilities of observation.

Chapter II: Deepening Critical Awareness of Science

- Even quality journalists cannot and need not know everything. Due to the perpetual and immense production pressure of journalism, they are inescapably forced — in contradistinction to scientists and scholars — to play the role of ad-hoc experts and to practise a reasonable kind of dilettantism with regard to specialist questions, which can never be combated simply by increased and intensified demands of education. It is furthermore essential to encourage a fundamental attitude of scepticism in order to train the handling of uncertainty, and to develop a particular mind-set that is characterised, as has already been shown in detail, by the 'paradox of the non-committal commitment'.[4] Such scepticism may be gained from the example of the constructivist debate about the central instance of truth of the modern age, i.e. modern science. From a constructivist perspective, scientific knowledge is *culturalised* (referred to societal-cultural pre-dispositions), it is *temporalised* (given a time-index and thus labelled as finally provisional), it is *historicised* (embedded into the totality of historical circumstances), and it is *epistemologically relativised* (on the basis of scientific, in particular biological, research robbed of its claim to truth).

- Deepening critical awareness of science will certainly include the discussion of all the methods encountered in a curriculum of the study of journalism, which is based on social science. The acquaintance with quantitative and qualitative procedures and with the canon of methods current in the study of communication (content analysis, survey, observation, experiment), the occupation with the possible advantages of a combination of such methods (triangulation), and the analysis of basic philosophies of science, particularly with regard to methodologies and methods, are all additionally through the constructivist perspective turned into discussions of the cognitive consequences of *perspectivity*. The selected set of methods and its examination and application can therefore be experienced as a - inevitable and necessary — 'taming of the view'.[5]

---

4 Bolz (2001, p. 173) with reference to Luhmann.
5 This is the title of a book by Schmidt (1998).

- These considerations imply a particularly careful exposure and presentation of one's own methodical procedures (*requirement of transparency*), which naturally corresponds with current and accepted standards, anyway. What seems definitely required is the intensive and painstaking analysis of the process of research, which will transform individual action into an object of knowledge (*demand of self-reflection*). The important result of such intensified reflection of individual procedures in the acquisition of knowledge, which will always create awareness of things and events that have escaped observation in the process, is the fundamental insight: whatever is observed could always be observed in another way (*awareness of contingency*).
- The basic assumption is that scientific knowledge is necessarily observer-dependent. True knowledge becomes (temporarily) useful knowledge, descriptivity becomes problem-solving capability, and emphatically conceived objectivity becomes intersubjectivity. It is this newly grounded shaking up of scientific realism that is apt to create a more profound awareness of the possibilities and the limits, the methods and the structures, of modern science. This kind of critical examination and laying down of boundaries — and this is the meaning of the term *criticism* in this context — fundamentally immunises in an ideal way against premature judgements and a form of naive faith in experts and science that cannot do quality journalists any good.

Chapter III: Deepening Critical Awareness of Language

- The work of journalists is executed at the interface of spheres of communication, at a linguistic interface. It requires uptake with greatly varying speed, media-adequate transformation, and the target-related, audience-appropriate montage of highly different varieties that may be classified under different prototypes. Among the prototypes relevant to journalism are, for instance: specialised languages and sub-languages, dialects and doctrinal languages, and in particular the languages of the media which derive their forms and styles from a multi-layered catalogue of requirements based on conditions of production and reception (intelligibility, attractiveness, competition for attention, necessity of multiple address).
- Deepening critical awareness of language on the basis of constructivism aims at a more precise understanding and an improvement of linguistic communication. This goal may be approximated by first parting company with different varieties of linguistic realism, and then by registering with particular attention the observable differences of interpretation, and the competition between designations and meanings. The specific constellation of the use of varieties must be carefully monitored in order to identify possible problems of communication so as to be able to return to a situation-adequate use of language. Such an approach stimulates the analysis of language-immanent strategies of persuasion and manipulation, in

order to possibly immunise oneself against their exploitation and impact. Finally, it can be made clear that public and journalistic uses of language are frequently characterised by realist premises, and that language is generally a crucial instrument of reality construction. For whoever manages to establish their descriptions of reality, manages to universalise their particular conceptual creations and will also establish their views of things—and thus create reality to which others will refer, can refer, and in the extreme case will have to refer.

Chapter IV: Deepening Critical Awareness of Media-Epistemology

- Media-epistemology is not a term to be contrasted with media-ontology—of whatever kind—nor is it a special field of media-philosophy. It circumscribes a constructivistically grounded field of research which deals with a question that is also of relevance to journalistic practice: How do journalists and media construct reality, and how can the reality of their reality constructions be observed—i.e. on the basis of what theories, paradigms, presuppositions? The general goal is to investigate the reality-constitutive formative power of all media and all relevant journalistic programmes of construction and to present the results gained in the form of epistemological universal statements and/or as empirically interpretable trend hypotheses.
- This particular perspective of media-epistemology may be demonstrated by the example of news value research which is intended to reveal how and according to what rules journalists construct reality, select topics for their news reporting, scan events for key features in order to give them particular prominence. The result of such research is that there can be no *event in itself* and no ontic *solid body of news*, about whose properties something definitive could be stated in journalistic forms of presentation.
- Furthermore, it is made clear according to what rules and on what basis the study of journalism and communication observes these programmes of construction: realistically oriented scientists and scholars posit the event as the primary cause, describe journalists as rather passive, or characterise them with a media-critical intention as the people who actively *distort reality* or, by applying their selection rules, *estrange or alienate it*. Constructivistically oriented scientists and scholars tend to reverse such a logic of thought and attribute a strong power of influence to journalistic agents. It is the journalists, their assumption is, who access a relatively amorphous and shapeless field of phenomena, select so-called events from amongst these phenomena, and publicise a certain percentage of these events according to the conditions of the available medium so as to subject their selection to the final selection processes of their public.
- Media genre theory may be viewed as a specialist field within media-epistemology. It shows how and in what ways media genres,

patterns of news reporting and forms of presentation develop into orienting schemas (Jean Piaget). From the point of view of journalists, they function as commands of perception of the world, regulate the presentation and the arrangement of media offers, and thus make the contingency of journalistic communication manipulable in all its phases (production, distribution, reception).
- Media-epistemology possesses a central instrument of the reconstruction of construction in the form of the constructivist theory of distinctions that expressly includes the possibility of self-reflection. Media-epistemology is—in this view—an applied theory of distinction; it orients its own labour of interpretation by the questions why particular distinctions and designations become established, what makes these designations and distinctions visible and what makes them invisible, in what forms and for what reasons whole frameworks of distinctions are arranged into new constellations.

Chapter V: Deepening Critical Awareness of Ethics

- The occupation with a constructivistically grounded ethics of journalism is doubly loaded. On the one hand, critics of constructivism claim that the whole discourse legitimates forgery, arbitrariness and wilfulness, the mixing of facts and fictions. Constructivists respond, on the other hand, that it is their school of thought that has inspired the highest measure of self-responsibility and ethical-moral sensibility: the thesis is that everything said is said by people who could always say it in different ways and who are therefore responsible for their utterances.
- Heinz von Foerster's attempt to formulate a constructivist ethics, which is characterised by intellectual consistency and stylistic elegance, on closer scrutiny proves to be an *ethics of enabling ethics*. It defines a set of premises and rules of decision for arriving at a position of responsibility. His ethics of the second order may be understood as a theoretical frame for any kind of ethics—which is certainly also of importance for quality journalists. The offer comprises a strict logic of argumentation and decision, which inseparably connects means and purposes, reflexion and concrete procedure, theory and ethical-moral action. The presentation demonstrates that responsibility begins with the decision to construct freedom of choice as part of one's perception of the world. The assumption of personal freedom of choice (in the sense of a decision of a fundamentally un-decidable question) is an indispensable presupposition of ethical-moral action.
- The criticism of truth by constructivism can be reconstructed as a theory of truth, here called the *consequence theory of truth*. This theory of truth does not deal with the traditional questions of classical theories of truth that claim to explain the concept of truth and the emergence of truth (through correspondence, the experience of evidence, the internal coherence of statements within the system of statements etc.). The

topic of a constructivist criticism of truth, which may be seen as a theory of truth, are the possible consequences of the belief in truth, which may be coordinated with a logical-semantical and an individual-cognitive level, and a domain of relations. These consequences of the belief in truth extend to the legitimation of violence.
- Autonomy and dependence are frequently presented as reciprocally exclusive alternatives in the discussions of an ethics of journalism and the media. The discussions show that both alternatives of thought do not appear convincing as mutually exclusive points of view. The conception of ethics that styles the freely deciding and choosing individual a "moral hero", is context-blind; the structures of journalism that influence the activities of the individuals do not even become visible to such a conception. The attempt to tie ethics rigorously to a system of whatever kind cannot convince either because here the freedom of choice of the individual is rejected — and the condition of the possibility of responsible action is thus negated. The proposal advanced here is to unite or combine in thought autonomy and dependence, freedom and lack of freedom, i.e. fitting them into a dialectic that can be activated according to conditions and situations, and to consider them no longer as strict opposites. The perception of constraints and compulsions — in this view — can therefore be used to discover new playing spaces and new opportunities for action, and to win autonomy and increase degrees of freedom through the reflection of individual dependencies.
- Even a constructivist can use concepts like *dramatisation, staging, forgery, invention, lies* — at the centre of the conception of an ethics of journalism — but these concepts must be understood in a strictly observer-relative sense and be placed within a continuum of distinctions that extends between the unconscious construction, the inevitable forming and shaping of media offers, and the intentional goal-directed lie. The central premise of this argumentation is: whoever dramatises or stages reality, whoever forges, invents, and lies, knows what they are doing by actually doing it. In a constructivist ethics of journalism, this coupling with the minds of the agents replaces the recourse to an absolute reality, which in realist ontological thinking serves as a basis of reference for the diagnosis of staging, dramatisation and forgery. Responsibility is only applicable when what is done is done intentionally. The decisive thing is: those who forge and lie contradict their own assumptions about truth, break the ethical-moral *pact with themselves,* and land themselves in a contradiction to their own convictions and beliefs.
- The question of responsibility is *the key question of an ethics of journalism.* The claim, however, that someone is responsible, is highly charged with presuppositions. Responsibility presupposes freedom of choice and the possibility of perceiving mutually exclusive alternatives, and it must clearly be separated from causation (in the sense of

an ultimate calculability of action consequences). From a constructivist perspective, to act responsibly does not mean to achieve the desired results in every case. It means much rather that one carefully considers the *possible consequences* of personal action and orients one's actions by these imagined consequences according to the best of one's knowledge and in all conscience.
- Ethical-moral recommendations for action, in the framework of a consistent constructivistically formed sequence of arguments, should possess the character of meta-rules, certainly not the form of concrete prescriptions that would negate individual responsibility. The constructivist postulate of autonomy, the interest in difference, and the awareness of the plurality of realities, are the figures of thought providing the necessary orientation. They may also be reformulated as ethical-moral meta-rules of an ethics (of journalism): *maintain or enlarge the operational spaces for autonomy; spare or maximise differences; preserve or increase the plurality of reality designs.*

Chapter VI: Deepening Awareness of Autonomy

- Processes of education and training inevitably involve anthropological presuppositions, and are necessarily expressions of the ways and manners according to which human beings understand themselves and their actions. Such presuppositions shape concrete actions and activities, suggest a particular logic of interaction and the creation of relationships. The distinction between trivial and non-trivial machines may be used in order to elaborate the strictly formally arguing anthropology of constructivism. It provides the justification for abandoning simple control and regulation models and raises the awareness of the autonomy of all participants.
- The core problem of all the efforts of university didactics presents itself as a problem of a beginning that is no longer a beginning. Learning means here: follow-up learning. The teachers must work with what is made available, must take particular account of previous experiences, must connect their teaching with what is given. Learners move into the centre, teachers must orient themselves according to the interests of the learners.
- The constructivist epistemology of non-triviality and the so-called paradox of non-intervention must be made the point of departure for the reflection about teaching and learning that starts out from the autonomy of the learners and wants to raise the awareness of the learners for this autonomy. The key question is therefore: how can function-adequate inspirations be made possible—despite the autonomy of the learners?
- The general point is now that the ideal of knowledge transfer cannot be upheld and that ways and means must be discovered to refine the teachers' capabilities of communication in a situation-adequate way in order to stimulate their autonomous learner-partners. It is of deci-

sive importance to choose a guiding image adequate to the situation (Socratic maieutic techniques, moderator, research or expedition leader, ironist, irritation agent) and to orient teaching in a reflected way by the learners (*reading, flexing*), to attribute a different meaning to so-called mistakes, to listen in a comprehensive way and manner, and to employ dialogue as the elementary strategy of presentation (universalising of the dialogical principle).

- Many of the proposals offered may appear rather idealistic. They seem to have very little or nothing to do with the present situation of the universities that are depriving themselves of necessary resources of energy for research and teaching in a systematic way by engaging in hectic efforts of reform and immature definitions of objectives. However, observations of this kind cannot and must not justify resignatory silence, but they do indeed change the character of any kind of more or less programmatic description: the descriptions assume a utopian character. They turn into *one particular* possibility of thinking and action that derives its power precisely from the difference to what is experienced as reality.

Chapter VII: The Reality of the Study of Journalism

- The integration of theory and practice is the decisive promise of the study of journalism. The concepts of practice and theory in the debates within the field and outside it appear to be recognisably diffuse. They have become instruments of science politics and the subject of controversies in the study of journalism and communication, which will fundamentally influence the basic orientation of the discipline as a whole.
- In a constructivist view, the integration of theory and practice may be considered as the reciprocal irritation of the system of science and the system of application. The study of journalism can therefore be conceived of as a hybrid system that combines different levels of observation in the *simulation* of practice, in the *reconstruction* of contents, and in the *deconstruction* of dogmas and beliefs that appear all too dominant.
- The concept of irritation that is used by different constructivist and systems-theoretical authors for the characterisation of the relationship between theory and practice or also for the description of the core task of the study of journalism as a whole is not precise enough. Every influence impinging on a system — within the framework of these meta-theories — may be seen as an irritation. This means that the concept of irritation in this unspecific interpretation can all too easily be used to repel any objection against curricula and preferred learning methods with the deflating statement that their design is only geared towards irritation. The thesis propounded here is, however, that the simple idea and will to irritation is not sufficient and that it is necessary *to practice informing irritation*, to confront the learners with distinctions that will prove viable and relevant in their worlds.

- The central strategy of investing distinctions with relevance and irritating others in an informing manner consists in what is called *problem design*, i.e. in the most skilful illustration of contradictions, paradoxes and aporias that structure the daily routine work of journalists. Such problem design ends, however, with the staging and the dramatisation of possible contradictions between ideal and reality, between the desire for independence and the external compulsion, between moral and economic orientation etc., due to the respect for the autonomy and capability of the individual to take decisions. The management of contradictions is left to the individuals and must be left to them. The imposition of convictions and beliefs is not the business of the study of journalism. But its task must certainly be to keep alive the *great discourse* on the quality of journalism and the quality of ways and means of the education and training for journalism.

Bibliography

Ackermann, Edith (1995): Construction and Transference of Meaning Through Form. In: Leslie P. Steffe/Jerry Gale (Ed.): Constructivism in Education. Hillsdale, NJ/Hove, UK: Lawrence Erlbaum Associates, 341–54.
Altschull, J. Herbert (1990): Agenten der Macht. Die Welt der Nachrichtenmedien – eine kritische Studie. Konstanz: Universitätsverlag. [Agents of Power: The Media and Public Policy. Longman Publishers USA].
Arndt, Adolf (1966): Die Rolle der Massenmedien in der Demokratie. In: Martin Löffler (Ed.): Die Rolle der Massenmedien in der Demokratie. München/Berlin: Beck, 1–21.
Arnold, Rolf/Horst Siebert (2003): Konstruktivistische Erwachsenenbildung. Von der Deutung zur Konstruktion von Wirklichkeit. Baltmannsweiler: Schneider Verlag Hohengehren.
Attems, Rudolf (1996): Es lebe der Widerspruch! In: Alfred Gutschelhofer/J. Scheff (Ed.): Paradoxes Management. Widersprüche im Management – Management der Widersprüche. Wien: Linde, 523–48.
Bachem, Rolf (1979): Einführung in die Analyse politischer Texte. München: Oldenbourg.
Baecker, Dirk/Norbert Bolz/Wolfgang Hagen (2004): Über das Tempo der Massenmedien und die Langsamkeit ihrer Beobachter. In: Wolfgang Hagen (Ed.): Warum haben Sie keinen Fernseher, Herr Luhmann? Letzte Gespräche mit Niklas Luhmann. Dirk Baecker/Norbert Bolz/Wolfgang Hagen/Alexander Kluge. Berlin: Kulturverlag Kadmos, 109–44.
Baraldi, Claudio/Giancarlo Corsi/Elena Esposito (1997): GLU: Glossar zu Niklas Luhmanns Theorie sozialer Systeme. Frankfurt am Main: Suhrkamp.
Bardmann, Theodor M. (1991a): Vorwort. In: Theodor M. Bardmann/Heinz J. Kersting/H.-Christoph Vogel/Bernd Woltmann (Ed.): Irritation als Plan. Konstruktivistische Einredungen. Aachen: Kersting, 7–9.
Bardmann, Theodor M. (1991b): Der zweite Doppelpunkt. Systemtheoretische und gesellschaftstheoretische Anmerkungen zur politischen Steuerung. In: Theodor M. Bardmann/Heinz J. Kersting/H.-Christoph Vogel/Bernd Woltmann (Ed.): Irritation als Plan. Konstruktivistische Einredungen. Aachen: Kersting, 10–31.
Bardmann, Theodor M. (1997): Unterscheide! Ein Vorwort. In: Theodor M. Bardmann: Unterscheide! Konstruktivistische Perspektiven in Theorie und Praxis. Aachen: Kersting, 7–20.
Bardmann, Theordor M./Torsten Groth (2001): Die Organisation der Organisation. Eine Einleitung. In: Theordor M. Bardmann/Torsten Groth (Ed.): Zirkuläre Positionen 3. Organisation, Management und Beratung. Wiesbaden: Westdeutscher Verlag, 7–20.
Baum, Achim/Armin Scholl (2000): Wahrheit und Wirklichkeit. Was kann die Journalismusforschung zur journalistischen Ethik beitragen? In: Christian Schicha/Carsten Brosda (Ed.): Medienethik zwischen Theorie und Praxis. Normen für die Kommunikationsgesellschaft. Münster: LIT, 90–108.
Beck, Ulrich/Wolfgang Bonß (1989): Verwissenschaftlichung ohne Aufklärung? Zum Strukturwandel von Sozialwissenschaft und Praxis. In: Ulrich Beck/Wolfgang Bonß (Ed.):

Weder Sozialtechnologie noch Aufklärung? Analysen zur Verwendung sozialwissenschaftlichen Wissens. Frankfurt am Main: Suhrkamp, 7-45.

Bentele, Günther (1993): Wie wirklich ist die Medienwirklichkeit? Einige Anmerkungen zum Konstruktivismus und Realismus in der Kommunikationswissenschaft. In: Günther Bentele/Manfred Rühl (Ed.): Theorien öffentlicher Kommunikation. Problemfelder, Positionen, Perspektiven. München: Ölschläger, 152-71.

Bentele, Günther/Manfred Rühl (Ed.) (1993): Theorien öffentlicher Kommunikation. Problemfelder, Positionen, Perspektiven. München: Ölschläger.

Berger, Peter L./Thomas Luckmann (1997): Die gesellschaftliche Konstruktion der Wirklichkeit. Eine Theorie der Wissenssoziologie (reprint of 5th edition). Frankfurt am Main: Fischer. [The Social Construction of Reality: A Treatise in the Sociology of Knowledge, Penguin Group].

Blöbaum, Bernd (2000): Zwischen Redaktion und Reflexion. Integration von Theorie und Praxis in der Journalistenausbildung. Münster: LIT.

Boghossian, Paul (1997, January 24): Sokals Jux und seine Lehren. Der postmoderne Schwindel – über den Niedergang wissenschaftlicher Standards und den Verlust intellektueller Verantwortung. In: Die Zeit. No. 5, 49-50.

Bohm, David (1998): Der Dialog. Das offene Gespräch am Ende der Diskussion. Herausgegeben von Lee Nichol. Stuttgart: Klett-Cotta. [On Dialogue, Routledge Classics].

Böhme, Gernot (1998): Der Typ Sokrates (2nd ed.). Frankfurt am Main: Suhrkamp.

Bolz, Norbert (1993): Am Ende der Gutenberg-Galaxis. Die neuen Kommunikationsverhältnisse. München: Fink.

Bolz, Norbert (2001): Weltkommunikation. München: Fink.

Bolz, Norbert (2005): Blindflug mit Zuschauer. München: Fink.

Boventer, Hermann (1992): Der Journalist in Platons Höhle. Zur Kritik des Konstruktivismus. In: Communicatio Socialis, 25 (2), 157-67.

Breed, Warren (1973): Soziale Kontrolle in der Redaktion: eine funktionale Analyse. In: Jörg Aufermann/Hans Bohrmann/Rolf Sülzer (Ed.): Gesellschaftliche Kommunikation und Information. Forschungsrichtungen und Problemstellungen. Ein Arbeitsbuch zur Massenkommunikation. Frankfurt am Main: Athenäum, 356-78.

Bresser, Klaus (1992): Was nun? Über Fernsehen, Moral und Journalisten. Hamburg/Zürich: Luchterhand Literaturverlag.

Bucher, Hans-Jürgen (2005): Verständlichkeit. In: Siegfried Weischenberg/Hans J. Kleinsteuber/Bernhard Poerksen (Ed.): Handbuch Journalismus und Medien. Konstanz: UVK, 464-70.

Buchloh, Stephan (2003): Eingriffe in die Freiheit des Journalismus und der Kunst. Eine Typologie von Zensurformen. In: Wolfgang Donsbach/Olaf Jandura (Ed.): Chancen und Gefahren der Mediendemokratie. Konstanz: UVK, 82-94.

Burkart, Roland (1999): Alter Wein in neuen Schläuchen? Anmerkungen zur Konstruktivismus-Debatte in der Publizistik- und Kommunikationswissenschaft. In: Gebhard Rusch/Siegfried J. Schmidt (Ed.): Konstruktivismus in der Medien- und Kommunikationswissenschaft. DELFIN 1997. Frankfurt am Main: Suhrkamp, 55-72.

Cissna, Kenneth N./Rob Anderson (2002): Moments of Meeting. Buber, Rogers, and the Potential for Public Dialogue. Albany, NY: State University of New York Press.

Dayan, Daniel/Elihu Katz (1994): Media Events. The Live Broadcasting of History. Cambridge, MA/London: Harvard University Press.

Debatin, Bernhard (1997): Ethische Grenzen oder Grenze der Ethik? Überlegungen zur Steuerungs- und Reflexionsfunktion der Medienethik. In: Günther Bentele/Michael Haller (Ed.): Aktuelle Entstehung von Öffentlichkeit. Akteure – Strukturen – Veränderungen. Konstanz: UVK Medien, 281-90.

Debatin, Bernhard (2002): Zwischen theoretischer Begründung und praktischer Anwendung: Medienethik auf dem Weg zur kommunikationswissenschaftlichen Teildisziplin. In: Publizistik, 47 (3), 259-64.

Dieckmann, Walther (1964): Information oder Überredung. Zum Wortgebrauch der politischen Werbung in Deutschland seit der Französischen Revolution. Marburg: Elwert.

Diekmann, Andrea (2004): Empirische Sozialforschung: Grundlagen, Methoden, Anwendungen (12th ed.). Reinbek bei Hamburg: Rowohlt.
Donges, Patrick (2005): Medialisierung der Politik—Vorschlag einer Differenzierung. In: Patrick Rössler/Friedrich Krotz (Ed.): Mythen der Mediengesellschaft—The Media Society and its Myths. Konstanz: UVK, 321-39.
Donsbach, Wolfgang (2005): Rollenselbstverständnis. In: Siegfried Weischenberg/Hans J. Kleinsteuber/Bernhard Poerksen (Ed.): Handbuch Journalismus und Medien. Konstanz: UVK, 415-20.
Eckoldt, Matthias (2002): Von der Lehrbarkeit des Schreibens. Umsetzung des Studienmoduls 'Schreibpraxis'. In: Matthias Schneider (Ed.): Schreiben lehren und Schreiben lernen an der Universität. Greifswald: Ernst-Moritz-Arndt-Universität, 18-24.
Ernst, Heiko (2000): Die Ausweitung der Spielzone. Borderline-Journalismus: Zwischen Wahrheit und Dichtung. In: Message, 2 (3), 64-7.
Fischer, Hans Rudi (1992): Zum Ende der großen Entwürfe. Eine Einführung. In: Hans Rudi Fischer/Arnold Retzer/Jochen Schweitzer (Ed.): Das Ende der großen Entwürfe. Frankfurt am Main: Suhrkamp, 9-34.
Fischer, Hans Rudi (1993): Information, Kommunikation und Sprache. Fragen eines Beobachters. In: Hans Rudi Fischer (Ed.): Autopoiesis. Eine Theorie im Brennpunkt der Kritik (2nd rev. ed.). Heidelberg: Carl-Auer-Systeme, 67-97.
Fleck, Ludwik (1983): Erfahrung und Tatsache. Gesammelte Aufsätze. Mit einer Einleitung hg. von Lothar Schäfer und Thomas Schnelle. Frankfurt am Main: Suhrkamp.
Fleck, Ludwik (1993): Entstehung und Entwicklung einer wissenschaftlichen Tatsache. Einführung in die Lehre vom Denkstil und Denkkollektiv. Mit einer Einleitung hg. von Lothar Schäfer und Thomas Schnelle (2nd ed.). Frankfurt am Main: Suhrkamp. [Genesis and Development of a Scientific Fact, University of Chicago Press].
Floyd, Christiane (1997): Das Mögliche ermöglichen: Zur Praxis der Realitätskonstruktion am Beispiel Softwareentwicklung. In: Albert Müller/Karl H. Müller/Friedrich Stadler (Ed.): Konstruktivismus und Kognitionswissenschaft. Kulturelle Wurzeln und Ergebnisse. Heinz von Foerster gewidmet. Wien/New York: Springer, 107-24.
Foerster, Heinz von (1981): Gregory Bateson. In: The Esalen Catalogue, 20 (1), 35.
Foerster, Heinz von (1993a): Wissen und Gewissen. Versuch einer Brücke. Hg. von Siegfried J. Schmidt. Frankfurt am Main: Suhrkamp.
Foerster, Heinz von (1993b): KybernEthik. Berlin: Merve Verlag.
Foerster, Heinz von (1993c): Das Gleichnis vom Blinden Fleck. Über das Sehen im Allgemeinen. In: Gerhard Johann Lischka (Ed.): Der entfesselte Blick. Symposion, Workshops, Ausstellung. Bern: Benteli, 15-47.
Foerster, Heinz von (1994): Das Konstruieren einer Wirklichkeit. In: Paul Watzlawick (Ed.): Die erfundene Wirklichkeit. Wie wissen wir, was wir zu wissen glauben? Beiträge zum Konstruktivismus (8th ed.). München/Zürich: Piper, 39-60. [THE INVENTED REALITY: How Do We Know What We Believe We Know? Norton].
Foerster, Heinz von/Bernhard Poerksen (2002): Understanding Systems. Conversations on Epistemology and Ethics. Heidelberg/New York: Carl-Auer-Systeme Verlag/Kluwer Academic Publication/Plenum Publishers.
Foerster, Heinz von/Monika Bröcker (2002): Teil der Welt. Fraktale einer Ethik. Ein Drama in drei Akten. Heidelberg: Carl-Auer-Systeme.
Frerichs, Stefan (2000): Bausteine einer systemischen Nachrichtentheorie. Konstruktives Chaos und chaotische Konstruktionen. Wiesbaden: Westdeutscher Verlag.
Frerichs, Stefan (2005): Gatekeeping. In: Siegfried Weischenberg/Hans J. Kleinsteuber/Bernhard Poerksen (Ed.): Handbuch Journalismus und Medien. Konstanz: UVK, 74-7.
Fuchs, Peter (2000): Die Skepsis der Systeme. Zur Unterscheidung von Theorie und Praxis. In: Helga Gripp-Hagelstange (Ed.): Niklas Luhmanns Denken. Interdisziplinäre Einflüsse und Wirkungen. Konstanz: UVK, 53-74.
Garrison, Jim/Stefan Neubert (2005): Bausteine für eine Theorie des kreativen Zuhörens. In: Reinhard Voß (Ed.): LernLust und EigenSinn. Systemisch-konstruktivistische Lernwelten. Heidelberg: Carl-Auer-Systeme, 109-20.
Gerhards, Jürgen (2002): Öffentlichkeit. In: Irene Neverla/Elke Grittmann/Monika Pater (Ed.): Grundlagentexte zur Journalistik. Konstanz: UVK, 128-36.

Gipper, Helmut (1972): Gibt es ein sprachliches Relativitätsprinzip? Untersuchungen zur Sapir-Whorf-Hypothese. Stuttgart: S. Fischer.

Glanville, Ranulph (2004): Second Order Cybernetics. Unpublished manuscript, 1–40.

Glasersfeld, Ernst von (1991): Fiktion und Realität aus der Perspektive des radikalen Konstruktivismus. In: Florian Rötzer/Peter Weibel (Ed.): Strategien des Scheins. Kunst, Computer, Medien. München: Boer, 161–75.

Glasersfeld, Ernst von (1996): Radikaler Konstruktivismus. Ideen, Ergebnisse, Probleme. Frankfurt am Main: Suhrkamp. [Radical Constructivism. A way of Knowing and Learning].

Glasersfeld, Ernst von (1997): Wege des Wissens. Konstruktivistische Erkundungen durch unser Denken. Heidelberg: Carl-Auer-Systeme.

Gloy, Karen (2004): Wahrheitstheorien. Eine Einführung. Tübingen/Basel: A. Francke.

Gödde, Ralf (1992): Radikaler Konstruktivismus und Journalismus. Die Berichterstattung über den Golfkrieg – Das Scheitern eines Wirklichkeitsmodells. In: Gebhard Rusch/Siegfried J. Schmidt (Ed.): Konstruktivismus: Geschichte und Anwendung. DELFIN 1992. Frankfurt am Main: Suhrkamp, 269–88.

Görke, Alexander (1998): Ohne Titel. [Email October 10, 1998]. Retrieved March 18, 2003 from http://www.sbg.ac.at/autojour/mailneu2.html#n46, 3–4.

Groß, Bernd (1981): Journalisten – Freunde des Hauses? Zur Problematik von Autonomie und Anpassung im Bereich der Massenmedien. Saarbrücken: Die Mitte.

Großmann, Brit (1999): Der Einfluss des Radikalen Konstruktivismus auf die Kommunikationswissenschaft. In: Gebhard Rusch/Siegfried J. Schmidt (Ed.): Konstruktivismus in der Medien- und Kommunikationswissenschaft. DELFIN 1997. Frankfurt am Main: Suhrkamp, 14–51.

Haas, Hannes (2005): Mediengattungen. In: Siegfried Weischenberg/Hans J. Kleinsteuber/Bernhard Poerksen (Ed.): Handbuch Journalismus und Medien. Konstanz: UVK, 225–9.

Habermas, Jürgen (1973): Wahrheitstheorien. In: Helmut Fahrenbach (Ed.): Wirklichkeit und Reflexion. Walter Schulz zum 60. Geburtstag. Pfullingen: Neske, 211–65.

Hachmeister, Lutz (1992): Das Gespenst des Radikalen Konstruktivismus. Zur Analyse des Funkollegs 'Medien und Kommunikation'. In: Rundfunk und Fernsehen, 40 (1), 5–21.

Haller, Michael (1987): Wie wissenschaftlich ist der Wissenschaftsjournalismus? Zum Problem wissenschaftsbezogener Arbeitsmethoden im tagesaktuellen Journalismus. In: Publizistik, 32 (3), 305–19.

Haller, Michael (2000): Die zwei Kulturen. Journalismustheorie und journalistische Praxis. In: Martin Löffelholz (Ed.): Theorien des Journalismus. Ein diskursives Handbuch. Wiesbaden: Westdeutscher Verlag, 101–22.

Hannappel, Hans/Hartmut Melenk (1990): Alltagssprache. Semantische Grundbegriffe und Analysebeispiele (unchanged reprint of the 2nd edition 1984). München: Fink.

Hansen, Sandra (1996): Motive einer Kybernetik zweiter Ordnung. Ein Beitrag zur theoretischen Reflexion der Sozialen Arbeit. In: Theodor M. Bardmann/Sandra Hansen: Die Kybernetik der Sozialarbeit. Ein Theorieangebot. Aachen: Kersting, 35–101.

Hartmann, Frank (2000): Medienphilosophie. Wien: WUV.

Heims, S[teve] J[oshua] (1991): The Cybernetics Group. Cambridge/London: MIT Press.

Hejl, Peter M. (1995): Ethik, Konstruktivismus und gesellschaftliche Selbstregelung. In: Gebhard Rusch/Siegfried J. Schmidt (Ed.): Konstruktivismus und Ethik. DELFIN 1995. Frankfurt am Main: Suhrkamp, 28–121.

Hennig, Jörg (2005): Mediensprache. In: Siegfried Weischenberg/Hans J. Kleinsteuber/Bernhard Poerksen (Ed.): Handbuch Journalismus und Medien. Konstanz: UVK, 270–75.

Heringer, Hans Jürgen (1990): 'Ich gebe Ihnen mein Ehrenwort.' Politik, Sprache, Moral. München: Beck.

Hermanns, Fritz (1982): Brisante Wörter. Zur lexikographischen Behandlung parteisprachlicher Wörter und Wendungen in Wörterbüchern der deutschen Gegenwartssprache. In: Herbert Ernst Wiegand (Ed.): Studien zur neuhochdeutschen Lexikographie II. Hildesheim/New York: Olms, 87–108.

Hickethier, Knut (2002): Das Erzählen der Welt in den Fernsehnachrichten. Überlegungen zu einer Narrationstheorie der Nachricht. In: Irene Neverla/Elke Grittmann/Monika Pater (Ed.): Grundlagentexte zur Journalistik. Konstanz: UVK, 657-81.
Hillebrandt, Anke/Heiko Hungerige (1997); Überlegungen zu einer konstruktivistischen Methodologie. In: Journal für Psychologie, 5 (2), 3-20.
Hohlfeld, Ralf (2002): Journalismus für das Publikum? Zur Bedeutung angewandter Medienforschung für die Praxis. In: Ralf Hohlfeld/Klaus Meier/Christoph Neuberger (Ed.): Innovationen im Journalismus. Forschung für die Praxis. Münster: LIT, 155-201.
Hömberg, Walter (2002): Nachrichten-Dichter. Journalismus zwischen Fakten und Fälschung. In: Ute Nawratil/Philomen Schönhagen/Heinz Starkulla jr. (Ed.): Medien und Mittler sozialer Kommunikation. Beiträge zu Theorie, Geschichte und Kritik von Journalismus und Publizistik. Festschrift für Hans Wagner. Leipzig: Leipziger Universitätsverlag, 289-306.
Horster, Detlef (1994): Das Sokratische Gespräch in Theorie und Praxis. Opladen: Leske + Budrich.
Hug, Theo (2004): Konstruktivistische Diskurse und qualitative Forschungsstrategien. Überlegungen am Beispiel des Projekts *Global Media Generations*. In: Sibylle Moser (Ed.): Konstruktivistisch Forschen. Methodologie, Methoden, Beispiele. Wiesbaden: VS Verlag für Sozialwissenschaften, 121-44.
Humboldt, Wilhelm von (1964): Über die innere und äußere Organisation der höheren wissenschaftlichen Anstalten in Berlin. In: Wilhelm von Humboldt: Schriften zur Politik und zum Bildungswesen. Werke in fünf Bänden IV. Hg. von Andreas Flitner und Klaus Giel. Darmstadt: Wissenschaftliche Buchgesellschaft, 255-66.
Hungerige, Heiko/Kariem Sabbouh (1995): Let's Talk About Ethics. Ethik und Moral im konstruktivistischen Diskurs. In: Gebhard Rusch/Siegfried J. Schmidt (Ed.): Konstruktivismus und Ethik. DELFIN 1995. Frankfurt am Main: Suhrkamp, 123-73.
Kahl, Reinhard (2001): Lob des Fehlers. In: Spiegelreporter 3, 78-81.
Kahl, Reinhard (2004): Plädoyer für eine pädagogische Währungsreform. Ein Essay zum Film. In: Reinhard Kahl: Treibhäuser der Zukunft. Wie in Deutschland Schulen gelingen. Archiv der Zukunft, 103-30.
Kant, Immanuel (1983): Über Pädagogik. In: Immanuel Kant. Werke in sechs Bänden. Hg. von Wilhelm Weischedel. Band VI: Schriften zur Anthropologie, Geschichtsphilosophie, Politik und Pädagogik. Darmstadt: Wissenschaftliche Buchgesellschaft, 697-761.
Karmasin, Matthias/Carsten Winter (2002): Medienethik vor der Herausforderung der globalen Kommerzialisierung von Medienkultur: Probleme und Perspektiven. In: Matthias Karmasin (Ed.): Medien und Ethik. Stuttgart: Philipp Reclam jun, 9-37.
Kelle, Udo/Christian Erzberger (1999): Integration qualitativer und quantitativer Methoden. Methodologische Modelle und ihre Bedeutung für die Forschungspraxis. In: Kölner Zeitschrift für Soziologie und Sozialpsychologie, 51 (3), 509-31.
Kepplinger, Hans Mathias (1989): Theorien der Nachrichtenauswahl als Theorien der Realität. In: Aus Politik und Zeitgeschichte. Beilage zur Wochenzeitung *Das Parlament*. B 15/89, 3-16.
Kepplinger, Hans Mathias (1993): Erkenntnistheorie und Forschungspraxis des Konstruktivismus. In: Günther Bentele/Manfred Rühl (Ed.): Theorien öffentlicher Kommunikation. Problemfelder, Positionen, Perspektiven. München: Ölschläger, 118-25.
Klaus, Elisabeth/Lünenborg, Margret (2002): Journalismus: Fakten, die unterhalten — Fiktionen, die Wirklichkeiten schaffen. Anforderungen an eine Journalistik, die dem Wandel des Journalismus Rechnung trägt. In: Irene Neverla/Elke Grittmann/Monika Pater (Ed.): Grundlagentexte zur Journalistik. Konstanz: UVK, 100-13.
Klein, Josef (1998): Politische Kommunikation — Sprachwissenschaftliche Perspektiven. In: Otfried Jarren/Ulrich Sarcinelli/Ulrich Saxer (Ed.): Politische Kommunikation in der demokratischen Gesellschaft. Ein Handbuch mit Lexikonteil. Opladen/Wiesbaden: Westdeutscher Verlag, 186-210.
Knorr-Cetina, Karin (1989): Spielarten des Konstruktivismus. Einige Notizen und Anmerkungen. In: Soziale Welt, 40 (1/2), 86-96.
Knorr-Cetina, Karin (1992): Zur Unterkomplexität der Differenzierungstheorie. Empirische Anfragen an die Systemtheorie. In: Zeitschrift für Soziologie, 21 (6), 406-19.

Krainer, Larissa (2001): Medien und Ethik. Zur Organisation medienethischer Entscheidungsprozesse. München: KoPäd.
Krainer, Larissa (2002): Medienethik als angewandte Ethik. Zur Organisation ethischer Entscheidungsprozesse. In: Matthias Karmasin (Ed.): Medien und Ethik. Stuttgart: Philipp Reclam jun, 156–74.
Kramaschki, Lutz (1995): Wie universalistisch kann die Moralphilosophie diskutieren? Hinweise aus radikalkonstruktivistischer Sicht. In: Gebhard Rusch/Siegfried J. Schmidt (Ed.): Konstruktivismus und Ethik. DELFIN 1995. Frankfurt am Main: Suhrkamp, 249–275.
Kretzenbacher, Heinz L. (1995): Wie durchsichtig ist die Sprache der Wissenschaften? In: Heinz L. Kretzenbacher/Harald Weinrich (Ed.): Linguistik der Wissenschaftssprache. Berlin/New York: de Gruyter, 15–39.
Krippendorff, Klaus (1990): Eine häretische Kommunikation über Kommunikation über Kommunikation über Realität. In: Delfin, 13 (2), 52–67.
Krippendorff, Klaus (1993): Schritte zu einer konstruktivistischen Erkenntnistheorie der Massenkommunikation. In: Günther Bentele/Manfred Rühl (Ed.): Theorien öffentlicher Kommunikation. Problemfelder, Positionen, Perspektiven. München: Ölschläger, 19–51.
Krippendorff, Klaus (1994): Der verschwundene Bote. Metaphern und Modelle der Kommunikation. In: Klaus Merten/Siegfried J. Schmidt/Siegfried Weischenberg (Ed.): Die Wirklichkeit der Medien. Opladen: Westdeutscher Verlag, 79–113.
Krippendorff, Klaus (1995): Undoing Power. In: Critical Studies in Mass Communication, 12 (2), 101–32.
Krippendorff, Klaus (2004): Content Analysis. An Introduction to Its Methodology. Second Edition. Thousand Oaks u. a.: Sage.
Kummer, Tom (1997): Los Angeles. Die tägliche Jagd nach der Wirklichkeit. München: dtv.
Kummer, Tom (2004): Email: May 25, 2005. Unpublished manuscript 1–2.
Kummer, Tom (2005): Die Matrix der Wirklichkeitsentwürfe. In: Cover. No. 5, 10–12.
Landmann, Michael (1982): Philosophische Anthropologie. Menschliche Selbstdarstellung in Geschichte und Gegenwart (5th rev. ed.). Berlin/New York: de Gruyter.
Lenzen, Dieter (1999): Erziehungswissenschaft. Was sie kann, was sie will. Reinbek bei Hamburg: Rowohlt.
Lévy, Pierre (1996): Cyberkultur. Universalität ohne Totalität. In: Stefan Bollmann/Christiane Heibach (Ed.): Kursbuch Internet. Anschlüsse an Wirtschaft und Politik, Wissenschaft und Kultur. Mannheim: Bollmann, 56–82.
Liebert, Wolf-Andreas (2005): Wissenskonstruktion durch kooperatives Schreiben in Netzwerkmedien. In: Reinhard Voß (Ed.): LernLust und EigenSinn. Systemisch-konstruktivistische Lernwelten. Heidelberg: Carl-Auer-Systeme, 244–56.
Lindemann, Holger (2006): Konstruktivismus und Pädagogik. Grundlagen, Modelle, Perspektiven. München/Basel: Reinhardt.
Lippmann, Walter (1929): Public Opinion. New York: Macmillan.
Loosen, Wiebke (2004): Konstruktive Prozesse bei der Analyse von (Medien-)Inhalten. Inhaltsanalyse im Kontext qualitativer, quantitativer und hermeneutischer Verfahren. In: Sibylle Moser (Ed.): Konstruktivistisch Forschen. Methodologie, Methoden, Beispiele. Wiesbaden: VS Verlag für Sozialwissenschaften, 93–120.
Loosen, Wiebke (2005): Methoden der Kommunikationsforschung. In: Siegfried Weischenberg/Hans J. Kleinsteuber/Bernhard Poerksen (Ed.): Handbuch Journalismus und Medien. Konstanz: UVK, 299–306.
Loosen, Wiebke/Armin Scholl/Jens Woelke (2002): Systemtheoretische und konstruktivistische Methodologie. In: Armin Scholl (Ed.): Systemtheorie und Konstruktivismus in der Kommunikationswissenschaft. Konstanz: UVK, 37–65.
Luhmann, Niklas (1987): Archimedes und wir. Interviews. Hg. von Dirk Baecker und Georg Stanitzek. Berlin: Merve.
Luhmann, Niklas (1994a): Der 'Radikale Konstruktivismus' als Theorie der Massenmedien? Bemerkungen zu einer irreführenden Debatte. In: Comunicatio Socialis, 27 (1), 7–12.
Luhmann, Niklas (1994b): Die Wissenschaft der Gesellschaft (2nd ed.). Frankfurt am Main: Suhrkamp.

Luhmann, Niklas (1995): Die Behandlung von Irritationen: Abweichung oder Neuheit? In: Niklas Luhmann: Gesellschaftsstruktur und Semantik. Studien zur Wissenssoziologie der modernen Gesellschaft. Band 4. Frankfurt am Main: Suhrkamp, 55–100.

Luhmann, Niklas (2002a): Das Erziehungssystem der Gesellschaft. Hg. von Dieter Lenzen. Frankfurt am Main: Suhrkamp.

Luhmann, Niklas (2002b): Einführung in die Systemtheorie. Hg. von Dirk Baecker. Heidelberg: Carl-Auer-Systeme.

Luhmann, Niklas (2004): Die Realität der Massenmedien (3rd ed.). Wiesbaden: VS Verlag für Sozialwissenschaften.

Luhmann, Niklas (2005): Theoretische und praktische Probleme der anwendungsbezogenen Sozialwissenschaften. In: Niklas Luhmann: Soziologische Aufklärung 3. Soziales System, Gesellschaft, Organisation (4th ed.) Wiesbaden: VS Verlag für Sozialwissenschaften, 369–85.

Mack, Julian (2001): Softwareentwicklung als Expedition. Entwicklung eines Leitbildes und einer Vorgehensweise für die professionelle Softwareentwicklung. Berlin: Logos.

Maier, Michaela (2003): Der Wert von Nachrichten. Ein Modell zur Validierung von Nachrichtenfaktoren. In: Georg Ruhrmann/Jens Woelke/Michaela Maier/Nicole Diehlmann: Der Wert von Nachrichten im deutschen Fernsehen. Ein Modell zur Validierung von Nachrichtenfaktoren. Opladen: Leske + Budrich, 27–50.

Maresch, Rudolf (2000): Kummer über Kummer. In: Telepolis. Retrieved November 29, 2005 from www.heise.de/tp/deutsch/kolumnen/mar/8205/1.html, 1–5.

Margreiter, Reinhard (2003): Medien/Philosophie: ein Kippbild. In: Stefan Münker/Alexander Roesler/Mike Sandbothe (Ed.): Medienphilosophie. Beiträge zur Klärung eines Begriffs. Frankfurt am Main: Fischer, 150–71.

Maturana, Humberto R. (1985): Erkennen. Die Organisation und Verkörperung von Wirklichkeit. Ausgewählte Arbeiten zur biologischen Epistemologie (2nd rev. ed.). Braunschweig/Wiesbaden: Vieweg.

Maturana, Humberto R. (1998): Biologie der Realität. Frankfurt am Main: Suhrkamp.

Maturana, Humberto R./Francisco J. Varela (1992): Der Baum der Erkenntnis. Die biologischen Wurzeln des menschlichen Erkennens (4th ed.). München: Goldmann. [Tree of Knowledge, Shambhala].

Maturana, Humberto R./Bernhard Poerksen (2004): From Being to Doing. The Origins of the Biology of Cognition. Heidelberg: Carl-Auer-Systeme.

Mayring, Philipp (2003): Qualitative Inhaltsanalyse. Grundlagen und Techniken (8th ed.). Weinheim/Basel: Beltz.

Meckel, Miriam (2001): Die globale Agenda. Kommunikation und Globalisierung. Wiesbaden: Westdeutscher Verlag.

Merten, Klaus (1993): Kommentar zu Klaus Krippendorff. In: Günther Bentele/Manfred Rühl (Ed.): Theorien öffentlicher Kommunikation. Problemfelder, Positionen, Perspektiven. München: Ölschläger, 52–5.

Merten, Klaus (1996): Reactivity in Content Analysis. In: Communications, 21 (1), 65–76.

Merten, Klaus/Siegfried J. Schmidt/Siegfried Weischenberg (Ed.) (1994): Die Wirklichkeit der Medien. Eine Einführung in die Kommunikationswissenschaft. Opladen: Westdeutscher Verlag.

Meuron, Hannah de (2004): Tom Kummer. In: Faces, 5, 34–5.

Mitterer, Josef (1993): Das Jenseits der Philosophie. Wider das dualistische Erkenntnisprinzip (2nd rev. ed.). Wien: Passagen.

Mitterer, Josef (2000a): Der Radikale Konstruktivismus. 'What difference does it make?' In: Hans Rudi Fischer/Siegfried J. Schmidt (Ed.): Wirklichkeit und Welterzeugung. In memoriam Nelson Goodman. Heidelberg: Carl-Auer-Systeme, 60–4.

Mitterer, Josef (2000b): Aus objektiver Distanz. Notizen zum richtigen Abstand. In: Guido Zurstiege (Ed.): Festschrift für die Wirklichkeit. Wiesbaden: Westdeutscher Verlag, 243–8.

Mitterer, Josef (2001): Die Flucht aus der Beliebigkeit. Frankfurt am Main: Fischer.

Möhn, Dieter (1990): Das gruppenbezogene Wörterbuch. In: Franz Josef Hausmann/Oskar Reichmann/Herbert Ernst Wiegand/Ladislav Zgusta (Ed.): Wörterbücher. Ein internationales Handbuch zur Lexikographie. 2. Teilband. Berlin/New York: de Gruyter, 1523–31.

Möhn, Dieter (1998): Fachsprachen und Gruppensprachen. In: Lothar Hoffmann/Hartwig Kalverkämper/Herbert Ernst Wiegand (Ed.): Fachsprachen. Ein internationales Handbuch zur Fachsprachenforschung und Terminologiewissenschaft = Languages for special purposes. Berlin/New York: de Gruyter, 168-81.

Möhn, Dieter/Roland Pelka (1984): Fachsprachen. Eine Einführung. Tübingen: Niemeyer.

Morin, Edgar (2001): Seven Complex Lessons in Education for the Future. Paris: UNESCO Publishing.

Moser, Sibylle (2004): Konstruktivistisch Forschen? Prämissen und Probleme einer konstruktivistischen Methodologie. In: Sibylle Moser (Ed.): Konstruktivistisch Forschen. Methodologie, Methoden, Beispiele. Wiesbaden: VS Verlag für Sozialwissenschaften, 9-42.

Müller, Klaus (1996a): Erkenntnistheorie und Lerntheorie. Geschichte ihrer Wechselwirkung vom Repräsentationalismus über den Pragmatismus zum Konstruktivismus. In: Klaus Müller (Ed.): Konstruktivismus. Lehren–Lernen–Ästhetische Prozesse. Neuwied u. a.: Luchterhand, 24-70.

Müller, Klaus (1996b): Wege konstruktivistischer Lernkultur. In: Klaus Müller (Ed.): Konstruktivismus. Lehren, Lernen, Ästhetische Prozesse. Neuwied u. a.: Luchterhand, 71-115.

Münker, Stefan/Alexander Roesler/Mike Sandbothe (Ed.) (2003): Medienphilosophie. Beiträge zur Klärung eines Begriffs. Frankfurt am Main: Fischer.

Musil, Robert (1996): Der Mann ohne Eigenschaften. Roman (rev. ed.). Reinbeck bei Hamburg: Rowohlt.

Müssen, Peter (1995): 'Gnothi seauton'. Konstruktivismus und die sokratische Methode der Maieutik. Versuch über konstruktivistische Fragen zur Ethik. In: Gebhard Rusch/Siegfried J. Schmidt (Ed.): Konstruktivismus und Ethik. DELFIN 1995. Frankfurt am Main: Suhrkamp, 178-209.

Nabrings, Kirsten (1981): Sprachliche Varietäten. Tübingen: Narr.

Nassehi, Armin/Irmhild Saake (2002): Kontingenz: Methodisch verhindert oder beobachtet? Ein Beitrag zur Methodologie der qualitativen Sozialforschung. In: Zeitschrift für Soziologie, 31 (1), 66-86.

Neuberger, Christoph (1996): Journalismus als Problembearbeitung. Objektivität und Relevanz in der öffentlichen Kommunikation. Konstanz: UVK Medien.

Ott, Klaus/Annette Ramelsberger (2000 May, 27/28): Ein Mann und sein ganz besonderer Draht. In: Süddeutsche Zeitung. No. 122, 21-22.

Ott, Konrad (1995): Zum Verhältnis von Radikalem Konstruktivismus und Ethik. In: Gebhard Rusch/Siegfried J. Schmidt (Ed.): Konstruktivismus und Ethik. DELFIN 1995. Frankfurt am Main: Suhrkamp, 280-320.

Pätzold, Ulrich (2000): Journalismus und Journalistik. Definitionsproblem und theoretische Perspektive. In: Martin Löffelholz (Ed.): Theorien des Journalismus. Ein diskursives Handbuch. Wiesbaden: Westdeutscher Verlag, 417-28.

Pfeffer, Thomas (2004): Die (Re-)Konstruktion sozialer Phänomene durch 'zirkuläres Fragen'. In: Sibylle Moser (Ed.): Konstruktivistisch Forschen. Methodologie, Methoden, Beispiele. Wiesbaden: VS Verlag für Sozialwissenschaften, 67-92.

Pias, Claus (2003): Cybernetics/Kybernetik. The Macy-Conferences 1946-1953. Volume I/Band I. Transactions/Protokolle. Zürich/Berlin: Diaphanes.

Pohla, Anika (2003): Eine verbindliche normative Medienethik–ein unmögliches Unterfangen? In: Bernhard Debatin /Rüdiger Funiok (Ed.): Kommunikations- und Medienethik. Konstanz: UVK, 65-79.

Poerksen, Bernhard (2000): 'Journalismus macht aus allem Journalismus.' Im Gespräch mit Siegfried Weischenberg. In: Communicatio Socialis, 33 (2), 132-50.

Poerksen, Bernhard (2002a): 'In einer Welt der Simulation wird das Reale zur Obsession.' Im Gespräch mit Norbert Bolz. In: Communicatio Socialis, 35 (4), 439-58.

Poerksen, Bernhard (2002b): Konturen digitaler Kommunikationswelten. Leitunterscheidungen eines interdisziplinären Forschungsfeldes–eine Einführung. In: Communicatio Socialis, 35 (4), 410-38.

Poerksen, Bernhard (2004): The Certainty of Uncertainty–Dialogues Introducing Constructivism. Exeter: Imprint Academic.

Poerksen, Bernhard (2004a): Journalismus als Wirklichkeitskonstruktion. Grundlagen einer konstruktivistischen Journalismustheorie. In: Martin Löffelholz (Ed.): Theorien des Journalismus. Ein diskursives Handbuch (2nd revised and expanded edition). VS Verlag für Sozialwissenschaften, 335-47.
Poerksen, Bernhard (2004b): Das Problem der Grenze. Die hintergründige Aktualität des New Journalism—eine Einführung. In: Joan Kristin Bleicher/Bernhard Poerksen (Ed.): Grenzgänger. Formen des New Journalism, 15-28.
Poerksen, Bernhard (2004c): The Circular View of the World. In: Bernhard Poerksen (2004): The Certainty of Uncertainty—Dialogues Introducing Constructivism. Exeter: Imprint Academic, vii-xiv.
Poerksen, Bernhard (2004d): 'Wir können von der Wirklichkeit nur wissen, was sie *nicht* ist.' Paul Watzlawick über die Axiome der Kommunikation, den heimlichen Realismus einer psychiatrischen Diagnose und das konstruktivistische Lebensgefühl. In: Bernhard Poerksen (2004): The Certainty of Uncertainty—Dialogues Introducing Constructivism. Exeter: Imprint Academic, 211-31.
Poerksen, Bernhard (2004e): ‚Wir selbst sind Konstrukte'. Gerhard Roth über die Entstehung der Wirklichkeit im Gehirn, eine bewusstseinsunabhängige Realität und die Verbindung von Neurobiologie und Philosophie. In: In: Bernhard Poerksen (2004): The Certainty of Uncertainty—Dialogues Introducing Constructivism. Exeter: Imprint Academic, 139-65.
Poerksen, Bernhard (2004f): ‚Wir beginnen nie am Anfang.' Siegfried J Schmidt über das Individuum und die Gesellschaft, die Wirklichkeit der Medien und eine konstruktivistische Sicht der Empirie. In: Bernhard Poerksen (2004): The Certainty of Uncertainty—Dialogues Introducing Constructivism. Exeter: Imprint Academic, 166-88.
Poerksen, Bernhard (2004g): ‚In jedem Augenblick kann ich entscheiden, wer ich bin.' Heinz von Foerster über den Beobachter, das dialogische Leben und eine konstruktivistische Philosophie des Unterscheidens. In: Bernhard Poerksen (2004): The Certainty of Uncertainty—Dialogues Introducing Constructivism. Exeter: Imprint Academic, 19-45.
Poerksen, Bernhard (2004h): ‚Was im Kopf eines anderen vorgeht, können wir nie wissen.' Ernst von Glasersfeld über Wahrheit und Viabilität, Sprache und Erkenntnis und die Prämissen einer konstruktivistischen Pädagogik. In: Bernhard Poerksen (2004): The Certainty of Uncertainty—Dialogues Introducing Constructivism. Exeter: Imprint Academic, 46-69.
Poerksen, Bernhard (2004i): ‚Wahr ist, was funktioniert.' Francisco J. Varela über Kognitionswissenschaft und Buddhismus, die untrennbare Verbindung von Subjekt und Objekt und die Übertreibungen des Konstruktivismus. In: Bernhard Poerksen (2004): The Certainty of Uncertainty—Dialogues Introducing Constructivism. Exeter: Imprint Academic, 112-38.
Poerksen, Bernhard (2004j): 'Die Freiheit, das Neue zu wagen.' Helm Stierlin über Schuld und Verantwortung im systemischen und konstruktivistischen Denken, die Dialektik der Beziehungen und das Ethos des Therapeuten. In: Bernhard Poerksen (2004): The Certainty of Uncertainty—Dialogues Introducing Constructivism. Exeter: Imprint Academic, 189-210.
Poerksen, Bernhard (2005a): Die Konstruktion von Feindbildern. Zum Sprachgebrauch in neonazistischen Medien (2nd expanded ed.). Wiesbaden: VS Verlag für Sozialwissenschaften.
Poerksen, Bernhard (2005b): Die Form und die Botschaft—Die kommunikative Matrix einer konstruktivistischen Hochschuldidaktik. In: Reinhard Voß (Ed.): LernLust und EigenSinn. Systemisch-konstruktivistische Lernwelten. Heidelberg: Carl-Auer-Systeme, 224-32.
Poerksen, Bernhard (2005c): Medienethik. In: Siegfried Weischenberg/Hans J. Kleinsteuber/Bernhard Poerksen (Ed.): Handbuch Journalismus und Medien. Konstanz: UVK, 211-20.
Poerksen, Uwe (1988): Plastikwörter. Die Sprache einer internationalen Diktatur. Stuttgart: Klett-Cotta. [Plastic Words: The Tyranny of a Modular Language. The Pennsylvania State University Press 1995].
Poerksen, Uwe (1997): Weltmarkt der Bilder. Eine Philosophie der Visiotype. Stuttgart: Klett-Cotta.
Queneau, Raymond (1990): Stilübungen. Frankfurt am Main: Suhrkamp.

Reich, Kersten (2002a): Konstruktivistische Didaktik. Lehren und Lernen aus interaktionistischer Sicht. Neuwied/Kriftel: Luchterhand.

Reich, Kersten (2002b): Systemisch-konstruktivistische Pädagogik. Einführung in Grundlagen einer interaktionistisch-konstruktivistischen Pädagogik (4th rev. ed.). Neuwied/Kriftel: Luchterhand.

Reus, Gunter (2002): 'Zum Tanze freigegeben.' Fiktion im seriösen Journalismus – ein illegitimes Verfahren? In: Achim Baum/Siegfried J. Schmidt (Ed.): Fakten und Fiktionen. Über den Umgang mit Medienwirklichkeiten. Konstanz: UVK, 77–89.

Reus, Gunter (2004): Mit doppelter Zunge. Tom Kummer und der New Journalism. In: Joan Kristin Bleicher/Bernhard Poerksen (Ed.): Grenzgänger. Formen des New Journalism. Wiesbaden: VS Verlag für Sozialwissenschaften, 249–66.

Rigotti, Francesca (1987): Der Chirurg des Staates. Zur politischen Metaphorik Mussolinis. In: Politische Vierteljahresschrift, 28 (3), 280–92.

Rorty, Richard (1992): Kontingenz, Ironie und Solidarität. Frankfurt am Main: Suhrkamp. [Contingency, Irony, and Solidarity, Cambridge University Press].

Roth, Gerhard (1997): Das Gehirn und seine Wirklichkeit. Kognitive Neurobiologie und ihre philosophischen Konsequenzen. Frankfurt am Main: Suhrkamp.

Rotthaus, Wilhelm (2000): Wozu erziehen? Entwurf einer systemischen Erziehung (3rd ed.). Heidelberg: Carl-Auer-Systeme.

Rühl, Manfred (1978): Journalistische Professionalisierung. Probleme der Integration von Theorie und Praxis. In: Walter Hömberg (Ed.): Journalistenausbildung. Modelle, Erfahrungen, Analysen. München: Ölschläger, 95–107.

Rühl, Manfred (2002): Wissenschaft kann nicht einer herrischen Praxis als Magd oder Hebamme dienen. In: Aviso. No. 31, 3–4.

Ruhrmann, Georg (1994): Ereignis, Nachricht und Rezipient. In: Klaus Merten/Siegfried J. Schmidt/Siegfried Weischenberg (Ed.): Die Wirklichkeit der Medien. Opladen: Westdeutscher Verlag, 237–56.

Ruhrmann, Georg (2005): Nachrichtenselektion. In: Siegfried Weischenberg/Hans J. Kleinsteuber/Bernhard Poerksen (Ed.): Handbuch Journalismus und Medien. Konstanz: UVK, 317–20.

Ruß-Mohl, Stephan (1985): Journalistik-,,Wissenschaft' und Wissenschafts-Journalistik. Anmerkungen zu Theorie und Praxis des Wissenschaftsjournalismus. In: Publizistik, 30 (2/3), 265–79.

Ruß-Mohl, Stephan (1987): Hochschulgebundene Journalistenausbildung. Von der Problemverstaatlichung zur Problemlösung? In: Publizistik, 32 (1), 5–22.

Sale, Joanna E. M./Lynne H. Lohfeld/Kevin Brazil (2002): Revisiting the Quantitative-Qualitative Debate: Implications for Mixed-Methods Research. In: Quality & Quantity, 36 (1), 43–53.

Sandbothe, Mike (2001): Pragmatische Medienphilosophie. Grundlegung einer neuen Disziplin im Zeitalter des Internet. Weilerswist: Velbrück Wissenschaft.

Sandbothe, Mike (2003): Der Vorrang der Medien vor der Philosophie. In: Stefan Münker/Alexander Roesler/Mike Sandbothe (Ed.): Medienphilosophie. Beiträge zur Klärung eines Begriffs. Frankfurt am Main: Fischer, 185–97.

Sandbothe, Mike/Ludwig Nagl (2005): Systematische Medienphilosophie. Berlin: Akademie Verlag.

Saxer, Ulrich (1992): Thesen zur Kritik des Konstruktivismus. In: Communicatio Socialis, 25 (2), 178–83.

Saxer, Ulrich (1993): Fortschritt als Rückschritt? Konstruktivismus als Epistemologie einer Medientheorie. Kommentar zu Klaus Krippendorff. In: Günther Bentele/Manfred Rühl (Ed.): Theorien öffentlicher Kommunikation. Problemfelder, Positionen, Perspektiven. München: Ölschläger, 65–73.

Saxer, Ulrich (1999a): Journalistische Ethik im elektronischen Zeitalter eine Chimäre? In: Adrian Holderegger (Ed.): Kommunikations- und Medienethik. Interdisziplinäre Perspektiven. 2nd revised and expanded edition of 'Ethik der Medienkommunikation'. Freiburg, Schweiz: Univ.-Verl./Freiburg [Breisgau]: Herder, 184–97.

Saxer, Ulrich (1999b): Entwicklung, Funktionalität und Typisierung journalistischer Textsorten. In: Daniel Ammann/Heinz Moser/Roger Vaissiére (Ed.): Medien lesen. Der Textbegriff in der Medienwissenschaft. Zürich: Pestalozzianum, 116–38.

Saxer, Ulrich (2000): Mythos Postmoderne: Kommunikationswissenschaftliche Bedenken. In: Medien & Kommunikationswissenschaft, 48 (1), 85–92.
Schiewe, Jürgen (1998): Die Macht der Sprache. Eine Geschichte der Sprachkritik von der Antike bis zur Gegenwart. München: Beck.
Schmidt, Michael (1993): Heute gehört uns die Straße... Der Inside-Report aus der Neonazi-Szene. Düsseldorf u. a.: Econ.
Schmidt, Siegfried J. (1987): Skizze einer konstruktivistischen Mediengattungstheorie. In: Spiel, 6 (2), 163–205.
Schmidt, Siegfried J. (1991): Der Radikale Konstruktivismus: Ein neues Paradigma im interdisziplinären Diskurs. In: Siegfried J. Schmidt (Ed.): Der Diskurs des Radikalen Konstruktivismus (4th ed.). Frankfurt am Main: Suhrkamp, 11–88.
Schmidt, Siegfried J. (1993): Kommunikation – Kognition – Wirklichkeit. In: Günther Bentele/Manfred Rühl (Ed.): Theorien öffentlicher Kommunikation. Problemfelder, Positionen, Perspektiven. München: Ölschläger, 105–17.
Schmidt, Siegfried J. (1994): Kognitive Autonomie und soziale Orientierung. Konstruktivistische Bemerkungen zum Zusammenhang von Kognition, Kommunikation, Medien und Kultur. Frankfurt am Main: Suhrkamp.
Schmidt, Siegfried J. (1995): Sprache, Kultur und Wirklichkeitskonstruktion(en). In: Hans Rudi Fischer (Ed.): Die Wirklichkeit des Konstruktivismus. Zur Auseinandersetzung um ein neues Paradigma. Heidelberg: Carl-Auer-Systeme, 239–51.
Schmidt, Siegfried J. (1996): Die Welten der Medien. Grundlagen und Perspektiven der Medienbeobachtung. Braunschweig/Wiesbaden: Vieweg.
Schmidt, Siegfried J. (1998): Die Zähmung des Blicks. Konstruktivismus – Empirie – Wissenschaft. Frankfurt am Main: Suhrkamp.
Schmidt, Siegfried J. (1999): Blickwechsel. Umrisse einer Medienepistemologie. In: Gebhard Rusch/Siegfried J. Schmidt (Ed.): Konstruktivismus in der Medien- und Kommunikationswissenschaft. DELFIN 1997. Frankfurt am Main: Suhrkamp, 119–45.
Schmidt, Siegfried J. (2000): Kalte Faszination. Medien – Kultur – Wissenschaft in der Mediengesellschaft. Weilerswist: Velbrück Wissenschaft.
Schmidt, Siegfried J. (2001): Mediengattungstheorie. In: Ansgar Nünning (Ed.): Metzler Lexikon Literatur- und Kulturtheorie: Ansätze – Personen – Grundbegriffe (2nd revised and expanded edition). Stuttgart/Weimar: Metzler, 412–14.
Schmidt, Siegfried J. (2003): Geschichten & Diskurse. Abschied vom Konstruktivismus. Mit einem Vorwort von Mike Sandbothe. Reinbek bei Hamburg: Rowohlt.
Schmidt, Siegfried J. (2005a): Selbstorganisation und Lernkultur. In: Reinhard Voß (Ed.): LernLust und EigenSinn. Systemisch-konstruktivistische Lernwelten. Heidelberg: Carl-Auer-Systeme, 99–108.
Schmidt, Siegfried J. (2005b): Lernen, Wissen, Kompetenz, Kultur. Vorschläge zur Bestimmung von vier Unbekannten. Heidelberg: Carl-Auer-Systeme.
Schmidt, Siegfried J./Siegfried Weischenberg (1994): Mediengattungen, Berichterstattungsmuster, Darstellungsformen. In: Klaus Merten/Siegfried J. Schmidt/Siegfried Weischenberg (Ed.): Die Wirklichkeit der Medien. Eine Einführung in die Kommunikationswissenschaft. Opladen: Westdeutscher Verlag, 212–36.
Schmidt, Siegfried J./Guido Zurstiege (2000): Orientierung Kommunikationswissenschaft. Was sie kann, was sie will. Reinbek bei Hamburg: Rowohlt.
Scholl, Armin (2002): Einleitung. In: Armin Scholl (Ed.): Systemtheorie und Konstruktivismus in der Kommunikationswissenschaft. Konstanz: UVK, 7–18.
Scholl, Armin (2004): Konstruktivismus und Methoden. Statements zur Podiums- und Plenumsdiskussion auf der Tagung 'konstruktivismus04' der Universität Siegen am 03.12.2004. Unpublished manuscript, 1–3.
Scholl, Armin/Siegfried Weischenberg (1998): Journalismus in der Gesellschaft. Theorie, Methodologie und Empirie. Opladen/Wiesbaden: Westdeutscher Verlag.
Schulz, Winfried (1989): Massenmedien und Realität. Die 'ptolemäische' und die 'kopernikanische' Auffassung. In: Max Kaase/Winfried Schulz (Ed.): Massenkommunikation. Theorien, Methoden, Befunde. [= Kölner Zeitschrift für Soziologie und Sozialpsychologie. Sonderheft 30]. Opladen: Westdeutscher Verlag, 135–49.

Schulz, Winfried (1990): Die Konstruktion von Realität in den Nachrichtenmedien. Analyse der aktuellen Berichterstattung (2nd ed.). Freiburg/München: Alber.

Schulz, Winfried (2003a): Mediatisierung der Politik oder Politisierung der Medien? Beitrag zum Symposium der Konrad-Adenauer-Stiftung 'Politische Kommunikation in der globalen Welt—Know-how-Transfer als Einbahnstraße?' in Mainz am 30./31.10.2003. Unpublished manuscript, 1–7.

Schulz, Winfried (2003b): Das Weltbild der Massenmedien prägt das Weltbild der Menschen. Ergebnisse der Wirkungsforschung. In: Uni.Kurier.Magazin, 29, No. 104, 38–40.

Schulz, Winfried (2004): Medialisierung. Eine medientheoretische Rekonstruktion des Begriffs. Beitrag zur Jahrestagung der DGPuK in Erfurt vom 19.–21. Mai 2004. Unpublished manuscript,1–19.

Schwanitz, Dietrich (2002): Bildung. Alles, was man wissen muss (13th ed.). München: Goldmann.

Seel, Martin (2003): Eine vorübergehende Sache. In: Stefan Münker/Alexander Roesler/Mike Sandbothe (Ed.): Medienphilosophie. Beiträge zur Klärung eines Begriffs. Frankfurt am Main: Fischer, 10–15.

Segal, Lynn (1988): Das 18. Kamel oder Die Welt als Erfindung. Zum Konstruktivismus Heinz von Foersters. München/Zürich: Piper.

Siebert, Horst (2003a): Didaktisches Handeln in der Erwachsenenbildung. Didaktik aus konstruktivistischer Sicht (4th revevised and expanded edition). München/Unterschleißheim: Luchterhand.

Siebert, Horst (2003b): Pädagogischer Konstruktivismus. Lernen als Konstruktion von Wirklichkeit (2nd revevised and expanded edition). München/Unterschleißheim: Luchterhand.

Siebert, Horst (2003c): Vernetztes Lernen. Systemisch-konstruktivistische Methoden der Bildungsarbeit. München/Unterschleißheim: Luchterhand.

Simon, Fritz B. (1997): Die Kunst, nicht zu lernen. Und andere Paradoxien in Psychotherapie, Management, Politik... Heidelberg: Carl-Auer-Systeme.

Simon, Fritz B. (1999): Unterschiede, die Unterschiede machen. Klinische Epistemologie: Grundlage einer systemischen Psychiatrie und Psychosomatik. Mit einem Geleitwort von Helm Stierlin (3rd ed.). Frankfurt am Main: Suhrkamp.

Sokal, Alan (1996): Transgressing the Boundaries: Toward a Transformative Hermeneutics of Quantum Gravity. In: Social Text 46/47, 14 (1–2), 217–52.

Sokal, Alan (2001a): Die Grenzen überschreiten: Auf dem Weg zu einer transformativen Hermeneutik der Quantengravitation. In: Alan Sokal/Jean Bricmont: Eleganter Unsinn. Wie die Denker der Postmoderne die Wissenschaften missbrauchen. München: dtv, 262–309.

Sokal, Alan (2001b): Die Grenzen überschreiten: Ein Nachwort. In: Alan Sokal/Jean Bricmont: Eleganter Unsinn. Wie die Denker der Postmoderne die Wissenschaften missbrauchen. München: dtv, 319–30.

Sokal, Alan/Jean Bricmont (2001): Eleganter Unsinn. Wie die Denker der Postmoderne die Wissenschaften missbrauchen. München: dtv.

Spencer-Brown, George (1997). Laws of Form. Gesetze der Form. Lübeck: Bohmeier.

Staab, Joachim Friedrich (1990): Nachrichtenwert-Theorie. Formale Struktur und empirischer Gehalt. Freiburg/Zürich: Alber.

Stachelhaus, Heiner (1989): Joseph Beuys (2nd ed.). München: Heyne.

Stäheli, Urs (2000): Poststrukturalistische Soziologien. Bielefeld: Transcript.

Steinfeld, Thomas (1991): Der grobe Ton. Kleine Logik des gelehrten Anstands. Frankfurt am Main: Hain.

Störig, Hans Joachim (1993): Kleine Weltgeschichte der Philosophie. Erw. Neuausgabe. Frankfurt am Main: Fischer.

Teichert, Will (1996): Journalistische Verantwortung: Medienethik als Qualitätsproblem. In: Julian Nida-Rümelin (Ed.) Angewandte Ethik. Die Bereichsethiken und ihre theoretische Fundierung. Ein Handbuch. Stuttgart: Kröner, 751–76.

Thissen, Frank (1997): Das Lernen neu erfinden—konstruktivistische Grundlagen einer Mulitmedia-Didaktik. In: Uwe Beck/Winfried Sommer (Ed.): LearnTec. Europäischer

Kongreß für Bildungstechnologie und betriebliche Bildung. Tagungsband. Karlsruhe: Karlsruher Kongress- und Ausstellungs-GmbH, 69-79.
Thomaß, Barbara (1998): Journalistische Ethik. Ein Vergleich der Diskurse in Frankreich, Großbritannien und Deutschland. Opladen/Wiesbaden: Westdeutscher Verlag.
Thomaß, Barbara (2003): Fünf ethische Prinzipien journalistischer Praxis. In: Bernhard Debatin/Rüdiger Funiok (Ed.): Kommunikations- und Medienethik. Konstanz: UVK, 159-68.
Timmerberg, Helge (1988): Das Glück des Süchtigen. Helge Timmerberg über Gonzo-Journalismus. In: Medium Magazin, 2, 18-19.
Varela, Francisco J. (1994): Ethisches Können. Frankfurt am Main/New York: Campus. [Ethical Know-How: Action, Wisdom, and Cognition, Stanford University Press].
Varela, Francisco J./Evan Thompson/Eleanor Rosch (1995): Der mittlere Weg der Erkenntnis. Der Brückenschlag zwischen wissenschaftlicher Theorie und menschlicher Erfahrung. München: Goldmann. [The Embodied Mind: Cognitive Science and Human Experience, The MIT Press].
Virchow, Fabian (1996): '... über die Trümmer der KZ-Gedenkstätten.' Von Auschwitzleugnern und anderen Geschichtsfälschern. In: Jens Mecklenburg (Ed.): Handbuch deutscher Rechtsextremismus. Berlin: Elefanten Press, 666-91.
Voß, G. Günter (2000): Unternehmer der eigenen Arbeitskraft — Einige Folgerungen für die Bildungssoziologie. In: Zeitschrift für Soziologie der Erziehung und Sozialisation, 20 (2), 149-66.
Voß, Reinhard (Ed.) (2005): LernLust und EigenSinn. Systemisch-konstruktivistische Lernwelten. Heidelberg: Carl-Auer-Systeme.
Watzlawick, Paul (1993): Wie wirklich ist die Wirklichkeit? Wahn, Täuschung, Verstehen (21st ed.). München/Zürich: Piper.
Watzlawick, Paul (Ed.) (1994a): Die erfundene Wirklichkeit. Wie wissen wir, was wir zu wissen glauben? Beiträge zum Konstruktivismus (8th ed.). München/Zürich: Piper. [THE INVENTED REALITY: How Do We Know What We Believe We Know? Norton].
Watzlawick, Paul (1994b): Bausteine ideologischer 'Wirklichkeiten'. In: Paul Watzlawick (Ed.): Die erfundene Wirklichkeit. Wie wissen wir, was wir zu wissen glauben? Beiträge zum Konstruktivismus (8th ed.). München/Zürich: Piper, 192-228. [THE INVENTED REALITY: How Do We Know What We Believe We Know? Norton].
Watzlawick, Paul (1994c): Epilog. In: Paul Watzlawick (Ed.) Die erfundene Wirklichkeit. Wie wissen wir, was wir zu wissen glauben? Beiträge zum Konstruktivismus (8th ed.). München/Zürich: Piper, 310-15. [THE INVENTED REALITY: How Do We Know What We Believe We Know? Norton].
Weber, Max (1995): Wissenschaft als Beruf. Stuttgart: Philipp Reclam jun.
Weber, Stefan (1995): Nachrichtenkonstruktion im Boulevardmedium. Die Wirklichkeit der 'Kronen Zeitung'. Wien: Passagen.
Weber, Stefan (1996): Die Dualisierung des Erkennens. Zu Konstruktivismus, Neurophilosophie und Medientheorie. Wien: Passagen.
Weber, Stefan (1999a): Wie journalistische Wirklichkeiten entstehen. Salzburg: Kuratoriums für Journalistenausbildung, Band 15, Schriftenreihe Journalistik.
Weber, Stefan (1999b): Was können Systemtheorie und nicht-dualisierende Philosophie zu einer Lösung des medientheoretischen Realismus/Konstruktivismus-Problems beitragen? In: Gebhard Rusch/Siegfried J. Schmidt (Ed.): Konstruktivismus in der Medien- und Kommunikationswissenschaft. DELFIN 1997. Frankfurt am Main: Suhrkamp, 189-222.
Weber, Stefan (2000a): Was steuert Journalismus? Ein System zwischen Selbstreferenz und Fremdsteuerung. Konstanz: UVK Medien.
Weber, Stefan (2000b): Ist eine integrative Theorie möglich? Distinktionstheorie und nicht-dualisierender Ansatz als Herausforderungen für die Journalismustheorie. In: Martin Löffelholz (Ed.): Theorien des Journalismus. Ein diskursives Handbuch. Wiesbaden: Westdeutscher Verlag, 455-66.
Weber, Stefan (2001): Medien — Systeme — Netze. Elemente einer Theorie der Cyber-Netzwerke. Bielefeld: Transcript.

Weber, Stefan (2002a): Doppelte Differenz. Schritte zu einer 'konstruktivistischen Systemtheorie der Medienkommunikation'. In: Irene Neverla/Elke Grittmann/Monika Pater (Ed.): Grundlagentexte zur Journalistik. Konstanz: UVK, 73–88.

Weber, Stefan (2002b): Konstruktivismus und Non-Dualismus, Systemtheorie und Distinktionstheorie. In: Armin Scholl (Ed.): Systemtheorie und Konstruktivismus in der Kommunikationswissenschaft. Konstanz: UVK, 21–36.

Weber, Stefan (2003a): Einführung: (Basis-)Theorien für die Medienwissenschaft. In: Stefan Weber (Ed.): Theorien der Medien. Von der Kulturkritik bis zum Konstruktivismus. Konstanz: UVK, 11–48.

Weber, Stefan (2003b): Konstruktivistische Medientheorien. In: Stefan Weber (Ed.): Theorien der Medien. Von der Kulturkritik bis zum Konstruktivismus. Konstanz: UVK, 180–201.

Weber, Stefan (2003c): Systemtheorien der Medien. In: Stefan Weber (Ed.): Theorien der Medien. Von der Kulturkritik bis zum Konstruktivismus. Konstanz: UVK, 202–23.

Weber, Stefan (2003d): Komparatistik: Theorien-Raum der Medienwissenschaft. In: Stefan Weber (Ed.): Theorien der Medien. Von der Kulturkritik bis zum Konstruktivismus. Konstanz: UVK, 325–45.

Weber, Stefan (2003e): Under Construction. Plädoyer für ein empirisches Verständnis von Medienepistemologie. In: Stefan Münker/Alexander Roesler/Mike Sandbothe (Ed.): Medienphilosophie. Beiträge zur Klärung eines Begriffs. Frankfurt am Main: Fischer, 172–84.

Weck, Roger de (2002, June 15): Die wahren Populisten sind die Journalisten. In: Frankfurter Allgemeine Zeitung. No. 136, 58.

Weischenberg, Siegfried (1990): Das 'Paradigma Journalistik'. Zur kommunikationswissenschaftlichen Identifizierung einer hochschulgebundenen Journalistenausbildung. In: Publizistik, 35 (1), 45–61.

Weischenberg, Siegfried (1992): Der blinde Fleck des Kritikers. Zu den 'Wahrheiten' einer Konstruktivismus-Rezeption. In: Comunicatio Socialis, 25 (2), 168–77.

Weischenberg, Siegfried (1993): Die Medien und die Köpfe. Perspektiven und Probleme konstruktivistischer Journalismusforschung. In: Günther Bentele/Manfred Rühl (Ed.): Theorien öffentlicher Kommunikation. Problemfelder, Positionen, Perspektiven. München: Ölschläger, 126–36.

Weischenberg, Siegfried (1995): Journalistik. Theorie und Praxis aktueller Medienkommunikation. Band 2: Medientechnik, Medienfunktionen, Medienakteure. Opladen: Westdeutscher Verlag.

Weischenberg, Siegfried (1998): Journalistik. Theorie und Praxis aktueller Medienkommunikation. Band 1: Mediensysteme, Medienethik, Medieninstitutionen (2nd revevised and expanded edition). Opladen/Wiesbaden: Westdeutscher Verlag.

Weischenberg, Siegfried (2001a): Nachrichten-Journalismus. Anleitungen und Qualitäts-Standards für die Medienpraxis. Unter Mitarbeit von Judith Rackers. Wiesbaden: Westdeutscher Verlag.

Weischenberg, Siegfried (2001b): Das Ende einer Ära? Aktuelle Beobachtungen zum Studium des künftigen Journalismus. In: Hans J. Kleinsteuber (Ed.): Aktuelle Medientrends in den USA. Journalismus, politische Kommunikation und Medien im Zeitalter der Digitalisierung. Opladen/Wiesbaden: Westdeutscher Verlag, 61–82.

Weischenberg, Siegfried (2004a): Kurt Koszyk und das Dortmunder Modell. Laudatio zum 75. Geburtstag des Institutsgründers, Dortmund, 18. Juni 2004. Unpublished manuscript, 1–10.

Weischenberg, Siegfried (2004b): Zeitgeister. In: Journalist, 54 (11), 10–16.

Weischenberg, Siegfried/Armin Scholl (1995): Konstruktivismus und Ethik im Journalismus. In: Gebhard Rusch/Siegfried J. Schmidt (Ed.): Konstruktivismus und Ethik. DELFIN 1995. Frankfurt am Main: Suhrkamp, 214–40.

Wellershoff, Mariane (2000, May 22): 'Implosion des Realen.' Tom Kummer über fingierte Interviews mit Hollywood-Stars und sein Verständnis von 'Borderline-Journalismus'. No. 21, 110.

Welsch, Wolfgang (1996): Vernunft. Die zeitgenössische Vernunftkritik und das Konzept der transversalen Vernunft. Frankfurt am Main: Suhrkamp.

Weßler, Hartmut (2002): Journalismus und Kommunikationswissenschaft: Eine Einleitung. In: Otfried Jarren/Hartmut Weßler (Ed.): Journalismus—Medien—Öffentlichkeit. Eine Einführung. Wiesbaden: Westdeutscher Verlag, 17–38.

Whorf, Benjamin Lee (1963): Sprache, Denken, Wirklichkeit. Beiträge zur Metalinguistik und Sprachphilosophie. Hg. und übersetzt von Peter Krausser. Reinbek bei Hamburg: Rowohlt. [Language, Thought, and Reality: Selected Writings of Benjamin Lee Whorf, The MIT Press].

Willke, Helmut (1987): Strategien der Intervention in autonome Systeme. In: Dirk Baecker/Jürgen Markowitz/Rudolf Stichweh/Hartmann Tyrell/Helmut Willke (Ed.): Theorie als Passion. Niklas Luhmann zum 60. Geburtstag. Frankfurt am Main: Suhrkamp, 333–61.

Willke, Helmut (2004): Einführung in das systemische Wissensmanagement. Heidelberg: Carl-Auer-Systeme.

Wimmer, Rudolf (1999): Wider den Veränderungsoptimismus. Zu den Möglichkeiten und Grenzen einer radikalen Transformation von Organisationen. In: Soziale Systeme, 5 (1), 159–80.

Winter, Wolfgang (1999): Theorie des Beobachters. Skizzen zur Architektonik eines Metatheoriesystems. Frankfurt am Main: Neue Wissenschaft.

Zschunke, Peter (2000): Agenturjournalismus. Nachrichtenschreiben im Sekundentakt (2nd rev. ed.). Konstanz: UVK Medien.